MANITOWOC RIVER →

Beck & Pauli, Lithographers, Milwaukee, W

# OC, WIS.
## 83.

urch.
h.
eran Church.
odist Church.
ch.
h.
n Church.
ist Church.

Church.

A. J. Patchen, Dentist, 212 North Eighth St.
H. F. Gillett, Meat Market, 214 North Eighth St.
William Gale, Dry Goods and Notions, 216 North Eighth St.
A. Landreth, Seeds, wholesale and Retail, Buffalo cor. Eighth St.
Henry Esch, Dry Goods, Clothing, Boots and Shoes, Hats and Caps and Groceries, 421 and 423 Jay St.
W. H. Wernecke, Farm Machinery and Sewing Machines, 313 South Eighth St.
F. Becker, Saloon, Billiards and Bowling Alley, 319 South Eighth St.
Joseph Pfeffer, Harness, Saddles, Trunks, &c., 504 Washington St.
Eggert & Howard, Boots and Shoes, 104 South Eighth St.
Chas. Gauger, Blacksmith and Wagon Shop, 905 Washington St.
John Schaefer, Meat Market, 999 Washington St.
Chas. Hartwig, Saloon, Groceries and Crockery, 1002 and 1004 Washington St.
E. Siegismund & Son, Furniture, 515 Washington St.
F. Schultz, Saloon, Main St.
Chas. H. Paulus, Justice of Peace, Insurance, Land and Passenger Ag't, Main St.
G. G. Lade, Sewing Machines, Crockery, Notions and Picture Frames, South Eighth St.

G. G. Sedgwick, Attorney, Torrison's Block.
Cota & Anderson, Barbers, 101 North Eighth St.
M. J. Kern, Fancy Goods, Toys, Wall Paper, Zephyr, &c., 512 York St.
Simon Schurr, Saloon and Billiards, 523 York St.
John G. Bahr, Saloon and Restaurant, 824 Franklin St.
Ignatz Bradl, Wagon and Carriage Builder, State and Ninth Sts.
Fred. Hine, General Blacksmithing, State and Ninth Sts.
M. Christiansen, Bakery and Confectionery, 506 Buffalo St.
R. K. Paine, Physician and Surgeon, 312 North Eighth St.
Chas. Schaefer, Custom Tailor, York St.
Chas. Bock, Dry Goods, Clothing, Boots and Shoes, Hats and Caps, Groceries, &c., 209 North Eighth St.
Geo. B. Guyles, Lumber, Lath and Shingles, Main cor. Commercial St.
Zeman & Krajnik, Lumber, Lath and Shingles, Main cor. Commercial St.
H. Hentscher, Photographer, 314 North Eighth St.
Nagle & Borcherdt, Editors, Manitowoc Pilot, Torrison's Block.
Haukohl & Baensch, Editors, Lake Shore Times, 102 South Eighth St.
Adolph Wittmann, Editor, Manitowoc Post, 107 South Eighth St.
Henry Sandford, Editor, Manitowoc Tribune, 212 North Eighth St.
C. H. Schmidt, Editor, North Western, Main near Quay.

# MANITOWOC COUNTY

## A *Beacon* on the *Lakeshore*

Partners in Progress by
Robin E. Butler, Rachel Young, and MaryBeth Matzek

Photo Researcher Marie O'Brien
Historical Consultant Bob Fay

Produced in cooperation with the
Manitowoc/Two Rivers Area Chamber of Commerce

Milwaukee Publishing Group
Milwaukee, Wisconsin

# MANITOWOC COUNTY
## *A Beacon on the Lakeshore*

by Ellen D. Langill

*For Ross*

*Editor*  Karen Story
*Photo Editor*  Doug O'Rourke
*Editorial Assistant*  Kathy B. Peyser
*Indexer*  Teri Greenberg
*Designer*  Ellen Ifrah

Milwaukee Publishing Group
David Turner, Publisher

Library of Congress Catalog Card Number: 99-74517
ISBN: 0-9650759-2-3

**MANITOWOC
TWO RIVERS**
— AREA —
Chamber of Commerce

*Special thanks to the Manitowoc/Two Rivers Area Chamber of Commerce for spearheading this project and to those chamber members who, through their generosity, gave this wonderful gift to the community.*

*On the cover: Manitowoc Marina. ©Michael Thomas, PhotoTechnics*

*Frontispiece: The Two Rivers Coast Guard Station. ©Michael Thomas, PhotoTechnics*

*Endsheets: An 1883 bird's-eye view of Manitowoc. Lithograph by Beck & Pauli, Milwaukee. Published by J.J. Stoner, Madison. Courtesy, Manitowoc County Historical Society*

# Contents

*Lithograph by J. Knaube, Milwaukee.*
*Published by V.H. Vogt, Milwaukee.*
*Courtesy, Manitowoc County Historical*
*Society*

# Introduction

Although I have enjoyed my many visits to Manitowoc County during the past decade, I had not had the opportunity to concentrate on the richness of its history until I began to work on this book project. While the area reflects many of the historical trends of Wisconsin as a whole, about which I have written and taught, Manitowoc also has a unique heritage.

The tales of the lakeshore and the harbors, from the early fishing industry, to lumbering and shipbuilding, are a part of this special story. The area's prosperous farmlands, the variety of its immigrant settlers, and the ingenuity of its industrialists all blend to tell the economic story of Manitowoc County.

Moreover, the personal histories of early settlers, of pioneer judges, doctors, and businessmen, have been woven into the narrative to describe the human element of the local heritage. Not only was Manitowoc County a pioneer port and shipbuilding center, it also was a center of reform, wherein citizens took control of their local utilities and worked for better, more efficient government.

The emphasis on education is another part of the county's heritage, from the earliest schools to the development of higher education, both in teachers' courses, a private college, and a branch of the University of Wisconsin. The commitment to schools is a theme that comes through strongly in all of the local archives.

The maritime legends and the cultural growth of the county are matched by the citizens' commitment to their own history, so well exemplified by the strength, support, and membership of the Manitowoc County Historical Society. I owe many thanks to Bob Fay, its director, for his assistance with the project and his reading of the manuscript. The Society's numerous publications and its rich archives are a very valuable resource for historians. I also owe a debt of gratitude to the many librarians and communications personnel who assisted me in digging out specialized information about many of the county's institutions, both public and private.

The book would not have been possible without the careful shepherding and sponsorship of David Turner, through the Milwaukee Publishing Group. I am also grateful to Karen Story, whose careful editing and critical comments have greatly improved the text. Lastly, I am also blessed with the meticulous proofreading and critiques of my husband, Ross, to whom this book is dedicated.

*Ellen D. Langill*

# A Rich Heritage

## 1770 – 1840

Before the creation of what is today's Manitowoc County in 1836, the territory had a rich and fascinating history of native peoples and European explorers and settlers. The earliest inhabitants of Manitowoc were drawn to the scenic hills and valleys near the shore of Lake Michigan by their beauty, by the abundance of lumber, wildlife, and fish, the fertility of the soil, and by the rivers that provided ready access upstream from the natural lake harbors.

From the county's highest hill (in today's town of Schleswig), the first residents could look down at 359 feet across the forests and streams to the lakeshore. The native peoples could paddle their canoes from Lake Michigan all the way to Lake Winnebago to the west, making the area's greatest river, the Manitowoc, a useful highway for travel and trade. Despite its several rapids, the river flowed gently as it curved through the forests and valleys.

## Native Peoples

The pine forests were dense along the many waterways and tamarack and hemlock trees also filled the swampy areas. Locating their villages on high ground to avoid the spring floods, the native Chippewa and Ojibway peoples christened the largest river, "Munedoowk," which likely meant a "home of the good spirit." This good spirit that brought many native peoples to the area had existed since the days of the first prehistoric mound builders, whose ceremonial effigies were later excavated in the area north of Two Rivers. Skeletons from these mounds as well as copper implements were unearthed in 1893 and sent to the Smithsonian Institution in Washington, D.C., for further study and preservation.

Other tribal peoples also came to the area to partake of its "good spirit," including the Mescouten, Fox, Sac, Ottawa, Winnebago, Potawatomi, and the Menomonee. These indigenous peoples roamed the glacial bowls, or kettles, which had been created many thousands of years earlier by receding glaciers that left beds of limestone throughout the area. The clay and humus soils on top of the native bedrock were ideal for vegetation, while the sandy loam near the shore of the lake formed wide and beautiful beaches.

Inland, the limestone surface gave rise to many natural springs, creating creeks such as Meeme, Silver, Calvin, Point, and Centerville, and smaller rivers such as the Neshoto (or West Twin) and the Mishicott (or East Twin), named Twin or Two Rivers by the early natives.

The Chippewa people located their central village near Cato Falls on the upper Manitowoc River, near valleys where they planted corn and near forests where they gathered berries and hunted game. The leader of this tribe was a man named Waumegesako, called "Mexico," who later became renowned among the white settlers for his peacemaking skills.

Local legend told of several prolonged battles among the native peoples when the powerful Menomonee tribe moved into the area. The more hostile Sac and Fox and even Mescouten peoples were eventually pushed west across Lake Winnebago, with the assistance of the Chippewa, Ojibway, Ottawa, and Potawatomi. The Winnebago (who were related to the Sioux of the Great Plains in their language) migrated north and westward in Wisconsin sometime before the late 1600s, leaving the remaining tribes (all of the Algonquin group) at peace and prospering on the eve of French exploration.

## French Explorers

By the time the first Europeans reached the area, the dominant tribes were at peace and welcomed the explorers. Legend persists that Marquette and Joliet were the first to traverse the shore of the county in their southward trek mapping the western perimeter of Lake Michigan in 1673. However, there are no specific entries in their journal of camping or exploring farther inland in the Manitowoc or Two Rivers area.

*This Indian burial mound was found just outside Manitowoc County in the town of Rantoul. Surrounded by 10 "lizard" mounds, this particular mound offered a panoramic view of the Manitowoc River at its north fork. Burial mounds similar to this one were discovered near Two Rivers in 1893. Mound sizes vary and those built served different purposes such as for burial or as a totem. Courtesy, State Historical Society of Wisconsin*

It was almost a century later that more complete exploration took place along the lake's western shore as French fur traders arrived in the 1770s. One explorer noted in his journal that "Monsieur Fay" had established a fur-trading outpost "eighteen leagues north of Milwaukee" at Twin Rivers before 1780. Fifteen years later, in 1795, the arrival of Jacques Vieau, an agent of the Northwestern Fur Company, brought the Manitowoc area within the official network of its fur-trading empire. By that time America had won its Revolutionary War against Great Britain and had established ownership of what was to become Wisconsin at the Treaty of Paris in 1783. However, actual occupation by the Americans came only after a second war against Great Britain in 1812, and further land cessions by the Indian tribes in the upper Great Lakes region.

As an agent for the great fur company, Vieau's mission was to establish trading outposts wherever the native peoples were receptive and the trapping was good, particularly along the river tributaries to Lake Michigan. Landing at Two Rivers, Vieau and a companion traveled inland to set up the first post in the area near today's town of Gibson. He left an agent in charge, before walking farther south to set up a second fur-trading post near the rapids on the Manitowoc River.

Vieau then traveled south along the Lake Michigan shore to establish other posts, including the first one on the river in today's Milwaukee. Returning to his outposts each year, Vieau and his agents got to know the native peoples and learn their language. Vieau soon married a native Potawatomi woman in Milwaukee, becoming the first permanent settler in the region. His son-in-law, Solomon Juneau, later developed the east side and became the city of Milwaukee's first mayor in 1846.

Other fur-trading outposts were established in the area that is now Manitowoc County by agents on expeditions out of Mackinac, beginning in July 1795. These agents set up outposts at Larrabee and the Rapids. The fur-trading agents, called coureurs (or courriers) de bois, or runners in the woods, soon followed, making their pilgrimages through the Wisconsin waterways. These colorful men brought the native peoples into regular contact with the French, as the coureurs' red woolen hats and singing announced their arrival each spring in canoes.

As the contact between the French and the indigenous tribes continued, there was an increase in written accounts of the Indians' way of life. One such account described their manner of spearing whitefish from canoes at the mouth of the Manitowoc River where the fish swam in abundance each spring. The Indians relied upon a superb sense of balance while standing up in their canoes and hurling spears into the water at intervals.

From the native peoples, the French also learned the most direct paths through the dense forests that could serve as overland routes between outposts and forts. Along these paths, which closely follow today's highways, the French agents traveled from the fort at Green Bay to Manitowoc and back. These paths became even more important when the American army took over the old forts after the Treaty of Ghent in 1814, which finally forced the British to relinquish their hold on the Northwest Territory, including Wisconsin.

## An American Territory

By the early 1820s more Americans began to arrive at Fort Howard in Green Bay and to explore the surrounding territory. Descriptions of journeys to and through Manitowoc came from an American, Colonel J. Edwards, stationed at Green Bay, who noted the abundance of fish in the area's rivers. Another visitor, Colonel Ebenezer Childs, made frequent trips to the river's mouth to trade, as did Colonel William S. Hamilton, son of the famous Alexander Hamilton, who brought cattle on a trail through the county to supply the fort at Green Bay.

The path from Milwaukee and Sheboygan northward to the fort at Green Bay began to bring more settlers each year after 1830, but by this time the former good will between the French coureurs and the native peoples was beginning to break down. Problems emerged in part because the settlers did not bother to learn the native language. Moreover, the Indians were aware that their old friends, the French, had been defeated by the Americans and British and they resented the end of the more generous spirit displayed during the height of the fur-trading era.

As hostile feelings replaced the "good spirit," Manitowoc experienced its first murder in 1821, when an American army surgeon, Dr. Madison, was killed by a Chippewa. The murderer was tried under American law in a Detroit court (since Wisconsin was then part of the Michigan Territory) and executed. Even though the relations remained troubled, fur trading within Manitowoc County continued to be profitable until the late 1820s when an agent was murdered for refusing to give credit to a Chippewa in advance of receiving pelts.

In the early 1830s relations between settlers and the natives throughout Wisconsin deteriorated as Americans began to seek ever-greater cessions of land from the Indians. The area that includes all of Manitowoc County was signed over to the American government by the Menomonee tribe in 1831, but thereafter relationships worsened. The matter came to a head in the infamous Black Hawk War of 1832, following which most of southern and eastern Wisconsin was ceded by the native peoples to the American government in the Treaty of Chicago.

*Indian tribes roamed the countryside throughout Manitowoc County and beyond, living off the land carved out by prehistoric glaciers. The region was fertile and prime for planting. Courtesy, State Historical Society of Wisconsin*

*BACKGROUND: Numerous artifacts like this iron harpoon and spear were found in Manitowoc County in 1896. The harpoon was discovered in the Neshoto River and the spear was found in Newton. Courtesy, State Historical Society of Wisconsin*

*Jacques Vieau (above) established trading posts in Manitowoc County and also the first outpost in what would eventually become Milwaukee. Vieau married a native Potawatomi woman (above right) and their daughter later married Solomon Juneau—one of Milwaukee's founding fathers. Courtesy, Milwaukee County Historical Society*

*FAR RIGHT: An agent of the Northwest Fur Company, Jacques Vieau arrived in 1795 to bring fur trading along the western shore of Michigan into the fold of the industry. Vieau established his headquarters in Milwaukee on a hilltop near the Menomonee River. He also opened trading posts in the town of Gibson, another in Sheboygan, and yet another at Manitowoc Rapids. Courtesy, Milwaukee County Historical Society*

Even after the treaty, many tribes remained in the Manitowoc area, particularly around Cato Falls, where chief "Mexico" worked hard to keep peace. During an 1842 scare, when white settlers heard rumors of a pending Indian massacre, the chief had the courage to enter the white settlements to reassure them that they would come to no harm. In gratitude, the government awarded the chief a peace medal and, upon his death two years later, he was buried with honors in the town of Rapids. His portrait, painted by an Irish-American artist, was donated to the State Historical Society of Wisconsin when it was established in 1846.

However, the arrival of an increasing number of American settlers led to numerous land disputes and to the growing sale of liquor to the natives, once strictly forbidden. Together with cholera and smallpox, to which the Indians had no resistance, the use of liquor depleted the number of the tribal peoples and reduced many others to poverty. By 1850 there were only a few native peoples left in the county, dominated by the still-proud Menomonees.

Despite their dwindling numbers, the Indians were still the subject of wild rumors, as in 1862, in the middle of the Civil War, when the Sioux massacre occurred in New Ulm, Minnesota. Settlers in Manitowoc

County, many hundreds of miles away, heard about the massacre and rushed women and children to safety, despite the fact that there was no pending trouble with the few Menomonees who still lived nearby. Particularly frightened were settlers gathered for protection in the village of Branch, where women even boiled water to throw at any advancing war parties. However, when all of the rumors proved false, peace returned and, as one account of the event told of it, "the settlements soon took up their routine existence, albeit somewhat shamefaced over the affair."[1]

## Land Claims and First Settlement

Following the Indian land cessions of the early 1830s, a land office was opened in Green Bay in 1834, which soon began to do a "land office business." The first recorded land purchases for Manitowoc County were made the following year by two men, Louis Fizette and William Jones, followed by Francis Laframbois and William Jourdain. Land fever had arrived.

Later that same year, rumors of a gold strike near Kewaunee brought a rush of interest from investors. Several men of means from both Milwaukee and Green Bay bought up a number of tracts of land in case the rumors proved to be true. However, there was no gold and the most profitable use one could make of land purchased from the government at the going price of $1.25 an acre was to establish a town, because town lots sold well. Speculators soon claimed land along several rivers in the county in hopes of establishing a successful settlement and reaping huge cash rewards. In 1836 a newspaper report in Green Bay mentioned Manitowoc as a prime target for such land speculation as land prices began to soar.

As this frenzy continued a new venture, the Manitowoc Land Company, was formed in 1836 by Chicago investors led by the team of William and Benjamin Jones. The company bought up more than 2,000 acres and arranged for a team of men to begin to plat a future town site near the mouth of the Manitowoc River. However, of the large contingent assigned this task, only five men were hardy enough to begin the chore. The rest were frightened by the dark pine forests and forbidding wilderness and walked down the beach back to Sheboygan and on to Chicago.

Of those who remained, E.L. Abbott, Mark Howard, and a man named Farnham built a log cabin prior to cutting timber and beginning to lay out streets for a settlement. The company rewarded these stalwart men with a bonus of $100 each and began to construct the area's first sawmill, a necessary service if further settlement was to occur. By early 1837 a boatload of 40 prospective settlers arrived, carried north on the lake schooner *Elwellyn*. Some of the area's oldest families are descended from these arrivals who first came to the crude village and lived in one of these early log structures.

Soon Oliver C. Hubbard, D.S. Munger, Moses Hubbard, Benjamin Jones, and others began to build their own dwellings near the crude "Chicago Street" laid out by the first settlers. The area's first white baby was born to Munger and his wife that fall, in September 1837. Together with another settlement upriver at Rapids, the Manitowoc group survived the hard winter and even hung on during the great financial panic of 1837 that sent many other speculators back east bankrupt.

The panic was a crisis in currency that had been created by the demise of the first Bank of the United States, killed for political reasons by President Andrew Jackson. As the eastern banks began to call in their loans, banks throughout the country failed, making their currency worthless. Several banks had used the head of a wildcat on their dollar notes and this so-called "wildcat" currency had often been brought west by settlers to pay for land and supplies. When Jackson further announced, in the *Specie Circular*, that no paper money would be accepted in payment for federal land, thousands of settlers and land companies across the frontier had to declare bankruptcy.

Prior to the onset of the financial panic, some lots in the small settlement of Manitowoc had sold for an astounding $1,200

*As Indians, fur traders, and American settlers journeyed from Milwaukee to Sheboygan and north to Fort Howard in Green Bay, Manitowoc County became a heavily explored area. Those stationed at the fort were familiar with Manitowoc's well-stocked rivers. Fort Howard, as seen in this 1851 photo, was built in 1816 as part of the United States government's effort to regain control from the British who had a strong influence on the Indians and the fur trade. The need for the fort diminished over the years and the troops left in 1852. The buildings were removed in 1869. Courtesy, Neville Public Museum of Brown County*

*LEFT: This historical marker, erected in 1922, notes the site where Jacques Vieau built his trading post in Manitowoc County in 1796. Vieau was nicknamed "Jambo" by the Indians he befriended. The marker also documents the site as the location of the first "white man's house" in the county. Courtesy, State Historical Society of Wisconsin*

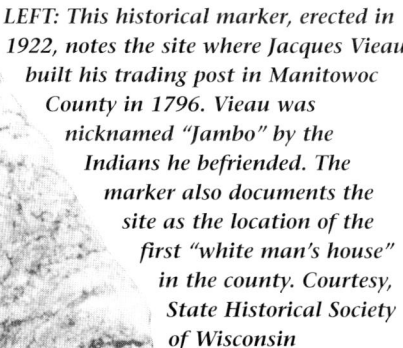

*ABOVE: As the needs of soldiers and settlers at Fort Howard increased, so did the traffic that passed through Manitowoc County. Cattle, a source of food for the dwellers at the fort, was often brought from Illinois along a well-worn trail from Chicago to Green Bay. Colonel William S. Hamilton, the son of U.S. statesman Alexander Hamilton, brought cattle through the area in 1825 on his way to the fort. Courtesy, State Historical Society of Wisconsin*

*RIGHT: Born in 1789, Chief Waumegesako, or "Mexico," became the leader of the Chippewa, Ottawa, and Menomonee Indian tribes. His village was located in Manitowoc County along the banks of the Manitowoc River. Chief Mexico's relationship with the white man was instrumental in keeping peace between the Native Americans and the settlers. He signed four treaties over a six-year span starting in 1827 and later received a peace medal from the U.S. government. Chief Mexico died in 1844. A stone monument was erected in 1909 to commemorate his contributions. This portrait, painted by artist Mark Robert Harrison, is currently housed at the State Historical Society of Wisconsin. Courtesy, State Historical Society of Wisconsin*

each, bringing vast profits to eager speculators. The population of the area had grown to 180, with 60 in Manitowoc, 40 in Two Rivers and Manitowoc Rapids, and approximately 20 at Thayer's Mill. However, six months later two-thirds of the settlers had left and the land was nearly worthless.

## Early Enterprises

During the late 1830s a hardy group of settlers hung on and began to establish the area's first economic concerns in lumber, sawmills, fishing, and farming. The Conroe family, which included five brothers who eventually settled in the area of Manitowoc Rapids, built a sawmill on the river in 1837 with "two upright saws, run by an old fashioned flutter wheel."[2] Downstream the first shipping concern, Jones, Clark & Co., contracted with the Conroes to buy all of its sawn lumber at the price of $20 per thousand board feet, "delivered at the mouth of the river."

In turn the company arranged to use some of the lumber to develop the new settlement of Manitowoc at the river's mouth and to ship the balance south to Chicago on lake schooners. It was the county's second exported product after furs. Soon the business employed more than 40 workers, many of them Frenchmen who had abandoned the life of fur trading to settle down in the area. Workers flocked to the river's mouth, where the settlement of Manitowoc began to grow again by 1838.

In Manitowoc, they were hired by the Jones company to build a large warehouse, 40 by 60 feet, and a number of other homes and business structures, as well as the first wharves for the lake schooners. At one end of this first warehouse, Benjamin Jones opened a small store from which he could sell or trade for provisions brought north, including food supplies, blankets, and tools. The rest of the structure was dedicated to storing these provisions and the lumber pending the arrival of yet another schooner.

The workmen themselves lived in shanties near the edge of the settlement. They were able to make extra money cutting and stacking "steamboat" logs for the newly arriving lake steamers that began to pull into the wharves to pick up loads of lumber for Milwaukee and Chicago. Records show that the unskilled laborers received between $30 and $40 a month in pay, whereas a skilled carpenter in the settlement could earn up to $70 a month.

One additional sidelight to the business of lumbering, which also proved to be profitable in the early years, was the production of wooden shingles. The first "finished goods" of wood produced in the county were shipped south to Chicago in return for provisions, food, and tools being sent north. The shingle business was one harbinger of the many wooden products companies that would later spring up across the area.

In addition to lumbering, the region's many rivers yielded a rich bounty of fish, particularly in Two Rivers. The settlement began to grow in 1837, after the arrival of Robert M. Eberts and John P. Arndt, who brought their families and recruited workmen for a new steam sawmill. In the summer of 1837 a recent arrival, Joseph Edwards, built a seine, or net, at the river to catch whitefish. Short of supplies, Edwards allegedly had to walk to Green Bay and back to purchase an adequate supply of heavy-gauge twine to make his seine.

Moreover, Edwards became the first local shipbuilder, inaugurating an industry that would later put Manitowoc on the map. In order to carry lumber in his schooner, as well as the harvest of fish on other voyages, Edwards had to build several small scows to transport the wood downstream from the rapids to the mouth of the river. Edwards' scows were valuable in bringing the cut lumber cheaply to the harbor where he could then have them loaded onto the lake schooners for shipment to the growing cities of Milwaukee and Chicago.

Soon thereafter, an entrepreneur from Detroit, J.P. Clark, established other fishing sites in the area, bringing his own schooner, *The Gazelle*, to ship the catch back to Michigan. Clark soon hired two dozen men to operate his seines and haul in the catch. These large nets, usually more than 150 rods (550 yards) long, were dragged from boats and hauled in by a crude hand-cranked windlass. Even though the work was difficult, the profits were enormous.

The bounty of fish in the waters off Manitowoc and Two Rivers yielded catches as large as 150 barrels (100 pounds each) at a time, which were then packed for shipment to either Chicago or Detroit where they sold for $12 each. In one early season, the Clark enterprise netted more than 2,000 barrels for reshipment. The small settlement at Two Rivers, composed mostly of fishermen, consisted of roughly 12 houses and 25 residents. Fish had become the area's third profitable export. With the growth in lumbering and fishing, and with the opening of several roads, more settlers began to pour into the area prior to 1840.

## The First Roads

Following its separation from Michigan into the Wisconsin Territory in 1836, the new territorial government began to create county governments in the settled areas and to draw the lines of the division of Brown County that would later become Manitowoc. In 1838 the territorial legislature officially separated Manitowoc County from Brown County and authorized the election of county officers with the power to levy taxes. In the newly created

*Benjamin Jones—one of Wisconsin's earliest settlers—is sometimes called the Father of Manitowoc. He arrived in 1837 to view his most recent acquisitions of land near the mouth of the Manitowoc River. Over the years Jones became very involved in the town of Manitowoc and held the office of county commissioner in 1841. Courtesy, Manitowoc County Historical Society*

*The lumber industry was one of the first to gain momentum as more and more settlers arrived in Manitowoc County. Early entrepreneurs soon realized the potential of lumbering and began to create wood products such as shingles. Manufacture of other wood items including clothespins, chairs, pails, and tubs soon followed. The horses in this photo are about to transport a large load of shingles that were produced at the mill in the background. Courtesy, State Historical Society of Wisconsin*

Manitowoc County, the first local elections were held in the various settlements for county commissioners in March 1839. (Court sessions for Manitowoc were still conducted in Green Bay to the northwest.)

At the first elections, the men from Manitowoc Rapids won out over the candidates from Manitowoc itself, with two of the Conroe brothers, Horace and John G. (with J. Rigby), elected as the first three commissioners. Another Conroe brother, Jacob, was elected county collector (treasurer) to bring in the first tax revenues. In the second election, held two years later, the results were reversed and Benjamin Jones and J.L. Edwards from Manitowoc took office.

This back-and-forth contest for dominance in both county government and in economic matters continued between Manitowoc Rapids and Manitowoc for another 14 years. The settlement at Manitowoc Rapids remained the designated county seat until 1853, when the site was changed to Manitowoc. These urban rivalries, even between tiny settlements, marked much of town entrepreneurship across the American Midwest during the 1830s and 1840s. The competition spurred civic leaders into focusing on ideas that would attract settlers, provide more jobs, and even develop a sense of community. Growth was good for those who had invested in land and town boosterism was part of the American spirit.

One of the first duties of the newly elected county officers was to survey and mark out several roads between settlements which would then be cleared with the help of county funds. A tax of "five mills per dollar of property" was assessed and $250 allocated for the construction of the first two roads, one going north from Manitowoc to Two Rivers and one going west to Manitowoc Rapids. Others soon followed.

These roads greatly aided both trade and settlement because the thickness of the timber and the rapids on the rivers had made inland travel very difficult. At that time the value of taxable property in the new county had risen to more than $210,000.[3]

One compelling reason for the building of roads was so that settlers could properly file their land claims at the federal land office in Green Bay, 35 miles to the northwest. An early story from county lore tells of a settler named Burnham who arrived in the Neshoto area from Detroit in 1837, but did not bother to file an official claim to his land. When two young men from Manitowoc, who had walked up the beach to bring him news, were roughly treated by Burnham, they decided to teach the squatter a lesson. They walked on to Green Bay, and filed a claim to his land for which they paid only the standard $1.25 an acre. They then returned to Burnham's cabin, showed him their claim and charged him $2,000 to receive title to the land he had settled and improved.[4]

Further roads were soon cleared inland, including the "River Road" upstream as far as Thayer, the main road to Green Bay, and other routes to developing farming settlements. However, these so-called roads were actually no more than crude paths, wide enough for two horses to pass at best. The new road to Green Bay was neither graded nor bridged, which meant that travelers had to ford streams and rivers along the way. By 1840 settlers made the trip to Green Bay with greater frequency, even though the journey took four days by this rough road. Green Bay had the area's only courts (until statehood), the closest federal land office, and the only flour mills in the area.

*The abundance of fish in the county's rivers provided settlers with yet another prosperous industry. The area's first fishery (established in Two Rivers in 1837) and others that soon followed were quite profitable. A large sturgeon caught at Two Rivers was recorded in this turn-of-the-century photograph. As one historian tells it, a fisherman, out fishing with his mates in the dark, was pulling in his catch by means of a rope tied to its tail. Not realizing the fish's size, the fisherman lost his grip, causing the sturgeon to fall and tear the net which was full of fish. The men lost their other fish, but eventually landed the great sturgeon. Courtesy, Wisconsin Maritime Museum*

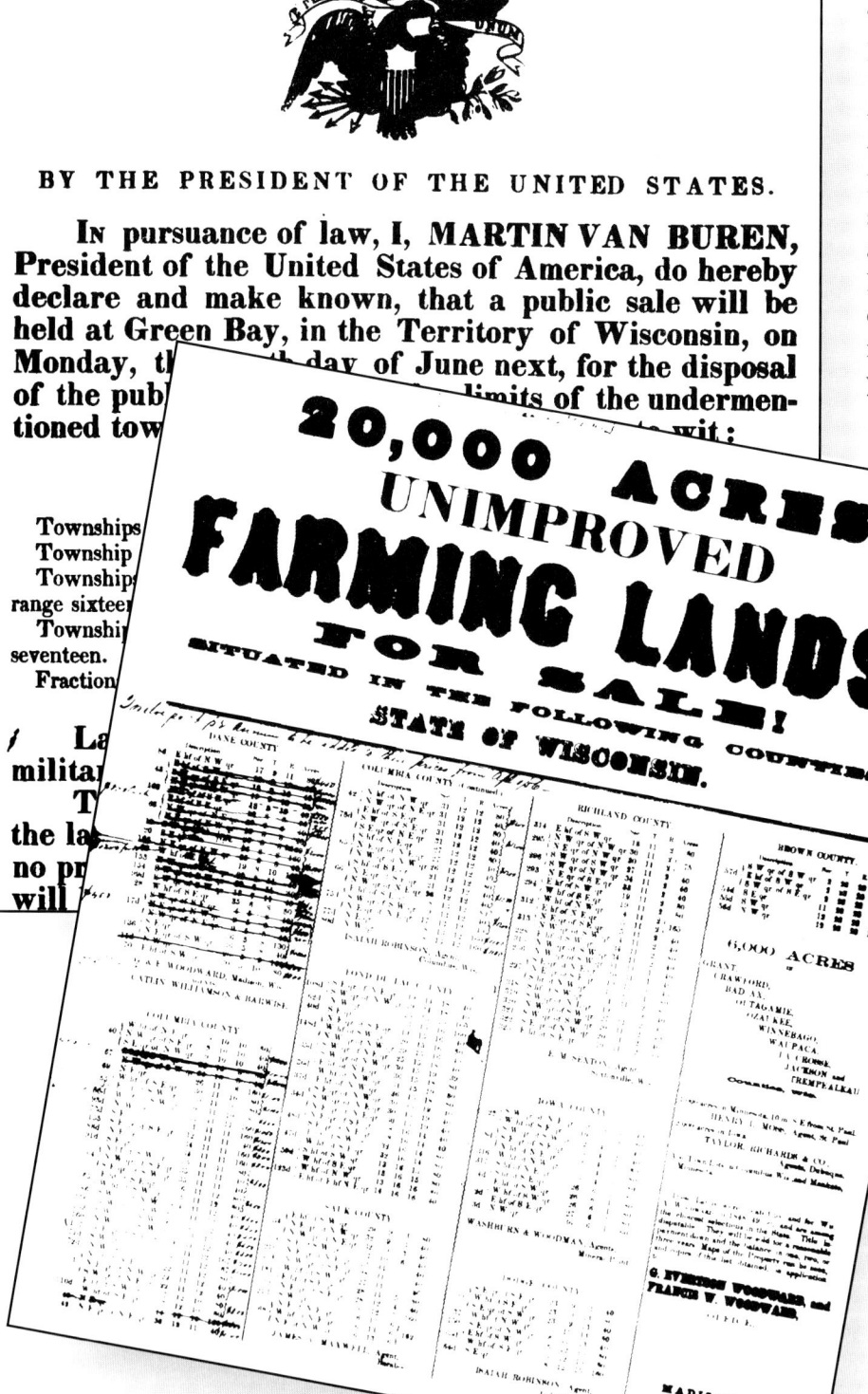

BY THE PRESIDENT OF THE UNITED STATES.

In pursuance of law, I, MARTIN VAN BUREN, President of the United States of America, do hereby declare and make known, that a public sale will be held at Green Bay, in the Territory of Wisconsin, on Monday, th⸍⸍⸍⸍ day of June next, for the disposal of the publ⸍⸍⸍⸍⸍⸍ limits of the undermentioned tow⸍⸍⸍⸍⸍⸍⸍⸍⸍ wit:

Townships
Township
Township
range sixteen
Townshi
seventeen.
Fraction

L⸍
milita
T
the la
no p
will

20,000 ACRES UNIMPROVED FARMING LANDS! SITUATED IN THE FOLLOWING COUNTIES, STATE OF WISCONSIN.

*ABOVE: When a new land office opened in Green Bay in 1834, land purchases began in earnest. Announcements like this one (top), issued in 1838, announced such public sales. Just 10 years later, a notice of 20,000 acres (above) shows that farming land was still abundant and parcels were being divided up by counties throughout the state. Courtesy, State Historical Society of Wisconsin*

Travel to the south was more difficult overland than to Green Bay. The first through road to Sheboygan, however, was not completed until 1843, and lake passage remained the preferred mode of transportation to both Milwaukee and Chicago. Prior to 1840 only a couple of lake schooners, primarily the *Milwaukee* and *Liberty*, made regular stops at Manitowoc or Two Rivers. The great era of shipping and the arrival of the first lake steamers was still several years away.

### Communication Patterns

Even with the regular visits of the lake schooners, the mail sent to the 240 residents of the county came overland. In 1838, when the county was officially established, the post office at Manitowoc Rapids received two deliveries a week, carried on foot on the Indian trail from Sheboygan to Green Bay. Two years later the increase in settlement and the volume of mail made it necessary for these biweekly deliveries to be carried on horseback.

Some of the commercial mail—directed to the lumbering and fishing concerns—was carried north on the lake schooners, which also carried bank drafts south to Milwaukee and Chicago. Trade had to be conducted on the basis of trust as the reissuance of paper money began and as bankers worked to recover from the earlier panic. Even copies of the area's first newspaper, the *Sentinel*, were brought north on shipboard from Milwaukee, bringing news from Wisconsin's territorial government in Madison as well as from around the country.

National news consisted of the growth of party and sectional conflicts in American politics. The Whig and Democratic parties traded election victories during the late 1830s and early 1840s, as issues such as the national bank, the future of slavery, and the growing quarrels with Mexico began to make headlines. Locally, the territorial government was busy erecting a new state capitol in Madison, and promising the development of more military roads to connect the territory's first four counties (Brown, Milwaukee, Dane, and Iowa).

Even though any news from the outside world was welcome, most of the settlers went many months with no word at all. Except in the small town settlements, most neighbors lived at least three miles apart and were virtually isolated during the worst of the winter weather. Land was difficult to clear and the early arrivals could only plant small garden plots on which they grew the dietary staple, potatoes, or a few oats. Unless they could receive provisions from more established farming areas, even bread and milk were in scarce supply during the early years.

Early settlers recalled that the winter of 1838-1839 was a particularly severe one, when most of the survivors lived on potatoes as small as nuts, venison, and some salted fish. What little wheat had been grown locally had become moldy. The rise of farming as a prosperous enterprise in the county did not occur for several more years. When the vast resources of lumber started to dwindle, immigrants moved into the county and began the process of clearing stumps and rocks from the rich farmland that lay beneath the one-time dense forests. They located in scattered settlements around the county, with perhaps only one or two families in each group at first.

With settlements so small and scattered, the opportunity to communicate even with one's neighbors was joyously welcomed. To this end, Benjamin Jones erected the county's first inn, which he called the National Hotel, in early 1838. A small roadhouse, the inn served the few transients who passed through, but mostly operated as a meeting place for area residents. The county's first recorded wedding, between E.L. Abbott and Maria Smith, took place later that year with Jones himself performing the ceremony as a justice of the peace, and then serving the wedding party and guests at his inn for the rest of the evening.

This early hostelry had only three rooms, two for overnight guests who were described as infrequent as "angel visits" and one that served as the bar and gathering room. Since it wasn't well supplied with beverages or even a variety of food, a local joke held that at Benjamin Jones' National Hotel all of the drinks—gin, brandy, or whiskey—came out of the same bottle![5]

Jones later recalled that his only real duties as justice of the peace were weddings, because there was, as yet, no crime in the county for him to deal with. As the population increased, both his wedding ceremonies and his duties as an innkeeper began to blossom.

By 1840 the Manitowoc area's 240 residents were still clinging to survival in small settlements on the river and the lakeshore. The census for that year listed only 11 horses and 80 head of cattle for the entire region. The few cleared acres of farmland yielded only several hundred bushels of wheat, keeping the settlers dependent on provisions being shipped in. Not until seven years later, in 1847, did the farms in Manitowoc County begin to produce sufficient foodstuffs to make the area self-reliant. The arrival of many more settlers in the 1840s and 1850s, including the first numbers of immigrants from Europe, changed the face of the county in the next decades.

*Postal carriers had the grueling task of bringing the mail on foot shortly after Fort Howard was established. Alexis Clermont, pictured here in 1893, traveled on a route through Manitowoc County when he delivered mail between Green Bay and Chicago from 1832 to 1836. In 1838, mail also came overland to Manitowoc County's residents. Courtesy, State Historical Society of Wisconsin*

# CHAPTER TWO

# *A Thriving Lake Port*

## 1840 – 1860

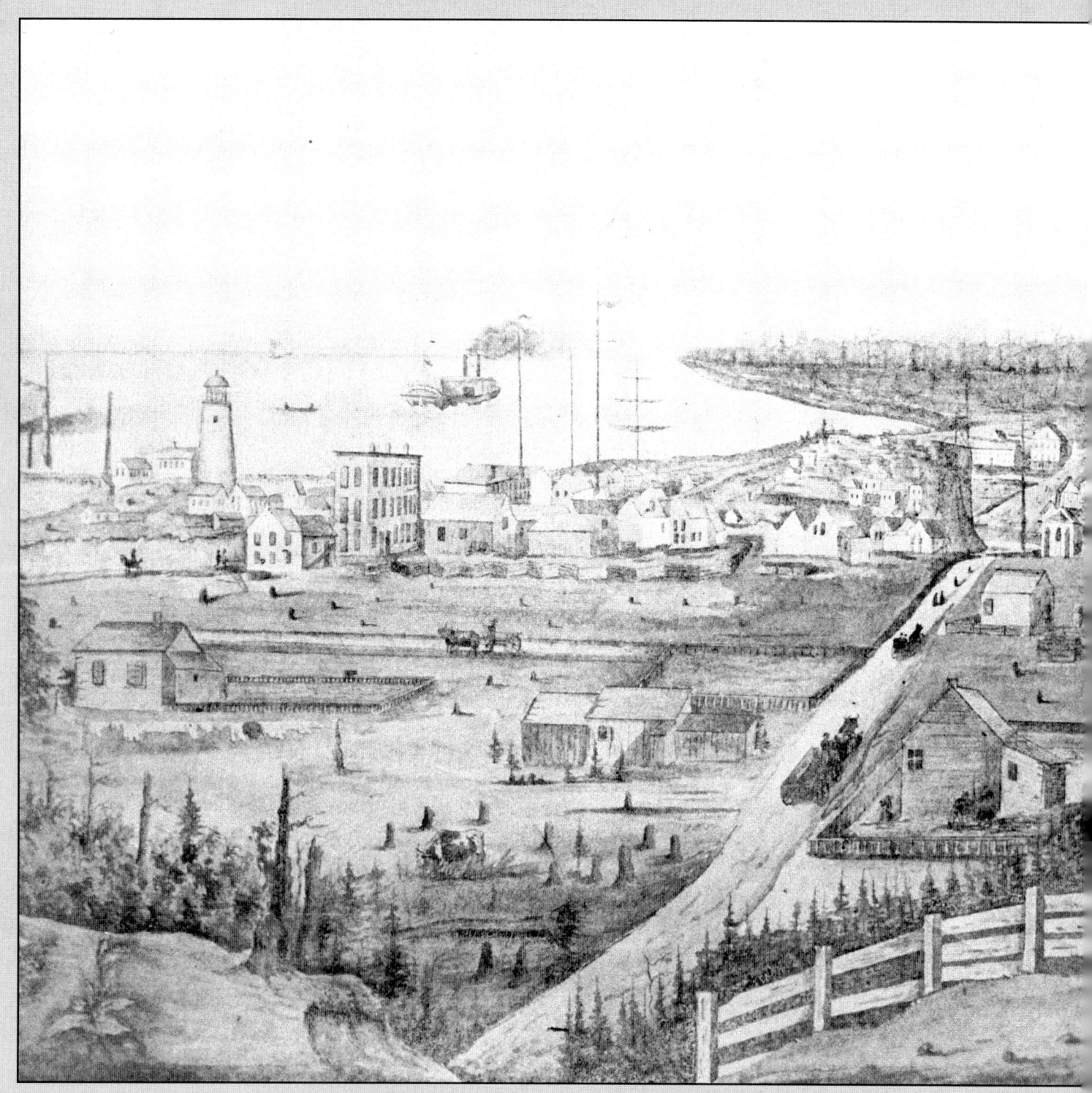

*Manitowoc in 1855, as seen in this early watercolor, was a growing melting pot, now home to German, Norwegian, and Irish immigrants. The area's first schools, churches, and businesses were becoming well established and the groundwork was being laid to begin what would become the area's successful shipbuilding industry. Courtesy, Rahr-West Art Museum*

*D*uring the 1840s and 1850s the few small settlements that were scattered around Manitowoc County began to attract both immigrants from Europe and settlers from the eastern United States, who came to build ships, buy farms, establish banks and newspapers, and to try to build roads and railroads. In the years before the Civil War, Manitowoc County witnessed the organization of many new businesses, a strong base of agricultural products, and two fine harbors for the new lake steamers to use in carrying settlers and shipping goods to ports across the Great Lakes.

## The Settlements Grow

From a population of only 240 in the census of 1840 when the county was just four years old, Manitowoc grew rapidly during the next decade. By 1850 the number had increased more than tenfold. While many of these new arrivals were of Yankee stock, others were European immigrants who also came west through the lakes via Buffalo and the Erie Canal.

Among the earliest settlers were Germans who were escaping the political troubles in central Europe during the 1840s. The first German settler, Frederick Borcherdt, arrived in 1841 and purchased a sawmill at Neshoto that he ran successfully for seven years. His letters home enticed other Germans to make the journey, including families with surnames such as Katzmeyer, Alsweide, Grube, Truettner, Meyer, and Schmitz. Coming from the various German states of Saxony, Bavaria, Holstein, and Prussia, these settlers bought land near Mishicot, Newton, and Two Rivers, where Borcherdt had relocated in 1848.

These early groups, which congregated in the eastern and southern parts of the county, were soon followed by Pomeranians, Mecklenburgers, and Hanoverians who settled in the growing town of Manitowoc or scattered westward into Centerville, Franklin, Maple Grove, Cato, and Rockland. In 1849 a pamphlet written by Gustav Richter, a recent immigrant, was circulated throughout Germany and brought many additional settlers who heeded the advertisement of cheap and fertile land in Wisconsin.[1]

Following the Germans, the Norwegians soon discovered the promise of county land. Between 1843 and 1848 the first three settlers from Norway, Soren and Allie Ballensted and Osuld Torrison, settled in Manitowoc Rapids where they initially became involved in lumber and trade. Others from Norway came shortly thereafter, finding homes and farms near Eaton and Liberty (originally called Buchanan). Families such as the Madsons, the Olsens, the Sulversons, and the Larsons drained the swampy areas and cleared stones from the fields to begin raising grain and potatoes in the rich black loam soil.

Part of the appeal of this area arose from its 100-acre lake, which soon became called Pigeon Lake and provided the water feed for a new sawmill, located on the 22-foot waterfall at its outlet. Because they were farther inland, the area's forests included more hardwoods such as maple and oak for lumbering, as well as the popular beech and pine woods.[2]

Next to arrive in the area were Irish settlers, who had come first to the East Coast of America following the onset of the tragic potato famine in the early 1840s. Towns such as Meeme, Maple Grove, Rockland, and Cato were settled by both Irish and English families with surnames such as Mulholland, Nagle, Doolan, and O'Shea. Small inns and breweries, as well as sawmills and stores, sprang up as the enterprising Irish took to business as well as farming.

The census of 1850 revealed the ethnic mix of the county, as a result of these various migrations during the previous decade. Of the county's 3,620 people, almost one half, or 1,378, were German; 246 were Norwegian, 175 Irish, 129 British, and 165 were Canadian born. Far fewer of the inhabitants had actually been born in Wisconsin (409), and only 1,118 were from other states (predominantly New York). The two largest towns were still Manitowoc

*RIGHT: The first German settler of Manitowoc County, Frederick Borcherdt established himself five miles northwest of Two Rivers at Neshoto in 1841. After purchasing a sawmill along the river, he ran a lumbering business for several years and befriended Chief Mexico, whose village was at the Rapids. Borcherdt's success in America did not go unnoticed—other German families followed suit and moved to the area after reading the letters Borcherdt sent back home. Borcherdt became a resident of Manitowoc Rapids and later of Manitowoc. Just six years before his death, he was appointed consul to Leghorn, Italy, by President Ulysses S. Grant. Courtesy, Manitowoc County Historical Society*

*ABOVE: Pamphlets produced by the State Board of Immigration of Wisconsin extolled the virtues of living in the state to European immigrants. The board, formed in 1867, published and distributed thousands of these booklets, which contained a wealth of information about Wisconsin including geology, location, native animals, manufacturers, wages, occupations, population, newspapers, churches, and schools. Courtesy, State Historical Society of Wisconsin*

Rapids, with 966 people, and Two Rivers, with 924. The settlement at Manitowoc itself, however, was gaining ground with 766, and would soon surpass the other two.[3]

One of the reasons for the ultimate predominance of Manitowoc was its location at the lakeshore where citizens began to work to develop wharves and dredge a better harbor to bring increased prosperity and to challenge the rival Two Rivers.

### Better Harbors for Trade

As the many new settlers arrived and as trade in agricultural commodities began to enhance the lumber and fishing industries, it became necessary to improve the harbor facilities. By the early 1840s many sailing ships, the lake schooners, sailed through the straits of Mackinac every week, braving the storms of Lake Michigan for the rich rewards of fish, fur, and lumber. It was essential, however, for any hopeful harbor to install some kind of navigational aid to beckon the ships to port.

The citizens of Manitowoc erected the first crude lighthouse just north of the harbor in 1840, made of brick and staffed by two local keepers. Even prior to the lighthouse, members of the Wisconsin delegation to Congress had begun to petition for federal monies to develop all of the territory's most promising lake ports. An early report, in 1837, asked Congress to survey the Manitowoc River. In response, the War Department (which ran the Army Corps of Engineers) sent a surveyor who reported back to Washington before Christmas.

This first survey of the harbor potential of Manitowoc made the claim for its great promise on the western shore. The Army Corps engineer announced: "I have the honor to transmit to you the map and report of the Manitowoc River, together with an estimate for its improvement." Declaring that the Manitowoc River was the next in size to the Milwaukee River on the west side of Lake Michigan, the report went on to describe the great safety offered by the bay formed by the river's mouth which would shelter boats in a well-protected harbor. The river mouth was "little obstructed by bars [of sand]…and there appears no deposit of any amount by the stream." The surveyor further outlined a series of recommended improvements, including piers and dredging a channel, at a projected cost of $82,979.44.[4]

The army's promising report, however, brought no federal funding and local citizens had to carry out what few improvements they could, building crude wharves and warehouses in the bay, as well as maintaining the small

lighthouse. Even with these primitive features, the many ship's captains passed the word among themselves about the safety of the Manitowoc dockage. One captain, whose ship *The Lady Elgin* would later be involved in a great disaster near Kenosha, praised Manitowoc, calling it "the only point on the west side of Lake Michigan where there was any real safety for vessels in a southwest gale."[5]

The legislature of the Wisconsin Territory added its appeal to the record, mentioning in 1843 that almost four million feet of lumber left the harbor each year, "taken on board vessels...at great risk and expense." The same year, frustrated by the lack of public support, the entrepreneurs Case and Clark erected their own bridge pier out into the lake and hired teenage boys to go out to the sandbars and scrape the sand down for ships to sail through.[6] This approach was difficult and dangerous at best.

After repeated petitions to Congress failed to bring the needed monies to dredge sandbars and build sturdy piers, in 1852 the citizens of Manitowoc

*ABOVE: In an effort to lure more settlers, the State Board of Immigration of Wisconsin created pocket maps like the one pictured to be inserted into the pamphlet titled, "The Emigrant's Friend." Courtesy, Milwaukee Public Library*

*FACING PAGE: Osuld Torrison, one of the first Norwegian settlers in Manitowoc Rapids, started a dry goods and general merchandise business in 1853. O. Torrison & Company, like many of its counterparts, experienced great success as the county's population grew in the mid- to late 1800s. Courtesy, Manitowoc County Historical Society*

*As the lumber industry began booming in Manitowoc County in the mid-1800s, schooners like this one hauled the goods to various ports along Lake Michigan's coast. Schooners, which usually had two or more masts and were designed to carry large cargoes, hauled the lumber whether it was in the form of cords of wood, railroad ties, or shingles. Courtesy, Wisconsin Maritime Museum*

decided to take matters into their own hands, pledging to raise $15,000 through a loan and a tax levy. Finally, Congress acted by allocating $8,000 (less than a tenth of the needed amount) in late 1852. The small sum, while providing hope of more federal aid to come, only went far enough to install a few cribs to hold off the sandbars and to dredge a 12-foot channel.[7] With debates in the federal Congress raging over the admission of Kansas and Nebraska to the Union and over the future of slavery, the repeated appeals for further assistance went unheeded until after the Civil War.

Even though their pleas for federal assistance went unheeded, the newly arriving settlers were resourceful enough to make most of the needed improvements themselves. This determination and enterprising spirit were particularly evident when it came to their development of their own schools and churches, which were soon sprinkled across the county, wherever small or large settlements arose.

### The Importance of Education

Just two years after the arrival of the first settlers came families with small children. By 1837 there was a sufficient population of children at the mouth of the Manitowoc River to establish the first school with a beginning enrollment of 12 students. The costs were paid by the parents themselves and supplemented by community support. Federal assistance to schools, which would turn over the

purchase money from section 16 in each town, did not go into effect until statehood in 1848.

The first teacher at this school, S.M. Peake, an educated citizen, virtually volunteered his time to teach at the school for the benefit of education. As one local writer noted of Manitowoc, "the interest shown in education in a community is, perhaps, the best test of the character of that community."[8] This first school was held in a sheltered corner of the Jones, Clark & Co. warehouse near the lakeshore at what was then the corner of North Sixth and Commercial streets. Through their location in this building, the young scholars were able to attend to their lessons as well as witness the growing commerce of their small settlement and celebrate the excitement of each new schooner's arrival, bringing provisions that were stored in the same warehouse.

The following spring a second school was opened in the county, at the Manitowoc Rapids County Courthouse. Many of the county's later leaders in business and politics, such as P.P. Smith, Giles and Erwin Hubbard, and Joseph La Counte, remembered being taught in these first two schools.

By 1844, with a growing population, the county board of commissioners set up three school districts, including these first two schools, plus Two Rivers, with elections to be held for officers to supervise instruction and the collection of funds for a school building in each area. District Number One, in

Manitowoc, raised $350 by 1848 to build a two-story frame school on North Seventh Street, which was also used for civic meetings and town functions.

The growth of schools was so substantial that by 1849, four more districts had been created across the county and seven schools were in full operation for an average of seven months each year. That same year all of the county's teachers met with State Superintendent of Public Instruction Eleazar Root at the village of Rapids to hear about the proposal for teacher training institutes and the plans for further state assistance to education following Wisconsin's admission to statehood in May 1848.[9] Following this meeting, a county-wide education organization was established to study the idea of introducing a "graded" plan for county schools to replace the one-room, no-grade-level distinctions under which they had been operating.

By 1850 there were nine more schools established in towns across the county, growing out of the demand for education from the great numbers of immigrants. In 1851 fully 633 out of the county's total 769 children were in attendance—at least part of the year—in a local school. The promised aid from the federal government, distributed through the state, had also increased to more than $560 that year.[10] The agreed-upon salary for teachers was among the state's highest at approximately $22 per month for male teachers and $15 for females, plus board if necessary.[11]

In addition to the public schools growing throughout the county, the many new immigrants began to establish their own parochial schools, both Catholic and Lutheran. In 1849, at the German settlements of Kossuth and Mishicot, the German Lutheran congregations set up their own classrooms in the first churches. In Manitowoc itself, the Reverend Hoyt of St. James Episcopal Church opened a small school for the children of parishioners. Irish settlers in Meeme and elsewhere similarly responded to the need to educate their children and founded parish schools during the first year after their arrival.

Manitowoc's great interest in education was evidenced both by the growth of its teachers' association, which continued to meet yearly to study ways to improve the schools, and by the sheer growth of its schools themselves. By 1860 the county had established 86 school districts, educating more than half of its 7,887 children for at least six months of the year. While the attendance statistics may appear to be low, it must be remembered that older children often took the spring and fall months off for planting and harvesting, and younger children stayed home in the most bitter weather of the winter.

## The Growth of Churches

Along with supporting the general growth of schools, the county witnessed the creation of a diversity of churches, each fashioned according to the settlers' particular spiritual creeds and immigrant traditions. Among the earliest of these church groups were the Methodists, who began holding services in

Manitowoc in 1843, in the upper story of the same Jones warehouse where the school classes were held (and moved in winter to a private home). Services were conducted by a circuit-riding minister, who also served settlements in Sheboygan County. By 1849 the Methodists in the county had three organized congregations (at Manitowoc, the Rapids, and at Two Rivers) and were able to support one full-time minister, the Reverend David Lewis, although they still met in either schoolrooms, homes, or a village hall. Finally, during the 1850s, with the growing number of Germans involved in Methodism, many of the settlements were able to erect the area's first permanent churches, at Manitowoc (St. Paul's), Two Rivers, Rapids, Maple Grove, and Newton.

*A leader in business and politics in Manitowoc County, Perry P. Smith arrived in Manitowoc in 1837 when he was just 15 years old. He traveled from New York on a schooner with his brother-in-law Benjamin Jones, who had purchased land in Manitowoc. Smith later built a mill, and in 1846 opened Manitowoc's first store with a few groceries and merchandise. Like other early settlers, he became a successful merchant as the city and its surrounding towns grew. Courtesy, Manitowoc County Historical Society*

Because of the many converts to Methodism among both the German and Norwegian populations, in 1860 there was only one Methodist church on the circuit with services in English. All of the Methodist parishioners, however, greatly benefited from the establishment in 1847 of Lawrence College in nearby Appleton, a Methodist school from which they would draw ministers, who were either faculty or young graduates.[12]

Older than the Methodist, but less prolific in evangelical efforts, the Episcopal congregation at Manitowoc was sustained as early as 1839 by the efforts of Bishop Jackson Kemper, who also established the mission outpost west of Milwaukee, called Nashotah House. Through Kemper, the new congregation at St. James Church in Manitowoc met the Swedish minister,

*The educational system in Manitowoc County was evolving by the late 1840s with the establishment of school districts and talk of "graded" schools, which would replace the system of having no set grade levels for students. Reedsville's school, as seen in this early photo, was one of many throughout the county that changed to the graded system. By 1860 some 86 districts handled the county's population of nearly 4,000 students. Courtesy, Manitowoc County Historical Society*

*As Methodist churches became established in Manitowoc County during the 1850s, they had the added benefit of recruiting ministers from Lawrence College, a Methodist school in Appleton. The college later became Lawrence University, when it merged with Milwaukee-Downer College in 1964. The Main Hall, as seen in the background of this early illustration, was completed in 1854, and was the college's only building until 1899. Courtesy, Lawrence University, Appleton*

Gustavus Unonius, a graduate of the Nashotah mission, who had settled on Pine Lake near Nashotah. In 1848 Unonius accepted the call from the new St. James congregation and came to Manitowoc to work with church leaders A.H. Edwards, Lemuel House, and Aiden Clark, early entrepreneurs in the area, to build the community's first church.

St. Paul's Church, begun in 1851 with a dedication by Bishop Kemper, was made possible by donations from eastern congregations. The building, located at the corner of North Ninth and Chicago streets in Manitowoc, could hold 250 people and had its own font, communion set, and liturgy, also from eastern donors. As with the Methodists, many ministers came to serve the growing church and to preach to newly developing congregations at the Rapids and Two Rivers.

Presbyterians and Congregationalists also organized new churches during the years of growing immigration after 1848. Through their Plan of Union, these two denominations had agreed to cooperate, rather than compete, in setting up churches across the Midwest. Beginning in 1851, they established churches at the Rapids, Two Rivers, and Manitowoc, with the first church building, called "the Tabernacle," erected in Manitowoc in 1855. Outlying congregations like those at Eaton and Cato were served by a circuit pastor in the early years.

Along with these denominations, the immigrant groups brought their own distinctive church forms. The German Lutherans formed a congregation at Newton in 1851, soon followed by others in Manitowoc (St. John's), Two Rivers, Centerville, Reedsville, Larrabee, Rosecrans, Eaton, Rube, Collins, and Mishicot. Norwegian Lutherans at Gjerpen organized a congregation in 1850, with churches at both Liberty and Eaton being formed soon thereafter. For both of these Lutheran groups, the ministers were men who often came directly from Europe to serve the immigrants' spiritual needs in America, and (like Unonius) were honored for their missionary efforts.

Other groups, such as the German Reformed and the Evangelical Association, also began services in the county during the 1850s, serving the newly arrived German immigrants. Baptists, too, began services among the many Welsh immigrants beginning at School Hill in 1856.

Many of the Irish and German immigrants were Catholic, and in 1850 the diocese of Green Bay sent the first priest to the area to establish parishes at French Creek, Two Rivers, Cooperstown, Meeme, Maple Grove, and the Rapids, where the first church was erected in 1852. Two years later the church of St. Boniface, capable of seating 700 people, was completed on Marshall Street in Manitowoc, with its own five-acre burial site and parsonage. St. Luke's Parish in Two Rivers, through the assistance of Bishop John Henni of Milwaukee, erected a church to serve its French Canadian, Irish, and German parishioners.

Also during the early 1850s a number of other Catholic churches—St. James' at Cooperstown and St. Anne's at Francis Creek, St. Joseph's at Kellnersville, St. Wenceslaus at Green Street, and St. Isidore's at Osman—were built. Each of these Catholic parishes, as with the Protestant congregations, reflected the specific language and customs of the immigrant settlers, so that on any given Sunday during the 1850s, voices were raised at churches across the county in English, Gaelic, German, Norwegian, Welsh, and a variety of other languages.[13]

*BOTTOM RIGHT: Sent to what was then known as the Northwest Territories, Bishop Jackson Kemper was given the task of providing midwestern settlers with Episcopal priests, churches, and a diocese. As a missionary bishop, Kemper established the mission outpost Nashotah House, just west of Milwaukee, and in the late 1830s he initiated efforts to begin an Episcopal congregation at Manitowoc. In 1851 he attended a dedication ceremony for St. Paul's Church in Manitowoc. Kemper, known as the first Episcopal bishop of Wisconsin, died in 1870. Courtesy, State Historical Society of Wisconsin*

*BOTTOM LEFT: Bishop Kemper attended the dedication of St. Paul's Church in Manitowoc, which was built and furnished with the help of donations from other congregations. Located on the corner of Chicago and North Ninth streets, St. Paul's could conduct a mass for as many as 250 people. Courtesy, Manitowoc Public Library*

FAR LEFT: Created of wood from the trees surrounding Two Rivers, St. Luke's Catholic Church was one of several churches constructed in the 1850s in Manitowoc County. This 1890 photo shows the original church and the addition that was built in 1863. In later years a portion of the original building was moved across the street and a new church for St. Luke's parishioners was completed in 1892. Courtesy, St. Luke's Parish, Two Rivers, Wisconsin

ABOVE: Manitowoc County's first Catholic church was erected in 1852 in Manitowoc Rapids. Other churches were built soon thereafter including Manitowoc's St. Boniface, which was completed in 1854. Courtesy, Manitowoc County Historical Society

## The Establishment of St. Nazianz

One of the most unique parishes in the county, at St. Nazianz, was the result of a unified movement of 114 parishioners from Baden, Germany, to the site in Wisconsin, led by the Reverend Ambrose Oschwald. His followers were united in their religious fervor and established a communalistic approach to the settlement of the 3,840 acres of land they purchased for $3.50 an acre in the town of Eaton in 1854. Working together, they cleared many acres for planting and erected their church, St. Gregory's, within a few months of their arrival.

Because of their belief that the single men and women in their congregation had to live separately, they later added both a convent and a Franciscan monastery to the site. The land in the settlement was owned and farmed in common, with all efforts directed by Father Oschwald himself. Oschwald also designed many of the settlement's buildings, including the pink convent, and the many "stations" of sacred scenes on boxes throughout the church grounds.

The community had plans to be completely independent of the outside world and so began to grow its own food, produce its own tools, and make its own clothing. Oschwald also took charge of the communal treasury until his death two decades later, at which time the harmony of the communalistic approach was threatened by dissension. Most of the problems stemmed from the fact that Oschwald had owned the property in his own name and then willed it to the community as a whole.

After his death, those who remained incorporated as the Roman Catholic Religious Society and operated under the governance of a board of trustees. Those who did not want to live under the new governance plan moved to other, independent farms across the county and in Sheboygan County, while those who remained continued their daily patterns and still wore the traditional German peasant outfits in their work.[14]

## Social Problems, Epidemic Diseases, and Community Service

For all of the county's diverse congregations, a sense of service and mission became of great importance as the county witnessed the growing problems of poverty and epidemic diseases during the 1850s. As early as 1839, there was a notation that some of the county funds were expended not just to build roads and pay commissioners, but also to help the poor. Ten years later, in 1849, the county's first jail was erected of wood in Manitowoc Rapids, which had to be remodeled after one year because it was deemed insecure. Spikes were added, as well as bars on the windows and a door of sheet iron.[15]

As the two ports where lake schooners brought goods from Milwaukee, both Manitowoc and Two Rivers were more susceptible to the arrival of epidemics. In 1850 the two lakefront settlements were visited by the dreaded cholera, resulting in 22 deaths in Manitowoc alone, including two small children in one family. At the settlement in Two Rivers, 12 of the victims were Indians who had been visiting the settlement for a summer celebration. An estimated 50 of the 300 settlers there were dead within the next two weeks.

The disaster at Two Rivers in August was of such enormous proportions that mill owner Hezikiah Smith provided the money to evacuate many of his workers to Sheboygan until the scare died down. When the ship arrived, there was a stampede by those who were in a panic to leave before the disease struck them. Smith had to place several ads in the Sheboygan newspapers, assuring his workers that the disease had subsided before they would agree to return. Some observers believed that Two Rivers never fully recovered from the disaster and its loss of population, while Manitowoc, just to the south, began to thrive even with the setback of disease.

*FACING PAGE, RIGHT: St. Joseph Parish was one of many Catholic churches that evolved during the 1850s throughout Manitowoc County. In the community of Greenstreet, early settlers from Bohemia gathered their resources to begin building a church. By 1860 they had completed the structure and dedicated it to St. Wenceslaus. Unfortunately, legal matters with the diocese were misunderstood by the members of St. Wenceslaus. The congregation rejected requests that the deed of the property and church be turned over to the diocese, because church members believed they had the right to sole ownership. After the second rejection, the bishop of the northeastern section of Wisconsin reestablished the parish at Kellnersville. In 1870 St. Joseph Parish was blessed and dedicated, and St. Wenceslaus was declared a mission of the parish. Courtesy, St. Joseph Parish, Kellnersville*

*ABOVE: In 1854 the Reverend Ambrose Oschwald, disenchanted with the changing economic and religious environment in Germany, arrived in Wisconsin to begin the colony of St. Nazianz. When Oschwald left Germany, about 114 parishioners followed him— eventually settling in the town of Eaton on a 3,840-acre site that Oschwald had purchased. The colony's dogma was to become independent of the outside world while also favoring a simple yet strong religious existence. Upon Oschwald's death in 1873, confusion over the property ownership was resolved after the community incorporated as the Roman Catholic Religious Society. Courtesy, St. Nazianz Historical Society*

With the second onslaught of cholera coming to both villages just four years later, in 1854, the citizens were somewhat more prepared and Manitowoc even had a physician, a Dr. Preston, who helped to tend the sick. This second epidemic also spread inland from the ports, reaching as far as Kossuth. As a result of the cholera, Manitowoc created its first board of health, although the commissioners, like the rest of America, weren't precisely certain what caused the disease or how to prevent its recurrence. It was several more years before the discovery that cholera germs bred in sewage and untreated water, but the county miraculously escaped the epidemics that raged through midwestern cities during the 1860s and 1870s.[16]

Caring for children orphaned by the epidemics and helping to assist families in need, or individuals who had fallen on hard times, various churches and community groups began to provide organized social service, a vital element in community welfare. Several of the county's earliest ministers had considered it a part of their calling to try to preach to the Stockbridge and Brothertown Indians on reservations to the northwest and north. When the need arose, food and blankets were also collected by settlers to aid the native peoples, whose own resources had become severely depleted by displacement.

Other efforts conducted by local congregations included assisting poor families with supplies, providing lodging for a short time for the jobless, and offering charitable medical care by the area's two physicians. In addition, both the Manitowoc Bible Society and the County Sunday School Association stood ready to supply Bibles and assistance to the more than 40 Sunday

schools in operation by 1861. Fraternal organizations, such as the Oddfellows (organized in 1851), the Good Templars (1855), the Masons (1856), and the Sons of Hermann, a German Lodge (1856), provided occasional services to local residents as well as a social outlet for their members.

With the good works of church groups and with the social fraternizing of the lodge members, citizens of the county recovered from the epidemic scares. Once the worst was over, residents could again settle into their many enterprises that brought productive wealth, employment opportunities, and many new settlers into the area in the decade before the Civil War.

## Forming New Businesses

Throughout the first several decades of the country's growth, until the forests were depleted, lumbering remained its most profitable export. The number of sawmills at advantageous spots on the various rivers continued to multiply as millions of board feet of lumber were shipped out each year. In 1854 alone, for example, the newly developing area of Neshoto exported more than 3.5 million feet of lumber, plus 50,000 feet of lath, 400,000 feet of pickets, 24,000 railroad ties, and 700,000 shingles.[17]

Even though lumbering and fishing were the dominant enterprises at this time, other smaller industries and businesses began to open their doors during the 1850s as the county's population expanded. The sawmills in Rapids, Two Rivers, and in Manitowoc itself were soon producing wood that could be reshaped into finished goods for export. In 1856 William M. Honey arrived in Two Rivers from his native Massachusetts and established the New

England Manufacturing Company, which began to produce high-quality wooden chairs for sale to the many new settlers across the county, as well as to the growing population in Milwaukee and Chicago.

That same year a new tub and pail factory, a wooden sash and door factory, and a wagon manufacturer were also established, all making profitable use of the ready supply of wood from the nearby sawmills. The large sawmill at Two Rivers, which supplied all of these concerns, had originally been set up with investment monies from Judge George Lawe and John P. Arndt from Green

ABOVE: Manitowoc County's early settlers thrived on the abundant trees and fish in the area by bringing to life the lumber and fishing industries. Both ventures contributed to the county's steady growth in the early to mid-1800s. The Two Rivers sawmill, as seen in this 1858 photo, was one of several in the county that not only exported the lumber, but also manufactured lumber for finished products such as chairs, scows, and doors. Courtesy, Wisconsin Maritime Museum

RIGHT: Manitowoc County's timber, particularly bark from hemlock and tamarack trees, was profitable for tanneries in the area. The Wisconsin Leather Company, founded in 1851 by Cyrus Whitcomb, used the tannic acid from the bark to tan leather hides shipped from Chicago and Milwaukee. The tanning industry continued in this area until about 1887, when the bark supplies waned and the expense of transporting the raw materials became too great. Courtesy, Manitowoc County Historical Society

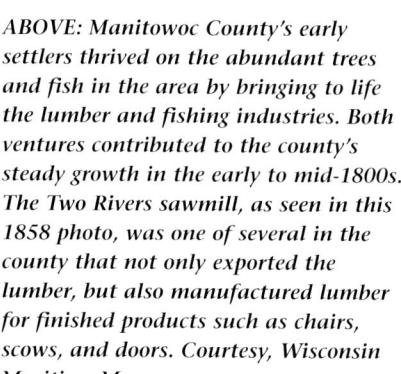

Bay, at the same time that speculators Daniel Wells, Jr., of Milwaukee and Morgan Martin of Green Bay had begun to buy up land in the area, just as they had farther south in Milwaukee. In fact, it was Martin who provided the financial backing for Solomon Juneau, the successful French fur trader, to develop the village of Juneautown, which became the east side of the city of Milwaukee.[18]

The wood from sawmills was not only used for chairs, scows, and doors, but also to construct the first ship built in Manitowoc, a city that would later become world famous for its shipbuilding industry. In 1847 Captain Joseph Edwards, father of one of the county's earliest settlers, decided to build his own ship right near the harbor's mouth. His 60-ton craft, christened *The Citizen*, was made of lumber sawn upriver at Conroe's mill in Rapids, as well as spikes, nails, anchor, ropes, and other metal parts that were imported from Chicago. Edwards' entire cost was only $3,000.

When completed, *The Citizen* could carry 150,000 board feet of lumber from Manitowoc to Lake Michigan ports, a very profitable enterprise. Edwards later sold the ship to investors from Chicago; it went down in a fierce Lake Michigan storm in 1857 off the eastern shore.

With all of these enterprises involving wooden products and with virtually all of the settlements' buildings made of wood, one essential skill was that of firefighting. As early as the 1840s the settled villages organized volunteer fire brigades that practiced so that they would know exactly what to do in case of fire. When the call came, the volunteers would form a line from the river to the building ablaze, each bringing at least two empty pails. Their ability to

fill and pass the pails of water along was successful in extinguishing several fires. Later, when horse-drawn fire wagons superseded this human-chain method, the success rate was even better.[19]

Another industry dependent on the county's rich supply of lumber, but not a producer of wooden wares, were the tanneries. As in Milwaukee to the south, the area near Two Rivers was full of tamarack trees, the bark from which produced tannin, an acid essential in tanning hides. During the winter of 1851 Cyrus Whitcomb arrived in Two Rivers and began to build a tannery that soon became known as the Wisconsin Leather Company. Together with several investors, Whitcomb opened the tannery in a brick structure on the east bank of the Mishicot River.

Soon the business had grown sufficiently for Whitcomb to hire 100 workers and to buy up about 1,200 acres of land full of tamarack trees. Hides were brought to the site via ships from Milwaukee and Chicago and turned into leather for harnesses, boot soles, and shoes. During the shipping season, these finished goods were carried south to the same cities for resale, but during winter, the tannery hired teams of oxen to pull them in wagonloads overland, a weeklong round trip at the very least.[20]

With so many workers coming to labor in the new tannery, Whitcomb had seven large houses constructed as living space, plus one boarding house for 40 men. He also helped to sponsor a small school for workers' children and operated a provisions store near the tannery. Following the success of this first enterprise, other tanneries soon followed, all of which prospered for several decades until the supply of tanning bark was completely exhausted during the 1880s.[21]

During the late 1840s several stores opened for business in Manitowoc to which settlers from nearby Rapids and Two Rivers could come for their hardware, tools, and other provisions. One of the most notable of these was George Dusold's General Store, established in 1845, which carried supplies as varied as shoes, yard goods, kerosene, nails, and food. The rival store, in Smith's warehouse, also boasted its own tailor shop operated by Manitowoc's first Norwegian settler, Christian Andrewson, in partnership with his son-in-law, one of the area's first pioneers, Perry P. Smith.[22]

In 1859 a large store on York Street was built by the Robinson brothers, followed by a retail establishment called the Platt and Vilas Store at the corner of Seventh and Commercial streets. Many others followed, both in Manitowoc and Two Rivers, as the port settlements became the emporia for

*As the farming industry grew in the county, so did the establishment of gristmills. Gristmills, such as Rock Mill, shown here in the late 1800s, operated on water power from a nearby river. Turbine water wheels moved the stone grinding machinery, which would grind grain into flour or grist. The flour was fed into sacks and distributed to Indians and farmers in the early years and later to merchants as communities expanded. Rock Mill, which is located near Maribel, is one of the oldest existing structures in Manitowoc County. Courtesy, Manitowoc County Historical Society*

*ABOVE: The wooded land of the county soon became a haven for successful farmers as more trees were cleared and soil was tended for crops. The Manitowoc Agricultural Society, established in 1856, provided a medium for farmers to exhibit their produce. Cattle fairs, like this one in Reedsville held in 1906, gave farmers the opportunity to exhibit their cattle and equipment. Courtesy, Manitowoc County Historical Society*

*RIGHT: An offshoot of the farming industry that would later bring Wisconsin its famous slogan, "America's Dairyland," was dairy farming. Several Manitowoc County cheese factories were exhibiting their products at the early exhibitions and fairs. Farmers in this early 1900s photo prepare to bring milk to the local cheese factory. Courtesy, Manitowoc County Historical Society*

trade and products needed by the hundreds of newly arriving immigrants.[23]

As European immigrants continued to clear more land, the area soon produced some thriving farms. In addition to the small gardens of the first settlers, with their crops of a few vegetables, potatoes, and a small patch of oats, wheat became a profitable crop during the 1850s. Between 1849 and 1855 the number of bushels of wheat grown in the county increased from 214 to 38,415. By 1860 the yield had grown to more than 135,000 bushels, forming a part of the remarkable production of the crop that would make Wisconsin the leading wheat-producing state in the union by 1865.[24]

Livestock, too, was introduced into county farms during the 1850s and the

Manitowoc Agricultural Society was formed in 1856 to stage exhibitions of the county's produce. In the 1859 cattle show and fair, prizes were offered for the best cattle, agricultural products, and farm equipment. Several local cheese factories, displaying their varieties of dairy products, were also in evidence at the fairs, as were the products of the growing number of local breweries, among them the W. Rahr Brewery (begun in 1848) and the Pautz Brewery (begun in 1849). These fairs soon became popular yearly events, held on the fairgrounds south of the Manitowoc River, near what became Washington Park.

Other festivals, held in the same location, featured speakers on patriotic themes (at Washington's birthday), and fireworks and a picnic on the Fourth of July, beginning as early as 1852. The fairgrounds became a favorite gathering spot for settlers who could come on horseback or by oxcart to spend a day or two in town, meeting neighbors and sharing news. The growing number of inns and taverns welcomed the arrival of people from around the county at such events, as did the storekeepers who enjoyed a substantial increase in sales during fairs and festivals.

### The Need for Banks

To service these developing enterprises, the county needed its own banks and the new State of Wisconsin, recognizing that need, lifted its ban on banking early in 1850. The first attempt at carrying on any of the functions of a bank occurred in 1853, when a local notary public established a depository in Manitowoc as part of his land business, and several other such businesses followed suit. However, the Panic of 1857 wiped them all out.

The following year, 1858, several small banks opened their doors, including the Lake Shore Bank, which had resources the next year of more than $61,000, and the Bank of Manitowoc, with a capital of $100,000. There were other smaller financial institutions as well, which failed in the unsteady economic climate in Wisconsin after the beginning of the Civil War. The Lake Shore and the Bank of Manitowoc, however, while suspending business temporarily, were able to survive the hard times and remain open.[25]

While the currency printed by sound banks proved an asset to the community, paper money was still a risky commodity before the Civil War. Even before the county's legal banks opened their doors, Manitowoc had to endure the danger of counterfeit currency, printed by a newspaper printer who had moved to Cato in 1845. After printing a certain number of fake bills, the felon packed them up in bundles and traveled to various towns to put them into circulation. On one of his trips, he was apprehended, tried, and jailed, after which his press was shut down permanently.[26]

### Courthouses, Roads, and Railroads

Following the admission of Wisconsin to the union on May 29, 1848, the legislature completed the establishment of Manitowoc as a full county, with its own courts and complete taxing powers. Once the county seat was transferred to Manitowoc in 1853, there were many discussions about the location and design of the new county buildings. Finally, the choice of John Meyer as architect resulted in the construction of the new county office and courthouse at a cost of $10,000.

During the early 1850s several local men were admitted to the state bar in front of Judge Alexander Stow, who had opened the first term of a local court in Manitowoc, beginning in 1848. The county citizens then elected one of the men, J.H.W. Colby, as the county's first circuit judge. In the same election, E.H. Ellis was chosen as district attorney, but these judicial offices experienced a high turnover with two deaths in the first four years. Colby, a native of Maine, died during the second cholera epidemic in 1854, as did two other young lawyers, who had subsequently served as judge or district

*The Manitowoc Savings Bank building, constructed in 1856, was one of two banks in the area that weathered the changing financial environment after the start of the Civil War. Many smaller banks, which opened about the same time, weren't so fortunate. Courtesy, Manitowoc Public Library*

attorney, Ezekial Ricker, age 33, and James L. Kyle, age 28.[27]

Under Colby's successor, Judge Gorsline, the county courts conducted the first murder trial, hearing the case of a newly arrived immigrant who was accused of killing the bartender at the Franklin Hotel after a fight broke out. Due to the lack of sober witnesses, the trial ended in an acquittal and the young German went free to begin a new life.[28]

With the judicial circuit well in operation and with the many county businesses growing rapidly, the 1850s witnessed a renewed push for better roads and transportation. The first attempts at improvement involved investors in companies to

*William Rahr & Sons opened the Eagle Brewery in 1849 at a plant on Washington Street in Manitowoc. Nearly 30 years later the brewery was producing about 4,000 barrels a year. The brewery remained in business until 1920, just after Prohibition laws were enforced. Rahr's malting business, which began in 1878, continued after the brewery closed. Courtesy, Wisconsin Maritime Museum*

construct plank roads, such as those in the southern part of the state that had shown a profit from charging five cents per five miles of travel, except on Sunday. When government efforts failed to complete road linkages between Manitowoc and points south, several private companies were chartered by the state legislature to try to accomplish the same task.

In 1850 the Calumet Plank Road Company was established with $100,000 capital to construct a road, using half-logs with the flat (or plank) side up. The road was intended to lead west from Manitowoc all the way to the state military road between Green Bay and Fond du Lac (today's Highway 41). However, the private stock subscriptions did not bring in sufficient money to finish the project and five years later the county took over the company and completed the road. A second effort at private enterprise, the Neenah and Manitowoc Plankroad Company, attracted several large investors from Milwaukee to its stock subscription of $200,000. One of the local board members, Hiram McAllister, the county's first successful farmer, planned the route northwest from Manitowoc. However, only the section up to the McAllister farm was completed with the available funds until the county also assumed control of the company and completed construction in 1857.

There were other unsuccessful plank road companies, but each met with a

*Plank road companies experienced short-lived success between 1846 and the mid-1860s as the need for better roads grew. In Wisconsin alone, 135 plank road companies were chartered. Planks, which were usually eight feet long and several inches thick, were laid side by side with a fine layer of gravel spread over the top. At the height of their popularity in 1850 about 2,000 miles of "highway" had been laid and tolls were charged to use them. However, Manitowoc County didn't see too much profit, because the next phase of transportation—the railroad—was about to reach Wisconsin. Courtesy, State Historical Society of Wisconsin*

similar fate. The road-building era in Manitowoc County came too late to realize profits because by the 1850s another breakthrough in transportation, the railroad, was coming to Wisconsin. As with the plank roads, all of the earliest endeavors to build railroads in the county depended on private investors, and most were not initially successful. One of the most promising, the Chicago, Milwaukee, and Green Bay Railroad, was chartered in 1851. This company's line was to connect at Manitowoc with a second, that of the Manitowoc and Mississippi Railroad, which would have its western terminus at LaCrosse on the river.[29]

As 1853 began, the residents of Manitowoc were still waiting for the northern linkage from Milwaukee to be built and several attended meetings there to argue for the extension to be completed as soon as possible. However, much to their disappointment, similar investors from Fond du Lac and Oshkosh were also at the meetings and brought in more shareholders to persuade the company to build its northern line farther west, going up the western shore of Lake Winnebago, instead of linking due northward along the lake to Manitowoc.

Efforts to push the western rail line toward Menasha, however, continued with an estimated cost of $924,326 for this first phase toward the Mississippi. Stockholders hoped that foreign investors, particularly from Germany, would

*This 1898 building, located at the corner of South 10th and Washington in Manitowoc, was one of several structures designed by John Meyer, a well-known architect in the mid- to late 1800s. Meyer was hired to design the new county offices and courthouse after the county seat was moved from Manitowoc Rapids to Manitowoc. At a cost of $10,000, the new courthouse was completed in 1857 and the county offices in 1860. Courtesy, Manitowoc County Historical Society*

be attracted to the bonds and engaged an agent, Charles Klingholz, to travel to Europe to sell at least $260,000 there. However, concern over other setbacks slowed the enthusiasm of stockholders and building came to a halt for lack of capital. One discouraged investor wrote, "It is our honest conviction that the M & M railroad when completed to Menasha will not pay for the oil necessary to lubricate its car wheels."[30]

To add to the problems of these companies, the financial panic of 1857 drove bonds and stocks across the country perilously low, as fears of pending Civil War and problems with the southern cotton crop struck across the country.

Several investors from New York and Canada came to Manitowoc to consider purchasing the railroad company to Menasha, but disputes between residents of the two cities discouraged them, as did the rumor that Manitowoc stockholders, fed up with the Menasha and Neenah people, had decided to direct the tracks west to Appleton instead. Investors from Two Rivers, also dismayed at the lack of progress in Manitowoc, had formed their own railroad company, the Two Rivers and Green Bay Railroad, but it met with the same dismal fate. When the Civil War broke out in 1861, the county still had no railroad and the matter was not resolved for nearly a decade.[31]

### The First Newspapers

Staunchly behind the efforts of banks, plank road builders, and railroad companies, the local newspapers in Manitowoc provided the boosterism and optimistic reports about local progress that was typical of the mid-nineteenth century. Even though the Green Bay and Milwaukee papers had reached the county by the slow mail prior to 1850, there was interest in starting a local operation. In November 1850 the the *Manitowoc County Weekly Herald*, owned by Charles W. Fitch, put out its first issue. Fitch, a native of New Jersey, was only 31 years old when he moved to Manitowoc, having already purchased a used printing machine from the Milwaukee *Evening Wisconsin* paper, which arrived on the ship *Champion*.

This first paper began publication with the admission by its young editor

*Without the luxury of a telegraph, Manitowoc's citizens waited anxiously for news from Milwaukee's papers, which arrived every other day on the sidewheel steamer the* Comet. *When the news that Fort Sumter had been fired upon arrived on April 19, 1861, meetings were held and Company A, Fifth Wisconsin Volunteer Infantry, was formed. Just two months later Company A volunteers boarded the* Comet *and headed to Milwaukee. A train transported them to Camp Randall at Madison. Courtesy, Wisconsin Maritime Museum*

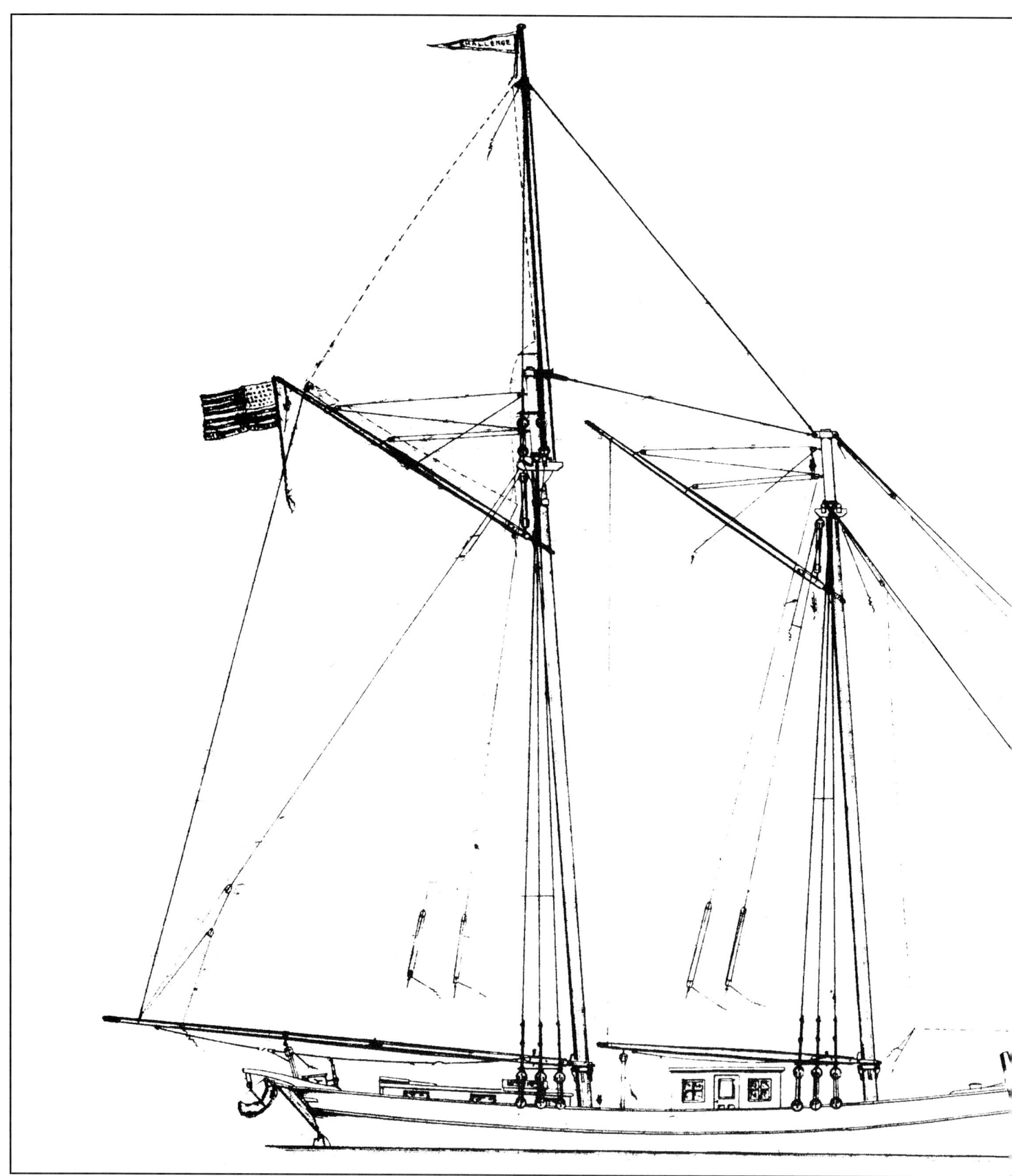

that, "When we decided to hazard the undertaking we had never set foot upon the soil of Manitowoc or seen an inhabitant of the county." Fitch announced that his paper would be "liberally Democratic" and would support the exclusion of slavery from the free states, a hot topic in national politics following the 1850 passage of the Fugitive Slave Law, which almost resulted in Wisconsin seceding from the union.[32]

Even the Milwaukee papers wished Fitch well in the "thriving village of Manitowoc," adding that "we trust that the people of Northern Wisconsin will give him a liberal support." The *Herald* was the county's only paper for almost five years, until a rival, the *Manitowoc Weekly Tribune*, began in 1855. It was published by S.W. Smith, who had just joined the new Republican Party,

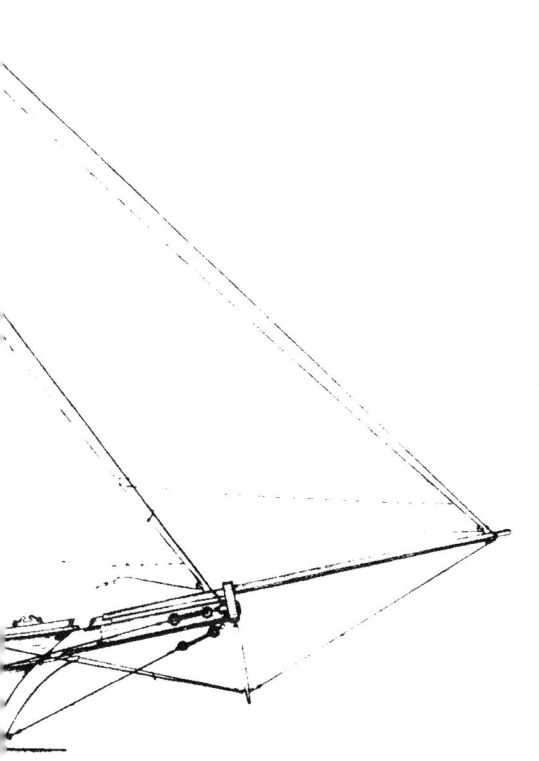

in nearby Ripon, Wisconsin. Shortly thereafter, one of Smith's associates, Carl Roeser, Sr., founded the county's first German-language newspaper, the *Wiskonsin Demokrat*. Soon this paper was followed by two other German-language weeklies, all of which hotly debated the questions of abolition, free soil, and the Dred Scott decision of 1857, which seemed to open up the free territories to the expansion of slavery.[33]

### The Road to Civil War

Thus, Manitowoc County residents were well served by a variety of newspapers during the last tumultuous years of political debate before the decisive election of 1860 that brought Republican Abraham Lincoln to the presidency and resulted in the secession of the first states of the Confederacy. By the time of that election, a majority of the county had enlisted in the Republican cause, including the large German vote, and Lincoln's victory was celebrated in polling places and later in taverns from Schleiswig to Mishicot.[34]

As the celebrations died out and the country faced the realities of a coming Civil War, the residents of Manitowoc were firmly tied into the economy of both Wisconsin and the region as loyal northerners. For eight years prior to 1860, shipbuilding had been a steadily growing enterprise. In 1852 alone, four schooners were built in Manitowoc, and double that number the following year. The *Weekly Herald* boasted that "Manitowoc is capable of furnishing more and better lake schooners than any town of its size west of Buffalo." Companies such as Bates & Son, Joseph Edwards, J. Hughes, E. Sorenson, and G.S. Rand of Manitowoc and James Harbridge of Two Rivers were beginning to build dozens of these ships by 1860, the largest of which, the *Mary Stockton*, had a capacity of 275 tons.[35]

However, even by the mid-1850s, the lake schooners were being replaced by steamships. In 1855 the port of Manitowoc hosted arrivals by 102 sailing vessels and 82 steamers, an illustration of the changing times. Five years later, on the eve of the war, Bates & Son, the local shipbuilder, received its first contract to build a steam vessel for the Goodrich line. It was on these steamships that the local volunteers for Lincoln's Grand Army of the Republic left their homes in Manitowoc County for battlefields in the Civil War.[36]

*ABOVE: Soon after Bates & Son established a shipyard, Greene S. Rand and a number of other professional shipbuilders came to Manitowoc. By 1853 Rand and his partner James Harbridge had built a steamboat, the* Menasha, *on nearby Lake Winnebago and Manitowoc had become one of the largest shipbuilding towns on Lake Michigan. Courtesy, Wisconsin Maritime Museum*

*LEFT: William Wallace Bates and his father Stephen formed Bates & Son, one of the county's early shipyards, in 1851, ushering in the era of professional shipbuilding in Manitowoc. William Bates designed and built innovative ships called clipper schooners—which were constructed to withstand the conditions of the Great Lakes. His first clipper schooner,* the Challenge, *was completed in 1852, and drew much attention. This endeavor and Bates' creativity in shipbuilding gave Manitowoc the nickname "Clipper City" and influenced Great Lakes shipbuilding for years to come. ©H.W. Potter 1944; courtesy, A.J. Fisher, Inc., Royal Oak, Michigan*

# CHAPTER THREE

# *The War Years and the Return of Prosperity*

## 1860 – 1890

*Peas became one of the primary foods of the canning industry as it grew during the 1880s and 1890s. In this early photo, workers load the peas for vining. After vining, the peas were hauled to the canning plant. While canneries existed in many states after the turn of the century, 1907 was the year that Wisconsin held the distinction of canning more peas than any other state. Courtesy, Lakeside Foods, Inc.*

On the eve of the Civil War, Manitowoc County was growing at a rapid pace, with hundreds of immigrants from across northern Europe, particularly Germans and Norwegians, arriving weekly. In the 1860 census, the county numbered 22,416 people, with the village of Manitowoc at 3,065 and the village of Two Rivers 1,340.

In the late 1850s a new county courthouse and adjacent office building brought recognition of the county's growing status and prosperity. However, the shadow of national politics during the early 1860s would result in turmoil for the largely Democratic population, which had to ponder switching allegiance to the Republican candidate, Abraham Lincoln, in the presidential election in November 1860. The resulting Civil War, on battlefields far from Manitowoc, nevertheless closely touched the county and the lives of its citizens.[1]

### The Election of Abraham Lincoln

The creation of the new Republican Party, in Ripon, Wisconsin, in 1854, had brought the issue of slavery and states' rights to the center of politics. While many people in Manitowoc County favored the "Little Giant," Stephen Douglas, the nominee of the Democratic Party, the question of slavery became paramount. A series of Republican clubs were organized throughout the county, which held bonfires and parades to offset the well-organized Democratic groups. Members of one club, the "Wide Awakes," wore oilcloth caps and old-fashioned helmets in their parades, a distinctive insignia. In one parade, farmers from Two Rivers and Cooperstown carried a wooden rail to symbolize their loyalty to their candidate the "railsplitter."[2]

In the November election, Lincoln won the county by a vote of 2,041 over Douglas' 1,947. It was one of the very few times that a Republican out-polled a Democrat in the presidential race.[3]

### Manitowoc County and Civil War

With Lincoln's election and the secession of southern states, the Civil War began the following spring on April 12, 1861, with the Confederate bombardment on Fort Sumter, in South Carolina, at 4:30 in the morning. Since Manitowoc was not part of the newly developed telegraph network that carried the news of the war's outbreak swiftly to all major cities, citizens did not receive word of the battle until the morning of April 17, five days later, when the steamer the *Comet* arrived in the port with the news.

Even though the Civil War's first battle was far away, support for the Union was strong in Manitowoc County. Several speakers mounted platforms as the Goodrich steamer was tied down, and gave "fiery orations" about supporting the Union cause to the "last dollar and the last feather bed." A long string of resolutions was read to a gathering crowd at the harbor "pledging support without respect to party." They were adopted by approving shouts. Even more vociferous was the oration by Perry P. Smith, saying that the government had no need of feather beds, but required "men that will fight...to wipe the... rebels off the face of the earth." As the shouting reached a crescendo of approval, many men in the crowd—including a judge, a leading Democrat, and a state senator—had signed their names to the first list of volunteers.[4]

This first band of county volunteers to answer Lincoln's call left Manitowoc just two months after Sumter on June 23, 1861, heading south on the same Goodrich steamer that had brought news of the war. They were bound for Milwaukee and then by train to Camp Randall in Madison, where they were formed into Company A of the Fifth Wisconsin Infantry. They were quickly sent east, where, with other raw Union recruits, they met the Confederates at the disastrous Battle of Bull Run in Virginia.[5]

Manitowoc's illustrious Company A soon became seasoned fighters, but only 36 of the original 104 volunteers returned home safely; 23 were killed, 27 were seriously wounded, and the rest were reported missing. Other com-

*Abraham Lincoln was elected in 1860, becoming the 16th president of the United States. In April 1861, just a few months after he took office, the Civil War began. During his tenure as president, Lincoln issued the Emancipation Proclamation in 1863 to free the slaves and he saw the end of the Civil War in 1865. A smiling Lincoln poses for this photo taken just after the war's end—and a few days before his death at the hands of the assassin John Wilkes Booth. Photo by Alexander Gardner; courtesy, State Historical Society of Wisconsin*

panies soon organized in the county, including Company E, in 1861, which participated in the bloody battle at Shiloh and at the siege at Vicksburg; and Company F (composed of Norwegians) and Company K, which fought with distinction in the battle for Atlanta under Sherman. Other volunteers from the county joined the Union forces at Gettysburg and on Sherman's march to the sea across Georgia. However, Lincoln's ability to entice volunteer soldiers soon waned as the war settled into a long and bitter struggle.[6]

In 1862 the first draft was instituted and each county in Wisconsin (as in other states) was given a draft quota to fill. Before the war's end in 1865, four companies of draftees were raised in the county to fill the semiannual quotas of almost 400 men. However, there was discontent over the war as well. Antiwar groups, sometimes called "Copperheads," "Butternuts," or "Knights of the Golden Circle," existed in the county, although they had to meet in secret to discuss their support of the Confederate cause. One Manitowoc newspaper, *The Pilot*, printed such virulent criticisms of Lincoln and the war effort that its offices were vandalized and parts of its press dumped into the river.[7]

Along with this turbulence, a frustration at the lack of Union victories and the appeal of the Democratic presidential candidate, General George McClellan, resulted in the county's voters deserting Lincoln in the presidential election of 1864. The incumbent Lincoln received only 1,179 votes to

*LEFT: Lincoln's opponent in the 1860 presidential elections was Democrat Stephen Douglas, a man short in stature but big in his accomplishments. Known as the "Little Giant," Douglas had defeated Lincoln just two years earlier in a run for the Senate. The two had engaged in seven debates during that time and much of the subject matter covered the issue of slavery extension to the territories. While Douglas was favored by many in Manitowoc County, Lincoln won an unprecedented victory by being the Republican who edged out the Democrat in the final county vote. Courtesy, State Historical Society of Wisconsin*

*The Manitowoc County Guards, the first military company from Manitowoc County to head off to battle during the Civil War, received their own flag—sewn by the women of Manitowoc. The red, white, and blue flag, emblazoned with the words, "Manitowoc County Volunteers," was presented to the men shortly before they left for training in Madison. The blue and red silks used to make the flag were purchased in Chicago, but no white silk was available because flag material had been bought up at the outset of the war. According to one soldier's account, the white in the flag was obtained from a soon-to-be bride who donated the material she had purchased for her bridal gown. The Manitowoc County Guards later became Company A, 5th Wisconsin Infantry. Miraculously, the flag survived many Civil War battles, and is currently on display at the Manitowoc County Heritage Center. Courtesy, Manitowoc County Historical Society*

McClellan's 2,248, although Lincoln carried Wisconsin and the Union to receive a second term.[8]

## The Boys in Blue

Even though the battlefields were far away, letters home from the boys in blue reached families across the county who were anxiously awaiting news. One young soldier wrote home from his encampment in Virginia in 1864 that, "we do not have as good beds, cannot go to church and know nothing of what is going on in the world." He also wrote poignantly of watching the wounded go by: "The wounded have been passing up the river [Potomac] for the last 3 days in great numbers...We helped 800 poor fellows... I saw more suffering in the five hours we were at work than ever before in my life...The men are badly hurt. Many of them cannot live but a few days."[9]

Another county boy, Frederic Charles Buerstatte, who was part of General Sherman's siege of Atlanta in 1864, wrote in his diary of the campaign: "18th May, We are extremely exhausted from the long march. 19th May, At noon, we engaged the enemy and the battle started. 22nd May, The heat is terrible and we are almost 'finished.' 3rd July, While we were on the march, the Rebs gave up their forward defenses and retreated with us on their heels. 19th Nov., Tonight we are about 45 miles from Atlanta. We began to live from that which we found on the plantations, such as potatoes, pigs,

*Manitowoc County voters changed their tune in the 1864 presidential election by voting Democrat. Candidate General George McClellan won countywide support by defeating Lincoln in the county vote. However, Lincoln did win the statewide vote as well as the support of the Union to start his second term. Just two years before, Lincoln (left) was photographed talking with McClellan after the battle at Antietam, where the advancement of Confederate troops was halted. Courtesy, State Historical Society of Wisconsin*

chickens, sheep, and cornmeal."[10]

On November 26, Buerstatte's comment is very brief, probably because of the shock of most of the Northern troops on the inhumane treatment of the prisoners at the Southern prison camp. He noted only: "Tonight we came upon Andersonville." After the fall of Atlanta just before Christmas in 1864, Sherman's troops began their famous "March to the Sea" during which they destroyed the heart of the Georgia farmland that supplied Confederate troops. Before the troops departed from their Atlanta encampment, his diary records a soldier's Christmas: "24th December, We cleaned our quarters. Each person planted a Christmas tree in front of his tent. 25th Dec., Christmas morning inspection. We received a 1/2 unit crackers, rice and meat."[11]

In early 1865 Buerstatte's unit marched across Georgia until April, when, with news of the war's end, they headed north across North Carolina and Virginia to Washington. There, on May 24, he recorded, "We marched past Alexandria, across the Potomac River, past the Capital, and up Pennsylvania Avenue through Washington... We were reviewed by Lieutenant

General U.S. Grant, Major General W.T. Sherman and other generals."[12]

Before the war's end, Manitowoc County could boast of sending more than 2,460 men to the Union army, a large percentage for an area that mustered only 3,988 total voters in the 1860 elections. All ethnic groups in the county were represented among the fighting men, including Native Americans, Germans, Irish, French, English, Norwegians, Bohemians, and others. One member of the volunteers was a Negro, who was an associate and friend of Manitowoc's Negro barber. Many county men reached high officer rank, including a major general, several brigade generals, colonels, and majors.[13]

## Manitowoc's Civil War Governor

In 1862, as the Civil War lengthened into a long and bloody combat, Wisconsin's gubernatorial race brought a young Manitowoc leader, Edward Salomon, into the forefront of state politics. The Salomon family, German Lutherans, had settled in Manitowoc during the 1850s after emigrating from Prussia and were staunchly Democratic. However, Edward, like his brothers, hated slavery and supported the Union cause. Three of the brothers fought in the Union army and Edward, who had changed to the Republican Party, became its nominee and at the young age of 33, was elected lieutenant governor of Wisconsin in November 1862.[14]

Following the election, Wisconsin Governor Louis P. Harvey undertook a journey to visit the troops fighting in the campaign in Tennessee. He traveled with supplies for the Wisconsin volunteers, but drowned during a storm on the Tennessee River, when the supplies were being transferred from his boat. When news reached Wisconsin, Manitowoc's native son, Salomon, was sworn in as governor after serving less than three months as second in command.

During his tenure as governor, Salomon became a skilled leader in dealing with the difficult questions of draft riots and Indian scares. Resistance to Lincoln's 1862 call for draftees was heated in several Wisconsin counties, where German Catholics violently opposed forceable enlistment. Salomon had to send troops to several towns to put down such riots, notably Port Washington, where the violence was so severe that several buildings were destroyed and a number of people were wounded in the upheaval.[15]

One of the problems, which Salomon addressed, was that Wisconsin had exceeded its state quota of volunteer enlistments and wanted to have that surplus applied to its draft requirement. In addition, Salomon worked to get the volunteer bonus per soldier raised from $100 to $302 as an inducement to join and he delayed the actual draft long enough to allow many more men to volunteer. These measures helped to defuse the anger of draftees, even though Salomon was disheartened that many of his fellow countrymen who had become citizens and voted still tried to claim that they were

*The communities of Manitowoc County sent hundreds of their men to fight during the Civil War. Loved ones at home received their own view of the battlefields when they read the letters their soldiers sent home over the years. One soldier, Two Rivers resident Charles Webster Knopp, described his encounters in detail. In the letter shown here, Knopp writes that he is "In the swamp— near Savannah, GA." and later makes reference to the "burning of Atlanta." Courtesy, State Historical Society of Wisconsin*

*The untimely death of Louis P. Harvey (top), Wisconsin's governor in 1862, led to the induction of one of Manitowoc's own into the position. Edward Salomon (above), son of a German Lutheran family in Manitowoc, was fulfilling his duties as the newly elected lieutenant governor when news of Harvey's death reached Wisconsin. Salomon, who then served as governor from 1862 to 1864, became known for trying to keep the peace when problems with the draft arose and for his efforts to get the Indian and "colored" troops accepted as volunteers for the war. Courtesy, State Historical Society of Wisconsin*

foreigners and not subject to military service.

He was more successful in persuading Secretary of War Edwin Stanton and through him President Lincoln to accept Wisconsin's 363 "colored" troops and 279 Indians (Menomonee, Oneida, and Stockbridge). He also succeeded in persuading the authorities to pay these men the same bonus as white volunteers.[16] These Indians who joined were from tribes along the lakeshore and had long enjoyed peaceful relations with the nearby white settlers.

In 1862 the people of Wisconsin were frightened by threats of Indian uprisings among other tribes. In neighboring Minnesota, Sioux Indians went on a rampage in August that left more than 100 settlers dead around New Ulm, and brought 40,000 terrified settlers across the Mississippi into Wisconsin seeking refuge. The panic spread and many settlers from Superior to Manitowoc took flight south for protection.

Keeping a level head during the crisis, Salomon listened to reports that Wisconsin's Indians were just as frightened and were flocking north en masse, fearful of white retaliation for the Minnesota events. Instead of diverting troops from the war effort, Salomon authorized the local militia to stand on alert for any signs of danger. Two incidents in Wisconsin, in which Winnebago Indians victimized farm families near the Minnesota border, led Salomon to call for federal help and a regiment was dispatched "for the protection of the Indians as well as the whites." By the end of the year, the scare was over and Salomon's cool head had kept matters under control.[17]

### Industry and Wartime

In addition to sending its young men to fight the war and dispatching Edward Salomon to the governor's office, Manitowoc County participated in shipping supplies to the Union cause and benefited from the prosperity of a wartime economy. Grain shipments to feed the Union army began as early as May 1861, with 8,000 barrels of wheat leaving the harbor at Manitowoc on the schooner *Joseph Vilas* for Buffalo. Just in time for this increased war trade, several new schooners and two new steamers, the *Union* and the *Victor*, were built at the shipyards to carry grain, lumber, and foundry metal products for the war effort.[18]

Between 1860 and 1870 Manitowoc County became one of the leading counties in the state in its manufacturing output with a total value of $2.3 million. One industry that was particularly stimulated by wartime purchases was that of tanning. The abundance of hides and hemlock bark made several Wisconsin lakeshore counties especially suited for the production of leather, a commodity in great demand for horses' saddles and soldiers' boots for the army.[19]

In 1861 a second large tannery was constructed by the Wisconsin Leather Company in Two Rivers adjacent to the first one and business flourished. During the shipping season at least two full loads were sent out every week, and during the winter months teams hauled the leather to Milwaukee for reshipment by rail to points east. The winter trip took three days and wagons returned to the area filled with hides from the company's warehouse in Milwaukee. By the early 1870s Manitowoc and Two Rivers had become leaders in the state in the output of leather with more than 60,000 hides annually, surpassed only by Milwaukee.[20] However, during the 1870s several tannery fires destroyed plants and the growing scarcity of hemlock bark brought an end to the dominance of the local tanning industry.

Another local industry that benefited from wartime demand was shipbuilding. From the first schooners built locally came the design for a fast cargo ship with a shallow draft that would not "yaw in the wind." These new ships, designed by William Bates in Manitowoc just before the war, became christened "clipper ships" and gave rise to Manitowoc's new nickname as the "Clipper City" in the postwar years. The firm of Bates & Son began to build

*Threats of Indian attacks between tribes and news of an attack on settlers in Minnesota left many Wisconsinites fearful in the early 1860s. However, many tribes in Wisconsin had established a peaceful relationship with settlers. Some of these Native Americans even went as far as joining in the war effort. Indian recruits in this photograph are being sworn in for Civil War duty. The 279 Indians—as well as the 363 "colored" troops—were recruited for the war effort and enjoyed receiving the same bonus pay that the "white" volunteers received. Photo copied from original by John Hunter, Madison, Wisconsin; courtesy, State Historical Society of Wisconsin*

propeller steamships for the Goodrich Steamship Line in 1860, developing the fast-moving coal-powered steamers.

Even after the development of steam vessels, the Manitowoc clipper ships remained dominant in shipping on the Great Lakes and the oceans of the world for several decades. Led by companies such as Bates, Edwards, Sorenson, Rand, Harbridge, and Burger, the shipbuilding industry was off to a start that would keep Manitowoc on the map for many decades as one of the leading shipbuilding ports in the nation.[21]

In 1866 Henry B. Burger, a native of Germany who had settled in the county three years earlier, took control of the firm of Greene, Rand and Burger and brought his nephew, George, into partnership. The new firm (later called Burger & Burger) was first located on a corner of Luep's Island near the harbor mouth, but moved upriver to provide a better turning basin for its boats. Along with the area's other shipbuilding concerns, Burger and Burger would soon become one of the most prominent shipbuilders in the United States, crafting both small and large boats out of wood and later out of iron, steel, and aluminum.[22]

Between this firm and the others, Manitowoc soon became known for the quality and size of its boats, as well as their swiftness. One observer noted that even during the early 1860s, he could stand at the harbor's mouth and count more than 50 vessels coming and going in their daily trade at the lakeshore. Between 1860 and 1870 Manitowoc's shipyards built 10 schooners, 7 steamers, and 2 tugboats. This output more than tripled in the next decade with 53 schooners, 9 steamers, 5 tugboats, and 2 barges. Between 1880 and 1900 the output increased once again with more than 150 ships of all sorts coming out of the shipyards. Before the turn of the century, however, most of the vessels were steamers, tugs, and barges, as reliance upon the old stalwart sailing schooners began to decline.[23]

All of the ships in the Great Lakes merchant fleets rivaled each other for speed and delivery achievements. Each spring, usually in April, ships loaded with grain stored in grain elevators from Wisconsin's fall harvest would line the piers of every harbor. As soon as the news came that the northern straits were clear of ice, the ships would embark on a virtual race to Cleveland or Buffalo. Even the crews got into the competitive spirit and all of the Great Lakes seamen knew which ships were the fastest and which crews and captains the most adept. In this way, a shipbuilder could gain a reputation for the swiftness of its crafts and earn more orders.

Occasionally, however, the straits would refreeze with a cold spell in late April. One year more than a dozen ships had to spend several days "frozen in" the ice near Mackinaw before they could break free on the southern run through Lake Huron to Detroit and beyond.[24]

One of the swiftest and largest ships was the *Chicago Board of Trade*, built at Manitowoc in 1862 with a capacity of 28,000 bushels of grain. However, the lack of rail transportation and adequate grain elevators meant that Manitowoc did not have the ability to rival other ports as a grain-shipping depot into the late 1860s or 1870s. Instead, that distinction went to Milwaukee, the leading wheat-shipping port in the world for several years, until wheat farming moved west to Minnesota and the Great Plains in the 1870s and 1880s.

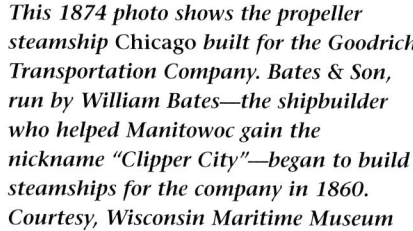

*This 1874 photo shows the propeller steamship* Chicago *built for the Goodrich Transportation Company. Bates & Son, run by William Bates—the shipbuilder who helped Manitowoc gain the nickname "Clipper City"—began to build steamships for the company in 1860. Courtesy, Wisconsin Maritime Museum*

## Wartime Improvements

Although the long-sought harbor improvements had been promised to Manitowoc during the 1850s, no substantial monies became available until 1859, when the old lighthouse was torn down and replaced by a new one. It was seven more years before the federal government finally released the funds to completely upgrade the harbor. In 1866, after the end of the war, the promised money for improvements was sent by the Republican Congress to the states and Manitowoc was able to completely dredge its harbor mouth, build a breakwater at the entrance, and upgrade its piers. The improvements and the federal funding of $52,000 came just in time for the great post-Civil War industrial boom that led to increased trade and ship-building during the 1870s.

Another breakthrough at war's end was the arrival of telegraph service to the county in 1865. In February, just two months before the end of the war, the United States Telegraph Company finally completed the line north from Milwaukee to Manitowoc. At last, the area's population could receive news of events from around the country and around the world within minutes, no longer awaiting the arrival of ships bringing day-old news from Milwaukee. Sadly, one of the first stories of national importance to arrive in the city was the tragic news of Lincoln's assassination on April 14, 1865, just five days after General Robert E. Lee surrendered.[25]

Soon the telegraph would control the shipping industry as dispatches were sent with ships' orders. Modern technology and competition in commerce had become the controlling spirit of the times by the 1870s. The United States had developed a "national market economy," bolstered by high-speed communication, by swift shipping fleets, and, of course, by the growing railroad network that soon spanned the country.

*A few sailing schooners still line Manitowoc's harbor in this 1887 photo. The harbor was a busy one as Manitowoc's shipbuilding companies continued to flourish. By the turn of the century, the antiquated sailing schooners would be used much less and replaced with steam-driven ships. Courtesy, State Historical Society of Wisconsin*

## Postwar Prosperity: The Coming of the Railroad

After several false starts, the first railroad line finally reached Manitowoc in the fall of 1873, four years after the entire continent was spanned by the Transcontinental Railroad in 1869. One reason that rail service came so late to Wisconsin's eastern lakeshore cities was corporate rivalry. Rail lines north from Milwaukee had earlier connected cities such as Appleton and Green Bay, but had only served the western shore of Lake Winnebago, leaving all of the eastern cities still reliant on the Goodrich Steamship Line.

Leading businessmen in the county had engaged in efforts to build a railroad since the early 1850s, but had always met with frustration and failure. One of their early railroad companies went broke during the Panic of 1857, and later attempts were postponed during wartime. Finally, a short-spur line between Manitowoc and Appleton was completed in 1872, but there was no direct or through freight or passenger service.[26]

Even after the Civil War, competition between the Milwaukee Road and Chicago's Northwestern Railroad slowed the efforts to connect cities such as Sheboygan and Manitowoc. Finally, in early 1873, the line to Sheboygan was completed and seven months later, on September 24, Manitowoc had a railroad at last! One year later the branch to Two Rivers, six additional miles, was also completed.

*Locomotives made their way to Manitowoc in the 1870s, with the very first one arriving by ship. This Soo Line locomotive, built in 1887, was typical of the engines seen at the time. It was donated to the Manitowoc County Historical Society by Robert Miller of Milwaukee. Courtesy, Manitowoc County Historical Society*

*The brick-making industry gained momentum as more cities began to construct roads and buildings with bricks. One well-known brickyard, located on the river banks in Manitowoc and Two Rivers, was the Bertler Yard. It dominated the brick production industry in the area by the turn of the century. This early 1900s photo shows a crew of brickyard employees, who include some members of the Bertler family. Courtesy, Manitowoc County Historical Society*

Even this achievement would not have been possible without the capital investments of New York entrepreneurs who bought railroad stock. Equally important was the substantial financial assistance of the City of Manitowoc, $75,000, the City of Two Rivers, $25,000, and the County of Manitowoc, $100,000. This line, which became known as the Milwaukee, Lakeshore, and Western Railroad, finally brought the county and its two largest cities into the national rail network.

During the next two decades additional rail service was completed by the Manitowoc and Western Railroad Company, which later became part of the Wisconsin Central network. The Chicago and Northwestern Railroad finally completed its system north to Green Bay in the early 1890s and soon absorbed the Milwaukee and Lakeshore company.

Ironically, the first train locomotive engine to arrive in Manitowoc came not by rail, but two years earlier by steamship. In 1871 a large schooner brought a train engine to the Manitowoc wharf where it sat for display and inspection until the railroad tracks reached town to utilize it. This first engine in town had actually been built in the East at least 20 years earlier. However, it was soon replaced by more powerful locomotives.[27]

Although trains were far more reliable than road travel and more constant than the seasonal lake shipping, even they could be held hostage to the weather. In 1881 Wisconsin suffered one of its worst blizzards during the first four weeks of the year. With no thaw, even during February, it was difficult to clear the tracks and keep the trains moving. Even though the county had rail service for only nine years, settlements had become dependent on supplies coming north from Milwaukee.

The crisis was reached in late February and early March, when another blizzard struck. Since the tracks were cleared by men with shovels, all work had to stop and it was nine days before the next train came through. Shortly thereafter, ice began to do its damage and the tracks buckled, derailing a large freight train and once again cutting the county off from badly needed supplies. Finally, by early April, the repairs were completed and the tracks were cleared. However, the blizzard of '81 and its resulting isolation was a memory that lingered long in local lore. The costs came close to bankrupting the young railroad company, but because the next winter was extraordinarily mild, it was able to recover profitability and remain in business.

### The Carferries

At the same time that Manitowoc County became a part of the great national railroad network, during the 1870s, there were already proposals to initiate a cross-lake railroad ferry service between Wisconsin's eastern shore and Michigan's western shore. The rail network in Michigan reached its western terminus almost due east of Manitowoc at a port then named Pere Marquette, soon renamed Ludington. The idea was to connect the Michigan railroad system, completed to Ludington in 1874, with Manitowoc's line to Menasha and west to Minneapolis-St. Paul. However, these early hopes were abandoned when the Civil War intervened and Manitowoc's own rail connection was put on hold.

By the late 1870s ships from the Goodrich line began to dock at Ludington to carry freight transferred from rail cars across the lake. However, this reloading of freight was costly and time consuming and an entrepreneur from Ludington, James Ashley, originated the idea of putting loaded railroad cars directly onto the ships for the cross-lake journey. In 1892 the dream became a reality as the first such ship, the *Ann Arbor*, was loaded with hopper cars full of coal for the journey west from Ludington. The ship had been especially designed for the railroad cars, with a 53-foot beam and a length of 260 feet. Each car was pushed aboard the ship's rails and then locked into place using its own air brakes, clamps fastened in front and behind each wheel, and chains

*This photo, dated 1880-1881, shows the buildup of snow at the corner of Eighth and Jay streets in Manitowoc after a snowstorm. A blizzard in January 1881 literally crippled the railroads in Wisconsin and temporarily isolated Manitowoc County's residents from their much-needed supplies, which regularly arrived from Milwaukee by train. Photo by A.B. Melendy; courtesy, Manitowoc County Historical Society*

*The* Ann Arbor, *shown at its dock in Frankfort, Michigan, provided regular carferry service to Manitowoc by the turn of the century. Previously, railroad car freight was unloaded onto ships, transported across the lake, and reloaded onto other railroad cars. In 1892, the* Ann Arbor *became the first ship to transport loaded railroad cars from one destination to another. The carferry industry quickly grew, and by the late 1890s Manitowoc had its own carferry dock. Courtesy, Wisconsin Maritime Museum*

fastening it to the ship's deck.[28]

Following this successful journey, the idea of railroad carferries caught on. Manitowoc became a favored destination because of its harbor and the great demand for coal from its growing industries. The system also had the advantage of putting Manitowoc into a lower-cost rail network in Michigan, called the Central Freight Association, which had a cheaper rate structure than that in Wisconsin. A large part of this savings came because the system could ship across Lake Michigan and avoid the higher costs of going through Chicago.[29]

By 1896 regular carferry service was established between Frankfort and Manitowoc, and that same year the city constructed its first permanent carferry dock. By the late 1890s the carferry runs had become steady and very profitable, with coal coming west and with grain from Minnesota heading east, all of it avoiding Chicago. The shipping tonnage on these ferries at Manitowoc became second only to Milwaukee by the end of the decade with the larger ferries carrying up to 32 railroad cars on each trip and making two round trips every 24 hours.[30]

To accommodate this increased freight traffic, the harbor was dredged to a depth of 20 feet, from its "improved" 13 feet in the 1870s. In addition, the company constructed special coal docks near the river's mouth to make the ferry service more efficient. However, the costs for maintaining these docks and the harbor continued to fall upon the city, which tried to assess the private shipping interests. Finally, through repeated pleas, the federal government once again extended funding at the turn of the century, to upgrade and maintain the harbors, both at Manitowoc and at Two Rivers, which had become the home of a Coast Guard Lifesaving Station for the Great Lakes fleet in 1878.[31]

## Industrial Growth

With a telegraph line in place and with rail transportation and carferry service secured at last, industrial growth in Manitowoc County boomed during the last three decades of the nineteenth century. Small companies, such as the lathe and pail works, the furniture factories, and even small machine shops and foundries, could now compete on a national scale and sell their wares to a national market, no longer dependent on the seasonal lake schooner shipping.

Since lumber and wooden products had already become a stable industry in the county, the development of the Schuetze Church Furniture Company was a logical outgrowth of existing skilled enterprises. Beginning in 1886, partners Hubbard and Noble opened a mill for the manufacture of wooden staves and tubs, to be shipped across the country. Two years later the name was changed to the Manitowoc Manufacturing Company, which prospered until a disastrous fire in the 1890s almost closed its doors.

However, the idea of using its existing expertise in woodworking emerged from the catastrophe and a new enterprise, the Manitowoc Seating Company, was opened in 1893, later to be known as the American School Furniture Manufacturing Company. Under this new name, the firm became a leading manufacturer of both church pews and school desks, which (following consolidation with similar concerns in Ohio and elsewhere) produced more than one-half of the national volume of these items during the next century.[32] Another furniture concern in Kiel, the Kiel Manufacturing Company, was organized in 1892 to produce high-quality wooden furniture, especially tables of all sizes.[33] This expertise in furniture production later led to the creation of the county's first metal furniture company in Kiel after the turn of the century.

Expertise in wood crafting and production also brought Frederick Eggers, of Two Rivers, to establish a business in 1884 that would produce plywood and veneer. Soon the company began to specialize in other wood-related products including desktops, wall paneling, doors, and later even gutters for bowling alleys. The wood for Eggers, as for the other wooden products companies in both Manitowoc and Two Rivers, came initially from the local lumber supply. As the forests in the eastern part of the state became depleted, the rail network brought wood from forests across the western part of the state and even specialized woods from California.[34]

In Two Rivers, another wooden products firm, the Hamilton Manufacturing Company, was established in 1881, just after the record-breaking winter storms had subsided. Growing out of an existing pail factory, the new enterprise was the creation of James E. Hamilton, who had been born in Manitowoc County in 1852 and became the sole support of his family following his father's death during the Civil War. He began work in a clothespin lathe factory that had been established several decades earlier by his maternal and paternal grandfathers in Two Rivers.[35]

Developing expertise as an engineer and mechanic, Hamilton worked on several projects where he became an expert pile driver, including the Sturgeon Bay Ship Canal and the Twin River Point Lighthouse. In 1877, hearing of gold discoveries in the Black Hills of South Dakota, he borrowed

INSET: Born in Manitowoc County in 1852, James E. Hamilton worked in Two Rivers before leaving in 1877. Hamilton had decided to seek his wealth in the Black Hills of South Dakota after hearing of gold discoveries there. Less than a year later, he was out of money and longing to come back to Two Rivers. He eventually found his fortune at home after establishing the Hamilton Manufacturing Company, which initially produced wooden printer's type and later specialized in the manufacture of items such as furniture for print shops and drafting tables. Courtesy, Manitowoc County Historical Society

ABOVE: Hamilton's foray into opening his own business resulted in the creation of wooden printer's type that could be produced locally to accommodate nearby businesses. The type for his first poster—which advertised the "Grand Ball at Turner Hall"—was called "logotype." The original wood type, shown here, details how the letters were carved into one piece of wood. The logotype, later christened "Hollywood Type," became popular among newspapers in Wisconsin and surrounding states, thus helping Hamilton's business to prosper in the coming years. Courtesy, Two Rivers Historical Society

*Before aluminum cookware became affordable, the newly formed aluminum companies in Manitowoc and Two Rivers produced what were called "novelty" items. Combs and matchboxes were among the popular products being manufactured by the Aluminum Manufacturing Company and the Manitowoc Novelty Company. In this 1905 photo, women at one of the plants are shown polishing the novelty items. Courtesy, Manitowoc County Historical Society*

$200 and headed west to find his fortune. One year earlier the Seventh Cavalry and General Custer had met defeat in Montana, not far from Hamilton's final destination of Deadwood, South Dakota, and the area was still part of the Wild West frontier. Just after getting off the train in Cheyenne, Wyoming, before catching the Deadwood stagecoach, Hamilton witnessed his first gun-fight, which resulted in the death of one of the assailants right in front of his hotel.[36]

His adventures continued, as he met the famous Calamity Jane on the Deadwood stagecoach, which was attacked en route by highwaymen who killed two of the passengers. The calm order of life in Two Rivers became increasingly more appealing, as Hamilton and his friends discovered that most of the gulches where they wanted to pan for gold had already been claimed by preemption. However, with his money gone, Hamilton had to work odd jobs in Deadwood before he could return home. During this time, "he learned to be wary of the ugly drunken bad man with the ever-ready guns…He saw death in many violent guises, life in the raw—and longed for the village on the lake."[37]

Coming out of the Black Hills by mule train, Hamilton caught a riverboat on the Missouri to St. Louis, then came by train to Milwaukee and by lake steamer to Two Rivers, where he was welcomed home broke and in debt, but still burning with ambition. Shortly after his return in late 1877, Hamilton courted and married the local schoolteacher, a graduate of Lawrence College, and decided to open his own business as a manufacturer of wooden printer's type. A local printer and newspaper publisher, William F. Nash, had turned to Hamilton, whose skill in wooden scrollwork was well known, and together they developed the idea of locally produced wooden type.[38]

The first poster, with type created by Hamilton on his foot-powered scroll saw in his mother's cottage, was an announcement for a local dance in Two

*The Kaltenbrun Company of St. Nazianz was another business that pushed Manitowoc County to the forefront of the agricultural equipment industry. Brothers Anton and Ambrose Kaltenbrun invented and received a patent for a safety feed cutter in 1896. The machine was made in their first factory, shown in this photograph. The feed cutters were so popular that the company had difficulty meeting the demand. In 1916 the Kaltenbruns also received a patent for a blower that transferred material into a silo more quickly and efficiently. Courtesy, Manitowoc County Historical Society*

Rivers, the "Grand Ball at Turner Hall." His work, called "logotype," was a series of carved wooden letters set into a single piece of wood. It became the foundation of his new business, Hamilton Manufacturing Company, and soon many other newspapers began to see the advantage of the system and sought to avoid the shipping costs from the East.

Advertising his logotype as "Hollywood Type" (from the kind of wood he used), Hamilton soon began receiving orders from newspaper publishers and printers across Wisconsin, Minnesota, and Michigan. During the next 10 years he took in several partners, incorporated under Wisconsin law (1889), and broadened the company's products to include furniture for an efficient print shop and a wider variety of print types on the wooden blocks. By the turn of the century the company had acquired other type shops, including one in Connecticut, and expanded its markets to a national scope. Further diversification followed with an expertise in wood leading to the creation of specialized cabinets for dentists, drafting equipment, and, later, steel products for use in wartime and for domestic appliances—including the first automatic electric clothes dryer.[39]

## Brick Making and Aluminum Production

The industries that began to grow in Manitowoc County before the turn of the century were not only those based on the local supply of wood. Just prior to the Civil War, the production of bricks began in the village of Manitowoc near the river when several small brickyards opened for business. Through postwar consolidation, several prominent yards emerged, among them the Bertler Yard. This change meant that more employees could be engaged and greater production numbers achieved.

The yards were located near the river banks in both Manitowoc and Two Rivers, taking advantage of the water, as well as the supply of clay and sand. The post-Civil War growth of cities, particularly Milwaukee and Chicago, meant that the demand for brick escalated rapidly. This demand was also fueled by the realization that the earlier wooden structures that dominated city building before the war were dangerously susceptible to massive fires. Following the horrible conflagration of 1871, called the Great Chicago Fire,

*Smalley Manufacturing, established in 1857 in Manitowoc, manufactured products for farmers that were not being heavily marketed by the larger companies. This strategy allowed Smalley to become a leader in the industry. The company also published a catalog that highlighted its many farm machines including those on which it held special patents. One catalog item—the Smalley Sweep Power for Two Horses—is shown priced at $35. Courtesy, Manitowoc County Historical Society*

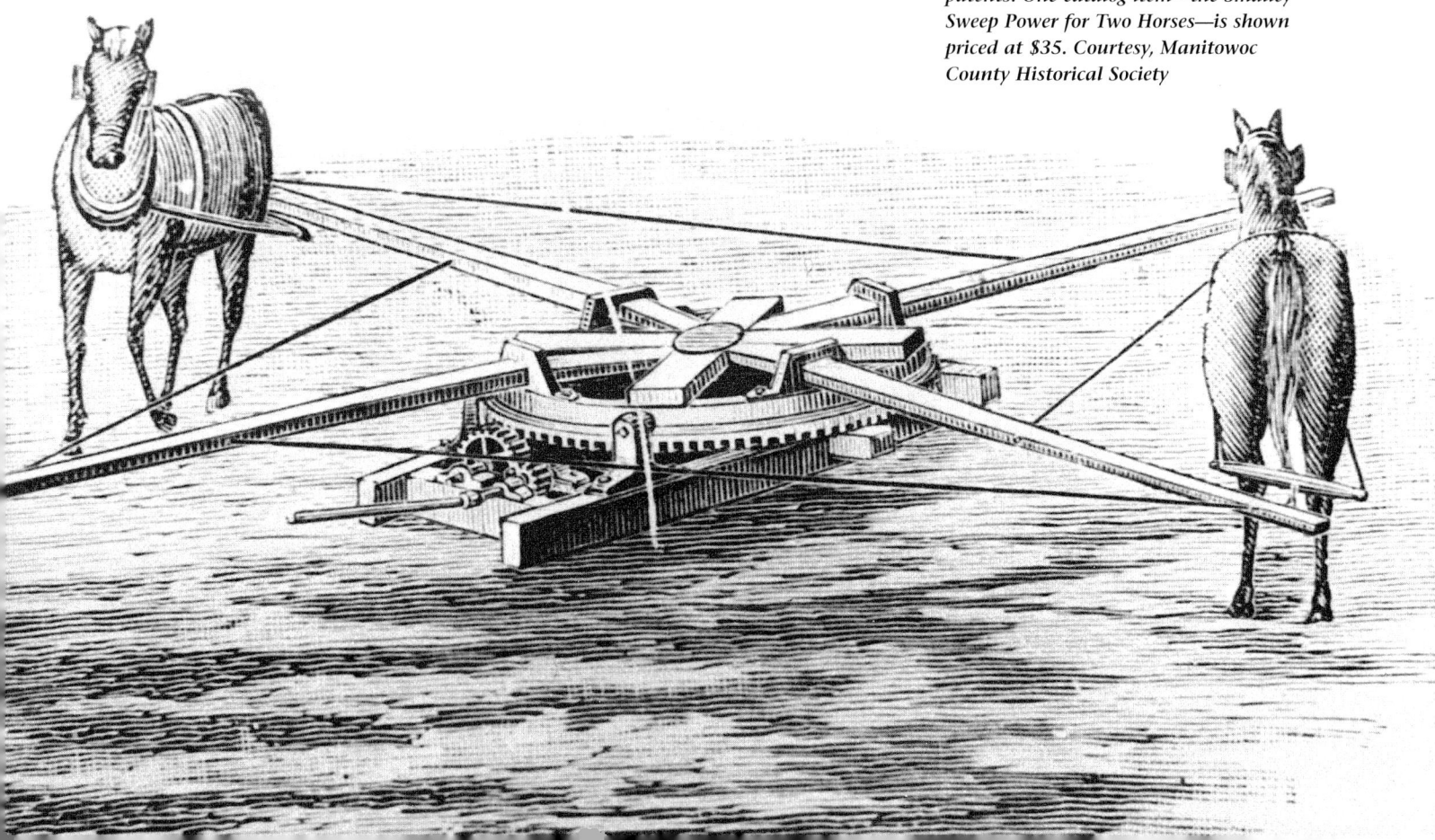

*The production of aluminum came to Manitowoc County in 1895 when Joseph Koenig (left) founded the Aluminum Manufacturing Company in Two Rivers and Henry Vits (right) opened the Aluminum Specialty Company in 1898. In 1909 the companies merged with another business to form the Aluminum Goods Manufacturing Company. While novelty items had been popular, the new corporation expanded production to include the manufacture of cooking utensils and pots and pans. Vits and Koenig, still leaders of the company, combined their names and VIKO cookware was born. Courtesy, Manitowoc County Historical Society*

city buildings began to consist increasingly of brick.[40]

This demand escalated during the next decades so that by 1890 the Bertler Yard alone was shipping almost 500,000 bricks south each season at a price of roughly six dollars per thousand. Shipping by rail was too expensive, so the proximity of the brickyards to the harbor was essential. Lake steamers carried thousands of these bricks since streets in these booming cities began to be made of this material. With further advances in production technology, including conveyor belts and high-powered cutting saws, the yards could produce 2,500 bricks an hour by the early years of the twentieth century.[41]

## Manufacturing and Farm Equipment

Another industry that grew up in the county following the Civil War was that of metalworking and metal production. Knowledge of the fabrication of aluminum had been developed in France during the 1850s, but its production did not begin in the United States until after the Civil War. In 1895 the Aluminum Manufacturing Company of Two Rivers was established to sell "useful and ornamental articles of aluminum or of other material or metals." Its founder, Joseph Koenig, had been inspired by exhibits of the new metal technology he had seen on a visit to the Columbian Exposition, or Chicago World's Fair, in 1893.[42]

Several years later, in 1898, Henry Vits, a tanner from Manitowoc, opened an aluminum plant and called it the Aluminum Specialty Company. Before the turn of the century both enterprises flourished as Americans came to recognize the many uses for the new metal, beyond that of toys or novelties. Just after 1900 the Two Rivers and Manitowoc companies were merged with a New Jersey aluminum venture to create the Aluminum Goods Manufacturing Company, which began to manufacture aluminum cookware, pots, and pans. Control of the firm remained with leaders from Manitowoc and Two Rivers, particularly with Vits and Koenig, who gave their combined names to the cookware, christened "VIKO." The rise of the automobile in the early twentieth century brought even further innovations, including the production of hubcaps, as profitability soared.[43]

One additional production company that put Manitowoc County on the map was Smalley Manufacturing. Edmund J. Smalley, a native of New York, had come to Manitowoc just before the Civil War in 1857, where he began to work as a schoolteacher and a blacksmith. Soon he became a dealer in farm equipment, tractors, and reapers from such newly booming companies as John Deere and McCormick.[44]

Realizing that the equipment manufactured by these large corporations did not provide all of the farmers' needs, Smalley and his two sons began to produce smaller farm items, such as feed cutters, burr mills, corn shellers, and root and vegetable cutters, as well as a wide variety of saws. Using their blacksmith shop at first, they installed a treadmill that used an ox for power. They also began to advertise their wares to farmers across the state, and soon across the Midwest, by printing a catalog with drawings of products upon which they held the sole patents.[45]

As Smalley Manufacturing grew, it bought electric-powered machines to continually refine production. The owners also stayed in close touch with the farmers of the county and the many local woodenware production companies so that they could create an ever-growing product line of vitally needed saws and farm equipment. Like other emerging companies, the Smalley concern realized that it needed national publicity to reach out to a national market. In 1893 the Smalleys submitted samples of their patented equipment for a display at the Chicago World's Fair and received an award that placed them on the map for the "general excellence of...farm machinery."[46]

Several other smaller farm equipment companies, located in St. Nazianz, contributed to the county's lead in this field. The Kaltenbrun Company specialized in the production of blowers and feed cutters, while three farm equipment sales concerns, Backhaus, Lulloff, and Miller, controlled franchises for machinery sales.

With all of these industries flourishing in the post-Civil War decades, several leading businessmen decided to band together to form the Manitowoc Industrial Association in 1883, to further promote the area's developing possibilities and to jointly work to attract additional labor and transportation to the county. Although industrial output continued to climb prior to 1900 and sales of agricultural equipment boomed, farming remained the mainstay of the area's economy for many years into the twentieth century.[47]

## Farming, Food Production, and Brewing

Like many Wisconsin farmers, the pioneers who settled in Manitowoc County prior to the Civil War turned to wheat production as a very successful cash crop. As the leading wheat-producing state in the Union during the

*Before milk bottles were delivered to homes by truck, the milkman delivered his product via horse-drawn carriage as seen in this photo taken during a milkman's rounds in Manitowoc. A large can of milk was taken from house to house and women would fill a container by dipping it into the can. Until the advent of refrigeration, a family could only take a day's worth of milk at a time. Courtesy, Manitowoc County Historical Society*

*No longer considered just "women's work," dairying in Manitowoc County had launched the cheese-making industry. Dairy farmers had to live within close proximity to the cheese factories because milk was often delivered by horse-drawn wagons. Without the luxury of refrigeration, farmers also had to transport the milk daily. In this early photo, Manitowoc County farmers bring their tins of milk to Klemm factories at Cato and Two Creeks. Courtesy, Manitowoc County Historical Society*

Civil War, Wisconsin enjoyed the prosperity of the increased demand for its leading crop, not only from the Union army and eastern cities, but from cities around the world. However, as the Homestead Act of 1862 opened up new fields for growing winter wheat in Minnesota, Nebraska, and the Dakotas, and as Wisconsin's soil began to give out, the post-Civil War period witnessed the center of wheat farming moving westward.

Wisconsin farmers had to find new sources of agricultural income and turned to a variety of new answers, the foremost of which was dairying. At first, the idea met with great resistance because milking was considered "women's work" and no one believed that owning a large number of cows could be profitable. However, through the efforts of William D. Hoard, later Wisconsin governor, and through the work of the College of Agriculture at the University of Wisconsin, the single-family "scrub cow" was phased out and farmers turned to Holsteins, Jerseys, and Guernseys.[48]

In Newton, the Rohde Dairy opened its doors in 1884, with cheese making as a very prosperous offshoot. Fifteen years later, in 1899, the Fischl Dairy began, adding a small creamery three years later called the Manitowoc Creamery. Deliveries were made by horse and wagon and milk was contained in large tin cans, until glass bottles were introduced after the turn of the century.

Similarly, the Stoelting Brothers Company of Kiel, which opened in 1905, entered the cheese-making business with few resources. Soon, however, like other growing food-processing concerns, the company was able to purchase the large-scale machinery that brought mass production and increasing profitability to the cheese industry. Additional cheese-making companies soon opened their doors in nearby Chilton and in Sherwood, as the county's production of dairy products soared. Soon butter and cheese became one of the leading exports from the ports at Manitowoc and Two Rivers.[49]

With the new dairies, an increasing number of farmers in Manitowoc County began to develop herds of milk cows. They also began to grow vegetables as a new cash crop. Sugar beets and peas, in particular, became staples as the canning industry developed facilities in the county during the 1880s and 1890s, with the opening of the Landreth Canning Company (forerunner of the Lakeside Packing Company, now called Lakeside Foods, a top 100 Wisconsin company), the Manitowoc Pea Packing Company, and the Northern Wisconsin Produce Company. In 1907, just after the turn of the century, more peas were canned in Wisconsin than in any other state.[50]

Another agricultural industry that developed in the county was malting. Like many areas in Wisconsin where German immigrants set up small breweries, Manitowoc County had its share of these small enterprises even before the Civil War. Included in the most memorable of these early breweries were the Rahr Brewery (Manitowoc), Muellers (Two Rivers), Pautz, Kunz (Branch), Scheibe (Centerville), and Gutheil Brothers (Kiel). Just before Prohibition became law in 1918, several of these local breweries merged to form the Kingsbury Breweries Company.[51]

The Rahr brothers decided to make their own malt, using locally grown grain, particularly barley. Just before the Civil War, William Rahr added a small malt house to his 1847 brewery and began to sell the excess to neighboring breweries. His location close to Lake Michigan in Manitowoc was ideal because the malting process requires great quantities of cold, clear water. In 1863 the company had grown sufficiently to build several grain elevators along the Manitowoc River to store the large quantities of barley being shipped in for processing.[52]

With barley, hay, and other feed crops replacing wheat by the early 1880s, these breweries stimulated the production of malt, first for local markets, and soon for the growing statewide and national demand.

## Toward the Century's Final Decades

By 1880 the county's population had surpassed 37,000 and the surge of prosperity in both industry and farmland continued to be strong. The coming of the railroads promised a bright industrial future for the area since it no longer had to suffer during the shutdown of lake shipping in winter. That same year the county voted Democratic once again, shaking off its wartime Republican leanings and giving presidential contender Winfield Scott Hancock 3,676 votes over the victorious Republican James A. Garfield's 2,988.

This Democratic pattern continued until just before the turn of the century in 1896, when Republican nominee William McKinley took the county by more than 1,000 votes over the "cross of gold" Populist Democrat William Jennings Bryan. By the late 1890s the county had two incorporated cities, a number of banks, newspapers, schools, and hospitals, in addition to its farms and growing industries.[53] The saga of the growing culture of the county, its new cities, utilities, stores, and professions is another story of progress in the last decades of the nineteenth century.

*Kunz, Bleser & Co., which began in 1858 as the Gottfried Kunz Brewery, was one of several breweries in Manitowoc County. This advertising poster from about 1885 shows the first beer that Kunz, Bleser & Co. produced—called Export Lager. When Prohibition took hold, the firm joined with the Rahr Brewery to form a new organization called the Manitowoc Products Co. In 1924 the company name was changed again—this time to Kingsbury Brewery. Courtesy, Manitowoc County Historical Society*

# CHAPTER FOUR

# *Urban Growth and County Culture*

## 1 8 6 0 – 1 8 9 0

**D**uring the same decades that Manitowoc County farmers and industrialists were creating local prosperity after the Civil War, the area's two leading settlements, Manitowoc and Two Rivers, were organized under Wisconsin law as cities. City status brought the benefits of urban utilities, as electric, gas, sewerage, and water facilities developed before the turn of the century.

Population growth throughout the county also meant that banks and schools grew in number, the professions of law and medicine developed, and hospitals were established. The last three decades of the nineteenth century also witnessed the growing popularity of cultural offerings from musical and theatrical societies to local theaters and traveling shows. Before the turn of the century, newspapers, the telegraph, and even the telephone brought the citizens of Manitowoc County into immediate contact with the outside world so that news of the outbreak of another war, this time in Cuba, reached them within minutes. The modern age of electronics and popular culture had begun.

## The County's First Two Cities

With a population of 5,168 in 1870, the village of Manitowoc could apply to become a city under Wisconsin law. City status brought multiple benefits in terms of taxing ability and the resultant offering of greater city services, from fire and police protection to a number of utilities. On March 12, 1870, the Wisconsin legislature officially granted the city charter and designated the first Tuesday in April as the date for municipal elections of mayor, constable, police magistrate, and aldermen.

With the new powers to tax, the city could hire its own harbor master, clerk, assessor, bridge tender, fire chief, city attorney, sealer of weights and measures, and street commissioner to be stewards of city property and take better care of the citizenry. Less than one month after the charter was approved, Manitowoc elected its first mayor, Peter Johnston, who presided over the construction of the city's first iron bridge, the creation of a new cemetery, sanitary cisterns for fresh water, and city sewers. One of the most important new city departments, however, was the recently expanded fire department, which purchased several horse-drawn engines during 1871 just in time for the greatest fire threat of the century.[1]

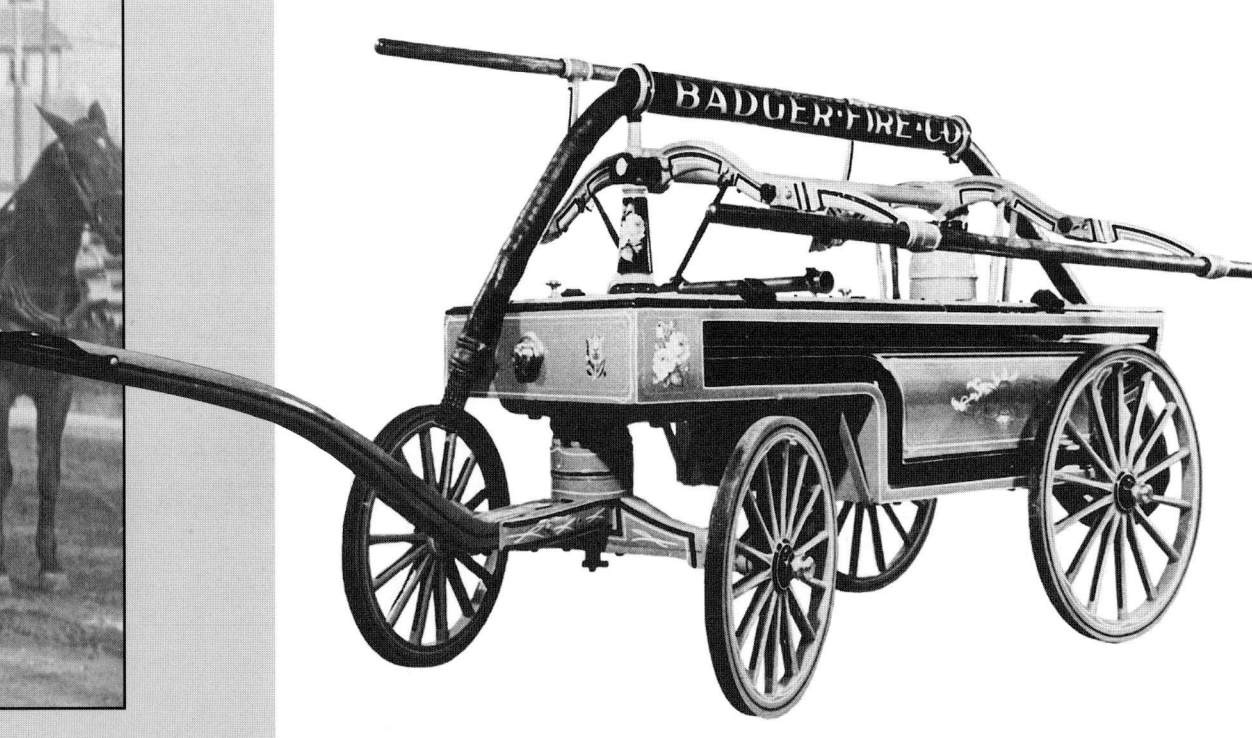

**65**

## The Threat of Fires

In 1871 the Peshtigo Fire burned thousands of acres to the north and brought the greatest loss of life of any fire in American history, occurring the same day as the highly publicized Chicago fire. Similar fires broke out throughout Manitowoc County that same October as forests, dry as tinder, burned out of control. In the county's northern towns, the blaze destroyed hundreds of acres, homes, and farmsteads as terrified residents hurried east to the lakeshore to try to save themselves.

The *Manitowoc Pilot*, one of the county's leading newspapers, chronicled this terror in its October 5th issue:

> **The fire which has been devastating the surrounding county for the past three weeks shows no abatement of its ravages…On Tuesday morning, a high wind from the west sprang up, and very soon our city was enveloped in smoke so dense as to obscure the light of the sun, and the wind, which seemed like the blast from a hot furnace, bore on its wings burnt leaves and other debris from the conflagration which seemed at that time to threaten with destruction everything within its reach.[2]**

Two days later the roaring inferno that became known as the Peshtigo Fire began.

However, when the worst of the fires took their toll to the north, most of the county was spared. Volunteer firemen raced to do what they could, as the report related. "The firemen were promptly on the ground and by fighting it inch by inch, we are happy to state that it was once more under control."[3] Nevertheless, while lives and villages were spared, many farmers in the northern part of the county lost all of their timber, including the valuable tamarack logs used by the tanneries.

*Nearly 10 years after the Electric Light Company began providing electricity to the city of Manitowoc, an electric trolley system was constructed to connect Manitowoc and Two Rivers—the county's main cities at the time. The Manitowoc & Two Rivers Railway, shown here, carried passengers between the two cities after the system was completed in 1899. Courtesy, Manitowoc County Historical Society*

One family, from just north of Two Rivers, had to use ingenuity, since the wells were almost dry in that rainless fall season. They threw the contents of their pickle barrels onto their outbuildings in order to save them. As a descendant later recalled, only one "log outbuilding was lost and deer came in later and ate the scattered pickles."[4]

Maple Grove, a settlement with many Irish farmers, posted a list of insurance losses that included "500 bushels wheat and oats and 15 tons hay…$1,000," and "barn, grain and hay…$1,200." However, those farmers who carried insurance were the lucky ones. Many others were wiped out by the fire's destructive power. One writer from Two Creeks described the 24-hour vigil kept by citizens who poured water on roofs to protect buildings from the flying sparks. "It was so hot the manure piles or rubbish heaps in farmers' yards caught fire," and people buried their furniture and valuables at the bottom of muddy streams to try to protect them.[5]

Finally, through the arrival of rain on October 9 (the first since early August), the fires were extinguished and the rest of the property saved. Relief supplies poured north, most heading to Peshtigo, but one ship brought clothing, blankets, and food to the citizens of Two Creeks, Mishicot, Cooperstown, and Gibson, where the worst damage had occurred. More than a century later naturalists reported that several charred stumps were still visible in forests at several northern locations in the county.[6]

## Waterworks and Electricity: Urban Improvements

One of the key problems during the fires was the great shortage of water. Wells had run dry during the drought of 1871, and few cisterns had been built. To address this problem, the new City of Manitowoc established a waterworks department that built more cisterns, and in 1889 chartered the Manitowoc Water Works Company. This company was bonded for $200,000 to erect a new waterworks plant at the lakefront, near the foot of Seventh Street, with the most modern machinery and pumps. The waterworks installed a 250,000-gallon reservoir so that no more shortages would threaten the city.[7]

For similar health reasons, the city built an extensive sewer system in 1893, which would drain all of the streets and alleys, as well as any other sewage from underground pipes. Before the turn of the century most of the city's main thoroughfares had been paved or set with local brick to reduce the dust and mud and to assist, with new drainage gutters, in making the sewers safer and more efficient.[8]

Another form of urban safety modernization came with the introduction of streetlights, which reduced crime and accidents in American cities. In many cities, such as Milwaukee, the first lights utilized gas, but in Manitowoc, the creation of the Electric Light Company in 1891 preceded the arrival of gas by almost 10 years. Streetlights, electricity to homes and offices, and soon an electric streetcar brought safety, efficiency, and mass transportation to the city for the first time during the "Gay Nineties." City life took on a whole new glow as nighttime entertainments became increasingly feasible and popular.[9]

Another utility that was greatly needed was a streetcar, or interurban, to connect the cities of Manitowoc and Two Rivers. More than a decade after

*When electricity arrived in Manitowoc in 1891, residents began to enjoy the comforts of electrical power in businesses, homes, and in the city streets. This image, taken prior to 1936, shows Manitowoc's streets lighted by single electric bulbs. The bulbs were housed in large glass globes and mounted to electric poles. In 1936 the electric wires were placed underground and the electric poles were replaced with more attractive light fixtures. Courtesy, Manitowoc Public Utilities*

*ABOVE: Lack of space for a growing collection of books prompted citizens to apply for additional funds to build a new library in Manitowoc. Completed in 1902, the Manitowoc Carnegie Library provided modern amenities and organized programs such as reading groups for children. Courtesy, Manitowoc Public Library*

*RIGHT: Reading circles and prominent, wealthy citizens played a role in jump starting the effort to open libraries in Manitowoc and Two Rivers in the late 1800s. Two Rivers built its first public library in 1892 and with money from the Carnegie Library fund, was able to build a larger facility—called the Joseph Mann Library—in 1914. Courtesy, Lester Public Library*

the arrival of train service, such an interurban was still only a dream. Finally, in late 1899, tracks were completed by the Manitowoc Traction Company and the first electric trolley connected the downtown depots of the two cities. Further plans were drawn up to take the line south along the lakeshore to Sheboygan, but this was never completed. However, at least the county's two main cities were connected for passenger travel and increased commercial cooperation.[10]

## The City of Two Rivers

Just eight years after Manitowoc became a chartered city, Two Rivers achieved that status as well. On March 18, 1878, the Wisconsin legislature created the county's second city with a similar election and government structure to that of Manitowoc. Like its sister city to the south, Two Rivers soon developed city-funded fire departments, a park system, and other offices that moved into a newly built city hall. The police "department" actually consisted of only two men: One, called the "chief," patrolled the streets by day, and the other by night.[11]

Soon Two Rivers also could boast of its own waterworks, electric lighting system, and other urban amenities. In fact, learning from the Manitowoc example, the Two Rivers utility was able to save money by combining the Two Rivers Water Works, Electric Light, and Power Company under one roof in 1901. The city also moved quickly to build sewers and to pave its streets, choosing the macadamized system (of crushed stones) over bricks.[12]

Two Rivers, with its strong base of industry from tanning to wooden and metal ware manufacturing, had become a part of the railroad network in 1874, just one year after the train arrived in Manitowoc. With its own local leadership, businesses, and civic pride, the new city was determined not to play second fiddle to its neighbor, but to establish its own distinct urban identity and culture with its own civic and educational institutions.

### New Libraries, Better Schools

As in other midwestern cities, the idea of a circulating library followed shortly after settlement when pioneers decided to pool their books and share them. In Manitowoc County, settlers in Kossuth, Meeme, Two Rivers, and Manitowoc organized these private, circulating book collections during the 1850s. In 1857 a group of young men in Manitowoc organized the first subscription library, whereby a formal collective actually owned books and members subscribed by paying a fee. However, these small private efforts did not provide reading materials to very many citizens.[13]

Finally, in 1868, town leader K.K. Jones donated a lot and a building on York Street in Manitowoc for the area's first semipublic library. Although circulating privileges were still restricted to members, the policy of who could join was wide open. However, the amount of the fees, $4 annually or $25 for

*Other forms of entertainment became popular in the years before the turn of the century, including the formation of bands. Some groups traveled around the county playing at dance halls while others gave public concerts. Members of one of the county's many bands take a moment to pose with their instruments in this circa 1885 photo. Courtesy, Manitowoc County Historical Society*

*Professional basketball games, held at the Opera House in Two Rivers, were well-attended events in the early 1900s. The Reach Athletic Club team, shown in this circa 1905 photo, was formed in 1902 and was one of several home teams that kept the Opera House packed with fans. From left to right (front row) are Billy Reed, Frank Lamach, Anton Lamach, (back row) Julius Belz, Dr. Joseph Eggers, and Gus "Shorty" Belz. Courtesy, Robert A. Niquette Collection*

*In the late 1860s baseball became more popular in the county as local teams formed and began to play other teams from nearby cities. Manitowoc's City Team is shown in this 1896 photo. Courtesy, Manitowoc County Historical Society*

a lifetime membership, kept poorer citizens from participating.[14]

During the next several years this "Jones Library Association" began to use its membership fees to develop a book-purchasing fund to enhance the collection. Benefit concerts and readings also built up the fund, until the collection of 1,600 volumes required the services of the first librarian, Alonzo D. Smith. In lieu of a salary for the first several librarians, the fund provided money for heat and free rent of the living rooms above the library.[15]

However, the old home soon fell into disrepair and the library closed its doors until members of a women's group, the Clio Club, took over its care. The club then lobbied leading businessmen and city fathers in order to convert the collection into a free public library such as those enjoyed in many other cities. Three of the women leading this effort, Mrs. William Rahr (of the malting family), Mrs. Lyman Nash (of the newspaper and printing concern), and Mrs. James S. Anderson (wife of the county judge), put together more than $4,700 in public subscriptions before taking their case to the city council in 1899.

The approach was successful, aided by the public support of Nash's newspaper and of William Rahr, then mayor of Manitowoc. The city agreed to take over the library with tax support, and secured new rooms above the post office, adjacent to the river on North Eighth Street. Finally, a salary was available for a full-time librarian, and Henrietta von Briesen, a graduate of the Illinois State University library school, became the city's first professional librarian. As the collection developed, however, the rooms over the post office became cramped and a citizen committee successfully applied to the

Andrew Carnegie fund, receiving money to build a new Carnegie Library in 1902.[16]

Acting earlier than Manitowoc, the citizens of Two Rivers were able to establish their own public library, the Joseph Mann Library, which also grew out of local volunteer efforts and citizen subscriptions. A Chautauqua Reading Circle in Two Rivers had begun the collection in 1888, and soon leading citizens took on the campaign to collect sufficient funding for a new building. In 1891 a new library was built, with the $3,500 fund, on 16th Street between Washington and Adams.

This citizen support, however, was not sufficient to pay for the mainte-

*Manitowoc's ships may have been frozen in, but this 1891 photo shows cold-weather activities enjoyed by local residents. Ice skating was one of the many popular forms of recreation for citizens, especially along the county's frozen rivers. Courtesy, Wisconsin Maritime Museum*

nance of the building or collection, and in 1895 the City of Two Rivers agreed to take over its support, pay for staff and expenses, and make it a free public library. With at least $500 annually in public funding, the library was able to build its collection to almost 4,000 books by the turn of the century.[17]

The growth of schools throughout the county was another top priority of its education-minded citizens. Beginning in the 1840s a number of small, one-room schools had been started in townships, benefiting from the Wisconsin and federal school fund, which set aside land sale receipts from one section, or 640 acres, for the support of public education. With the arrival of many immigrants, particularly Germans who wanted education in the German tongue, other small schools were also established. By 1860 the county could boast of 86 separate school districts, with more than 3,970 children enrolled.[18]

In the county's two cities, public education changed shape with the opening of both kindergartens and high schools during the 1870s, the latter mandated by the Wisconsin free public high school law of 1872. The larger schools were also "departmentalized" into various grades, instead of children of all ages studying together in one room. Boards of education and an elected county superintendent had oversight responsibilities for school quality, teacher qualifications, and safety.

Regulations included separate outhouses for boys and girls, and the use of individual drinking cups, instead of a single ladle, to cut down on the spread of diseases. Soon the larger schools were able to add specialized classes in music, vocational training, cooking, science, and business, in addition to the three "R's."

One continuing problem, however, was the shortage of qualified teachers, particularly for the smaller rural schools where boarding out the teacher was still very common. Teachers' salaries remained low, with the average male teacher receiving $22 per month and the average female $15. By 1870 the number of children enrolled in schools throughout the county had doubled

*Thanks to the efforts of the Ceske Slovanska Lipa, or the Bohemian and Slovakian Lodge, Manitowoc had a facility to conduct numerous events for citizens including balls and parties, musicals, plays, and dance classes. The association purchased property at North Eighth Street in 1884 for $700 and completed what would come to be known as the Opera House in 1889. By the time this photo was taken in 1975, the building was in the process of being razed because of extensive deterioration. Courtesy, Manitowoc County Historical Society*

to 7,810 and the shortage was critical. Even the opening of Lutheran and Catholic schools did not alleviate the problem, which grew steadily worse throughout the 1880s. By 1890 there were more than 110 public schools in the county and 19 parochial. Shortages were acute.

To address this problem, the county established its own teacher training institute in response to a state law offering support that passed in 1899. In 1901, by act of the county board, the Manitowoc Teachers' Training School was founded, with an initial enrollment of 44 students. As an incentive to potential teacher candidates, the county provided free textbooks and provided all classes tuition free. The school's first graduates of the one-year course numbered 32, a great boon to meet the needs for new teachers throughout the area.[19]

## Clubs and Culture

Just as industry and education were making strong gains in the county in this post-Civil War period, so too, the daily life of its citizens was filled with an increasing variety of social clubs and organizations and cultural outlets. One of the most prominent and popular organizations in the country in the nineteenth century, the Masonic order, was also a leader for men in Manitowoc County. Lodge 65 was organized in 1856, followed by Lodge 107, for German Masons, two years later.[20]

Another popular fraternal group, the Odd Fellows, had its origins in England as a pub club. In the United States, the Odd Fellows brought a social outlet and civic spirit to many small towns. In Manitowoc, the attempt to organize a lodge before the Civil War ran into difficulty and was revived immediately after the soldiers returned home in 1865. Thereafter, the organization began to thrive, with 114 members by 1880 who met in its own hall. Similarly, an Odd Fellows lodge in Two Rivers owned its own building, constructed in 1874. A member of the Two Rivers lodge, W. Aldrich, also became grand master of the state organization.[21]

Germans in the county followed suit with the creation of their own Odd Fellows chapter in 1871. Outlying areas also needed the social outlet provided by these groups and Kiel and Reedsville created their own chapters before 1900. In addition, women joined the "sister" lodge of the Good Fellows, with the creation of the Rebecca orders in several locations throughout the county.

Other similar fraternal organizations included the anti-alcohol society, the Good Templars, who worked for local temperance; the traditional German group, the Sons of Hermann; and the Knights of Pythias, founded on the principles of friendship, charity, and benevolence. Catholics in the county established the Order of the Foresters in 1894, succeeded by the Knights of Columbus eight years later, a group that enjoyed widespread support.[22]

All of these groups were largely social in nature, filling in the lonely evenings in the days before movies, radio, or television. They also worked for civic causes, offering support to charity drives, helping with the new orphans' home, and fulfilling the spirit of local boosterism so common in the post-Civil War decades.

One of the groups that also had a mission was the lodge of the Modern Woodsmen, created in 1890 in Manitowoc, with additional chapters in Kiel, Two Rivers, Reedsville, Cooperstown, Gibson, Centerville, Mishicot, Cato, Eaton, School Hill, and Two Creeks. This group became one of the most active lodges at the turn of the century, sponsoring county-wide conventions, establishing summer camps, and holding a yearly picnic for all members and their families.[23]

The women's organizations in the county also served several purposes, charitable as well as social. Two of the earliest, the South Side and the North Side Relief associations, were organized in 1880 and 1884, respectively, to help the families of Great Lakes sailors. Holding benefits to raise money,

*Two Rivers' old Turner Hall, shown in this 1900 photo, was built in 1873 and owned by the Turnverein Society (whose members are shown standing in front). The hall eventually became the Two Rivers Opera House, which became the center for community entertainment and events. Remodeled in the early 1900s to accommodate vaudeville shows, roller skating, dances, and basketball games, the building was eventually sold in 1931 to the government for use as a site for the U.S. Post Office. Courtesy, Robert A. Niquette Collection*

these relief organizations purchased food, medicine, and clothing for families in need, and later donated money for free milk for these children at the local schools.[24]

One leading women's club in town, which became part of the growing Women's Club movement nationally, was the Clio Club. Created in 1893, it included the wives of Manitowoc's most prominent business and civic leaders. Holding 20 regular meetings each year, the club divided its efforts between civic causes, including the public library, and literary gatherings. At the literary meetings, a favorite author was chosen each month for reading and discussion, with one member being responsible for leading the talk and for doing background work on the author's life and literary career. Closed in membership, the club joined the ranks of those elite women's organizations that later led to women's activism in a variety of social causes in the next century.[25]

Other clubs, usually organized separately by gender, included the Young Men's Institute (1856) which held lectures on education topics, including one at the turn of the century on the "Russian War" then being waged between the Czar and Japan. Other societies with more specific purposes were the Burns Society, of Scotch residents; the Norden, of Norwegians who wanted to keep alive the flame of their national literature; and the Monday Music Club (women), established in 1898 to study classical and modern composers.[26]

In addition to studying composers, the county came alive with the sound of its own singing societies and bands during these decades at the end of the nineteenth century. Germans figured prominently in several of the earliest groups, including the Manitowoc Musical Society, the Freier Saengerbund, the Concordia, and the Harmonia, all of which gave public concerts on holidays and enjoyed a wide following.[27]

Bands also organized in settlements small and large, as many immigrants enjoyed the opportunity of unpacking the musical instruments they had carefully brought from their homelands. Newton boasted one of the first such groups, the Schmidt Brothers Band, established just before the Civil War. This group was joined after the war by Professor Bieling's Band, the Lutheran Band, the Acme Band, Professor Weinschenk's Orchestra, the North

*Audiences were captivated by the many vaudeville shows, concerts, and other events that took place at local opera houses. This early 1900s photo depicts the interior of the Two Rivers Opera House, which could hold as many as 300 people for a performance. Courtesy, Robert A. Niquette Collection*

Side Brass Band, the Polish Band, the Lakeshore Mandolin and Guitar Club, and the Two Rivers Cornet Band. Together with impromptu groups, informal glee clubs, and the many church choirs of all denominations, music became a central part of popular entertainment and culture during the 1870s, 1880s, and 1890s.[28]

Theatrical groups, too, flourished in these decades when professional or electronic entertainment was lacking and people actively created the arts, rather than just passively watching outside performers. Once again, as in the musical groups, German immigrants took the lead. One newspaper reported that the county's first theatrical production, a German play, was performed in Manitowoc in 1848.[29]

Other performances followed—sometimes in English, sometimes in German—and groups such as the German Theatrical Association began to schedule regular offerings, given in a vacant room in a downtown store. Productions were very popular and were followed by social sessions that always included the celebratory drinking of "schnapps." Another theatrical group, the Bohemians, was founded during the 1860s, followed by the Manitowoc Dramatic Association in 1874 and the Young Peoples' Dramatic Club in the 1890s.[30]

### Recreation and Entertainment

Outdoor amusements for county residents consisted of the traditional ice skating on the frozen rivers and winter sledding, as well as spelling bees, quilting bees, and taffy pulls. Sport shooting was also popular and a number of shooting clubs were established for social as well as sporting purposes. Gymnastics was another favorite of the German residents, with the county's first Turnverein organized at Manitowoc in 1854, and a second at Two Rivers in 1857, with Centerville, Kiel, and Mishicot following soon after.[31]

During the warmer months the rise of baseball across the country was echoed in Manitowoc County when local teams competed with surrounding cities. In 1868 the Clipper's Boys team was organized, followed the next year by the Lakeside Baseball Club. Football also became popular at the high school level during the 1890s, as did the new sport of bicycling. The Manitowoc Bicycling Club was founded in 1884 for recreational cycling[32]

Boating and tennis were growing in popularity during these same decades. In 1885 the Manitowoc Boat Club was organized to hold regattas on the lake.

Club tennis became an organized sport for adults in the 1890s, as a social tennis club was established in Manitowoc. Horse racing for sport, bowling, and speed skating also became organized activities for recreation before the turn of the century.[33]

Along with these recreational outlets, one of the most popular forms of summer entertainment was the Manitowoc County Fair, which began during the early 1870s. When the County Agricultural Association was officially established in 1874, the annual fair was held in Clarks Mills, with three days of shows, racing, exhibits, and games. Ten years later the fair location was moved to Manitowoc, where a formal fairgrounds was built. Rules for fair-goers prohibited the use of intoxicating beverages, gambling, or any games of chance. For an admission price of 25 cents for adults and 15 cents for children, fair-goers could witness the best agricultural, livestock, and industrial products of the county; purchase food, jewelry, and souvenirs; watch the horse races; and visit exhibits of arts, crafts, canned food, bakery, quilts and handiwork of all sorts.[34]

In addition to the excitement of the fair, the county was visited annually by a traveling circus, the Billy Schultz Circus, an offshoot of the famous Ringling Brothers show. Schultz first came to Manitowoc from Milwaukee as a performer for the county fair in 1899. He caught the entertainment bug and moved to Chicago to train in minstrel shows and organize a company of his own. He soon began to travel around a circuit to many Wisconsin

cities, always including Manitowoc in his route. He became adept at musical comedy acts, clowning, and gymnastics and the annual visit of his variety show and circus became an event of great excitement for county citizens.[35]

One county group that was cohesive socially and very committed to the performing arts was the Ceske Slovanska Lipa, the Bohemian and Slovakian Lodge. In 1884 the group purchased its own building on North Eighth Street in Manitowoc for $700 and turned it into the Opera House. The first floor was used for gymnastics and tumbling until renovations created a stage and a small theater space, with an elaborate entryway protected by a red canopy that led to the street.[36]

The alley next to the Opera House was large enough for the liquor wagon from the nearby wholesale liquor dealer to pull his wagon alongside and unload the kegs of beer and wines for after-theater parties and for the many gala balls held there. One particular festivity, recalled by the daughter of the theater manager, was the Christmas ball. In preparation for the event, the green velvet theater seats were pushed to the side so that the whole floor could be polished. In the center of the dance floor stood a large Christmas tree decorated with apples, candy, and popcorn balls.

At 10:30 p.m., the lights were extinguished from the tree and only the ceiling Christmas lights shone down on the dancers and their families. At a signal, all of the children gathered around the tree (sometimes toppling it over) to take the candy and treats as their special Christmas gifts. Once the tree was stripped, the ball itself began, led by a grand march of couples from youngest to oldest. Santa Claus then appeared on the stage, awarding each promenading family more special treats. Afterwards, the children watched and listened to the music, or curled up with their gifts in the velvet box seats above while the dancing lasted late into the night below them. It was a special Christmas tradition.[37]

**ICE CREAM SUNDAE**

In 1881, George Hallauer asked Edward C. Berner, the owner of a soda fountain at 1404-15th Street, to top a dish of ice cream with chocolate sauce, hitherto used only for ice cream sodas. The concoction cost a nickel and soon became very popular, but was sold only on Sundays.

One day a ten year old girl insisted she have a dish of ice cream "with that stuff on top," saying they could "pretend it was Sunday." After that, the confection was sold every day in many flavors. It lost its Sunday-only association, to be called ICE CREAM SUNDAE when a glassware salesman placed an order with his company for the long canoe-shaped dishes in which it was served, as "sundae dishes."

Erected 1973

The Opera House became a community center of sorts, where dancing classes were held, traveling shows and bands could perform, and other community groups (who had no such facility) could hold their masked balls and parties. Joined by the Turner Hall, which also became a central community facility (later called the Orpheum), the Opera House hosted the early vaudeville shows that came to town beginning in the 1890s. At the turn of the century one visiting vaudeville troupe included the rising young boxer John L. Sullivan, whose fame was spreading across the country. When he signed the theater register, news spread quickly and soon boys from all over town were following him around. Several local chroniclers attribute the rise of youth boxing as a local sport to this exciting visit.[38]

Soon other theaters were built including the Crystal Theater at Eighth and Chicago streets, the Colonial Theater at 11th and Washington, and the Vaudette at York and Eighth.[39]

In Two Rivers, another opera house became the center of most of the city's entertainment activities. The old Turner Hall, complete with its "turn pole" around which German gymnasts had spun in the fine art of body building, was purchased in 1889 and remodeled into a theater for community use. From the 1890s through the 1930s this facility became the center of visiting minstrel shows, vaudeville shows, and frequent choral recitals and band concerts, as well as holiday balls.

Vivid posters were displayed around the city advertising the next show or event at Turner Hall. Celebrants often came early and had dinner in the rooms to the side of the stage, or stayed afterwards for sandwiches, snacks, and drinks. The hall was large enough to accommodate more than 300 people, including those who used chairs on the large balcony that encircled the first floor. The distance from the edge of the stage to the front doors was just over 100 feet, and a lower level was utilized for a boiler room and six dressing rooms for actors from the traveling shows.[40]

At times, these vaudeville shows included animal acts and another basement room had to be set aside to house them. On more than one occasion

animals escaped from their rooms and several theatergoers from the early 1900s recalled evenings when monkeys visited the audience or hung from the balcony railings overhead, stealing the crowd's attention from the act on stage. A list of shows that visited Turner Hall during its heyday, before it became a motion picture theater by 1911, include acts as varied as a German play, *Manfred's Marianne*; a rendition of *Uncle Tom's Cabin*; the Peak Family Bell Ringers; a magic lantern show; a band of Italian minstrels; and a concert by the Philharmonic Concert Company.[41]

Another popular entertainment that utilized Turner Hall even before the turn of the century was professional basketball. Seats would be placed around the perimeter and crammed into the balcony, while teams from other cities near and far came to town for matches against the local five—who called themselves the "Reach Athletic Team." Local companies, notably the Hamilton Manufacturing Company, would sponsor these visiting teams which included the Milwaukee "Bright Spots," the Beloit "Fairies," the Chicago "Big Five," and the New York "Nationals."[42]

When not being used for basketball and traveling shows, Turner Hall was the popular home of such local groups as the Gloe-Naidl Orchestra, which performed for weekend dances, and the Katzenjammer Kids, a musical group that enjoyed playing cards and drinking as much as playing ragtime and popular tunes. On other occasions, local teenagers used the hall for roller skating, and area high schools held their graduation exercises there. It was never without a daily event and served as the entertainment heartbeat of Two Rivers and its surrounding community for several decades until the innovation of the motion pictures replaced the old vaudeville theaters during the 1920s.[43]

While these opera houses and theaters hosted year-round entertainments, other traveling shows were more seasonal, particularly the annual summer Chautauqua lecture series. Many residents' earliest memories of summer included band concerts in Union or Washington Park, and attendance at the Chautauqua, where famous lecturers, artists, actors, explorers, and musicians

*RIGHT AND BELOW: Shopping became a favorite pastime as the cities in Manitowoc County prospered. Schroeder's Department Store opened in 1891 in Two Rivers. In 1899, in order to accommodate its growing customer base, Schroeder Bros. (as it was now called) constructed a large three-story building in 1899. The popular department store provided a wide variety of products including groceries and clothing. Schroeder Bros. also served many of its customers by providing home delivery of groceries via horse-drawn wagon. Courtesy, Schroeder's Department Store*

would put on public performances as part of their circuit tour from Chautauqua, New York. One summer, famous orator and politician William Jennings Bryan came to town and delivered his "Prince of Peace" lecture to a large crowd.[44]

Following the evening Chautauqua performances, families would often walk or go by buggy to nearby ice cream parlors. One story holds that it was at a Two Rivers parlor that the first ice cream sundae was served. One of the most popular parlors, Ed Berners, created a dish of ice cream with a choice of toppings and served it to the public in 1881. Soon the popularity of this dish spread widely and Berners became famous for its special holiday creations, including the Washington House Sundae with cherries on top.[45]

## The Shops and Stores
Part of the excitement of the growing cities of Two Rivers and Manitowoc was the increasing variety of the shops and stores that lined the downtown streets. Residents from across the county looked forward to coming to town both for the vaudeville shows and entertainment and for the fun of shopping. Weekend trips, or Friday night shopping events, became popular and the streets of both cities were lined with buggies as eager shoppers went from store to store.

One of the foremost stores of the area, Schroeder's Department Store in Two Rivers, boasted a three-story downtown building and a wide variety of merchandise. The store was founded by Peter Schroeder, whose family had farmed in the Two Creeks area after emigrating from Germany in the 1850s. Originally located at Washington and 18th streets, the first mercantile store was of wood, with a series of hitching posts in front for horses. Peter's three younger brothers joined the business in 1896 and it was renamed the Schroeder Bros. Department Store, relocating to the southeast corner of Washington and Walnut in a brand-new red brick building.[46]

As it expanded, the store featured dry goods, cooking equipment, men's clothing, shoes and boots, as well as groceries and produce—everything under one roof. The business office was located on the mezzanine level and all transactions were sent there by means of a "trolley," or pulley system, with the receipts returned to the customers the same way. Shopping was also a social pastime in those days, and customers enjoyed the extra time to chat while waiting the return of their receipt from the mezzanine. For those who could not come in person, Schroeder Bros. offered a horse-and-wagon delivery service that brought groceries and assorted items to a customer's home, including carrying all of the boxes or bags inside.[47]

Other specialty shops filled the downtown streets of both Two Rivers and Manitowoc, including the Urbanek and Wattawa Furniture Store, the Schuette Brothers Department Store, the Chapman Bakery, which specialized in pure rye bread, and the Manitowoc Iron and Metal Company, which advertised "rags, rubbers, hides, fur, wool, and scrap iron" for sale.[48]

The Manitowoc Music Company sold sheet music, organs, pianos, and other musical instruments, as well as sewing machines from its store on South Eighth Street, and one could get "meals at all hours" from the White Front Restaurant. Clocks and jewelry could be purchased from C. Liebenow & Son in Manitowoc and "superfluous hair, moles, warts…etc." could be "destroyed forever by the Electric Needle," at John M. Hoyer's office in the Williams Block. Those seeking wallpaper, toys, or guns could find them at J. Staehle & Son's store, near the seed plant.[49]

Ernest Hempel wove and sold rugs and carpets in his store at 1405 Washington Street and Schreiters Old Stand was the classic "5 and 10 cents store," offering hardware, hosiery, ribbons, laces, china, glassware, tinware, and stationery. Nearby, the store of Mendlik and Mulholland advertised that it was "strong on underwear," as well as notions of all kinds, coats, shawls, and men's furnishings. Rand and Roemer Hardware at York and Eighth streets sold iron stoves, paint, and tinware. In short, everything a household required could be purchased locally; there was no need for trips to shop in cities far away.[50]

### Financial Institutions

Underwriting this extensive commercial growth throughout the county, the leading banks and savings and loans also prospered during the post-Civil War period—with the single exception of the Panic of 1893 which took several into bankruptcy. Leading the way, the Manitowoc Savings Bank, organized in

1883, prospered with the growth of industry and city development in the area. Its capitalization grew from $25,000 at its founding to 10 times that amount 15 years later.[51]

At the turn of the century several other financial institutions were also making solid contributions to the stability of the local economy. The National Bank in Manitowoc, organized in 1894, built its new headquarters at the corner of York and Eighth streets and maintained a strong capital position, never lower than $100,000. Nearby, the German American Bank brought an ethnic flavor to area banking that appealed to wealthy German farmers and businessmen of the area.[52]

The bank that was hit the hardest by the national financial Panic of 1893, the T.C. Shove Banking Company, was actually driven under by the fire that destroyed the factory of its biggest client, the Manitowoc Manufacturing Company, which lost $175,000 worth of its capital property in the disastrous blaze of April 1892. Another local bank that succumbed to the panic, the Manitowoc State Bank, was found to be fundamentally unsound and legal action resulted that indicted several of its officers for embezzlement. The court cases involving claims against both banks went on for several years, before depositors were able to recover even a small amount of the money they had lost.[53]

The Bank of Two Rivers, established in 1891, included some of the leading industrialists of the city on its board, as did the Two Rivers Savings Bank, founded in 1902 by the Schroeder brothers and operating, at first, out of a booth on the first floor of their department store. Other smaller institutions that were able to weather the economic downturns included the Tisch Mills State Bank and the Mishicot State Bank, chartered under the Wisconsin banking laws of the 1890s.[54]

### The Professions: Law and Medicine

In addition to a strong banking network, Manitowoc County had enjoyed the services of a highly professional bar from its earliest years. While the first members of the bar in the county had to commute to Green Bay to attend court, the organization of the county's own separate court system in 1848

resulted in an increase in men who had "read the law" and who could put out a shingle as practitioners.

As in many counties, the judges took the lead in the organization of a local bar and in setting the standards for practicing law. A part of the state's fourth judicial circuit, Manitowoc County was fortunate to have a series of elected circuit judges who set very high standards and who would brook no unethical practices among the members of its bar. Beginning with Alexander W. Stow, the county's first judge, the subsequent leaders, judges Larrabee, Hoew, Gorsline, Taylor, McLean, and Gilson, enforced decorum and proper rules of procedure in the courtroom.[55]

In 1895 the Wisconsin legislature created the first municipal court for the City of Manitowoc, an action that brought cases involving city ordinances under local judicial control and relieved, somewhat, the 6,500-case burden handled by the county circuit bench. While the number of lawyers in the county was never large, and many who could practice law chose to enter business instead, leading practitioners such as P.J. Smalley, of the Smalley Manufacturing family, and Lyman Nash, who was also a printer and editor, were held in great esteem by the families and businesses they served. The law firm of Nash & Nash, the county's oldest, was founded in 1881 and continued with subsequent partners for more than a century.[56]

Medical practitioners, too, opened offices in Manitowoc in the decades following the Civil War, when breakthroughs in treatment brought an increased demand for their services. The pre-war epidemics had waned and the worst killers in these decades were diphtheria, typhus, and tuberculosis. One doctor, D.J. Easton, was self-taught and gave frequent lectures on the cures for various diseases. Even though there was no proof, other doctors considered him a charlatan and his practice slowly diminished.[57]

One problem, which got Easton into great trouble, was that he was a silent partner in a local pharmacy and began to write his prescriptions in code so that only that particular drugstore could fill them. This so angered other doctors and pharmacists in the area that one got himself elected to the legislature and helped to pass a state law mandating that all prescriptions had to be written in either English or Latin.[58]

Several years later, in 1882, the first medical society was organized in the county to try to enforce standards of medical practice and weed out alleged quacks. The society appealed to local newspaper editors to screen the advertisements from such phony practitioners who preyed upon an unsuspecting public and gave all doctors a bad name. Their appeal asked that newspapers in the area "debar the advertisements of medical charlatans…[avoiding] the falsity of the quack's claims, the cruelty of his promises, and the fraudulence of his methods."[59]

Other, more successful, healers included Franz Simon, a German immigrant, and Agnes Classon, the area's first female practitioner, who traveled to rural areas throughout the county caring for the sick and infirm. The first locally educated physician, F.W. Hammond, graduated from high school in Manitowoc before entering Milwaukee Medical College, paying the $150 entrance fees out of his earnings from three years of teaching. When his funds ran out, his family asked that he return to help on the farm, but a brother-in-law loaned him the $450 he needed to complete the next three years.[60]

Hammond recalled that there were few actual "cures" for diseases in the 1890s. Instead, he would try to diagnose an illness and prescribe ointments or potions to make his patients more comfortable. His first patient was a man who had a "jumping toothache," and handed Hammond a tool to extract the offending tooth. Although not a dentist, Hammond complied, the tooth came out, and the man paid him 25 cents and went away happy.

Another early patient told the doctor how he had cured himself of alcoholism by drinking a tonic called "Peruna." When Hammond read the label and saw that it was more than 30 percent alcohol, he told the man that 90 proof whiskey might have been better for him and much cheaper! Taking a sleigh across snowed-in roads in winter and bicycling to see his patients in summer, Hammond soon discovered that one of a country doctor's most important tools was a wire-cutter, to allow him to take shortcuts across farmers' fields when he was on an emergency visit.[61]

Even the profession of pharmacist involved a great deal of guesswork in these early years. Hammond recalled a local druggist who described physicians' prescriptions as "shotgun tonics." They contained such a variety of medications that one might be lucky enough to work! By the 1880s the State of Wisconsin began to regulate both the drug trade and licensing of pharmacists and physicians. During the 1880s and 1890s Manitowoc had only five pharmacies and fewer than 10 licensed physicians.[62]

ABOVE: Dr. F.W. Hammond, Manitowoc County's first locally educated doctor, often used wire cutters to get across farmers' fields in the event of an emergency. Hammond, born in 1873 near Cato in Manitowoc County, attended high school in Manitowoc and completed medical school in Milwaukee. He practiced medicine for 70 years. Courtesy, Manitowoc County Historical Society

LEFT: Lyman Nash, a printer and editor in Manitowoc who also held a law degree, was one of a small number of attorneys in the county. A prominent citizen, Nash was part of the county's oldest law firm, Nash & Nash, established in 1881. In addition, Nash's wife played a part in helping Manitowoc establish its first public library. Courtesy, Manitowoc County Historical Society

## The First Hospitals

Another great need was that of a community hospital. Following the leadership of Father Henry Jacobs of the St. Boniface parish, a citizens' group was founded to raise money for the first hospital in 1880. By the next year sufficient money had been raised to build a small, one-story frame facility that was named St. Mary's Hospital, with nursing care provided by the Sisters of Christian Charity.[63]

This first facility provided beds for 12 patients. Records revealed that its first patients included a man who had been shot in a hunting accident, a sailor injured in a storm on the lake, and a ragpicker who had been injured when a drunken farmer slammed into his sled. When patients were too poor to pay, the Sisters had to appeal to the County Poor Committee for relief assistance. However, ethnic conflicts between German and Polish Catholics over the hospital erupted and the small facility had to close its doors seven years later in 1888.[64]

It took another decade before the community rallied and unified behind another hospital fund, and the happy result was the establishment in 1898 of the Holy Family Hospital of Manitowoc, operated by the Sisters of Christian Charity. The total of funds collected, almost $4,000, was not enough but the Sisters decided to go forward on faith and a location of a high hill in Gerpheide's Park on the northwestern side of the city was secured for the building.[65]

The hill, on Western Avenue, was above property owned by the Rahr family, who made an exchange of acreage so that the Sisters could plant a small garden below the new structure.[66] The cornerstone was laid in September 1898, and the dedication of the new structure came just one year later at a final cost of $75,000, far more than the funds could cover. The new facility had 37 rooms and four wards and, with widespread community support, it was able to offer the most "modern" medical care available at the time. Built of stone and brick, it had modern elevators, an electric bell system, an operating room, as well as a dormitory for the Sisters, a chapel, and a large dining room.[67]

Under the leadership of Mother Alexa Fullmer, the hospital began to serve

*Construction of the county's second hospital began in September 1898, 10 years after St. Mary's Hospital had closed. When Holy Family Hospital opened its doors in Manitowoc just one year later, it was considered the most modern hospital in Wisconsin. The hospital's newest conveniences included a system of ventilation, electrical lighting, a passenger elevator, and electric bells. Courtesy, Holy Family Memorial Medical Center*

county residents of all faiths. While local residents were afraid to come to the hospital at first, its designation in 1899 as a marine hospital filled the beds with Great Lakes sailors. Gradually, the quality of care brought in more patients as hospitals all across the country began to spread the message that they were not places for just the poor, or places where people went to die.

By the beginning of the twentieth century, the hospital was serving more than 300 patients annually and needed to expand. The years before the world war also witnessed many advances in medicine and nursing, so that the hospital was able to establish its own nurses' training program to prepare for the new demands of the twentieth century.[68]

## Another War at the Century's End

At the end of the 1890s, the citizens of Manitowoc County could look back on the three decades since the end of the Civil War as a time of great prosperity and cultural development. Their county had two cities, profitable farms and industries, its own courts, a new hospital, many schools and libraries, and a variety of cultural institutions.

However, memories of the earlier war and the sacrifices of its soldiers were on the minds of many when the news came that the battleship *Maine* had blown up in the harbor of Havana, Cuba, and that America was once again at war in April 1898. Just one week later the local regiment, Company H, received its call to active duty on Thursday, April 28. The following morning, in pouring rain, the company boarded a train for Milwaukee, "amid the blare of bands and the shouts of hundreds of people who came to see them off."[69]

*The location for the new Holy Family Hospital—a former park and picnic ground—was cleared for construction in the spring of 1898. The cornerstone, placed in September 1898, was opened 75 years later by Sister Leovigild Spenner, assistant administrator, and Donald Orleans, administrator. Found were English and German newspapers of the day and religious relics. Courtesy, Holy Family Memorial Medical Center*

In Milwaukee, the regiment became part of the Second Wisconsin Infantry, which reported for duty in Washington, D.C., and was shipped to Puerto Rico for action in August. Their service in the ensuing battle to take the island from Spanish garrisons lasted for only two months, as American forces had little difficulty defeating the enemy in what Secretary of State John Hay called "the splendid little war." In fact, the onset of many fevers, from malaria to typhoid, brought more fatalities than did Spanish bullets. In September 1898 the Manitowoc regiment was returned to Washington for a parade and review before being dismissed and returned home by Christmas, a company of more than 100 men that had suffered only four casualties.[70]

This wartime service brought glory, few wounded, and many happy celebrations by the holidays. With their boys home, county residents settled down to the last year of the nineteenth century. The census of 1900 revealed the extent of growth in the preceding decades. The county had more than 42,000 residents, with its largest cities, Manitowoc, at 11,786, and Two Rivers, at 3,784, and its villages, Kiel, at 924, and Reedsville, 528.[71]

These county residents turned to a Republican nominee for president for the first time since Lincoln, when they gave William McKinley and his popular Vice President Theodore Roosevelt a resounding victory in the 1900 election. The citizens were also buoyed by the spirit of the "Gay Nineties," which celebrated the many advances in American industry, medicine, and the promises of more and better improvements in the exciting twentieth century to come.

# New Century, New Horizons

## 1900 – 1930

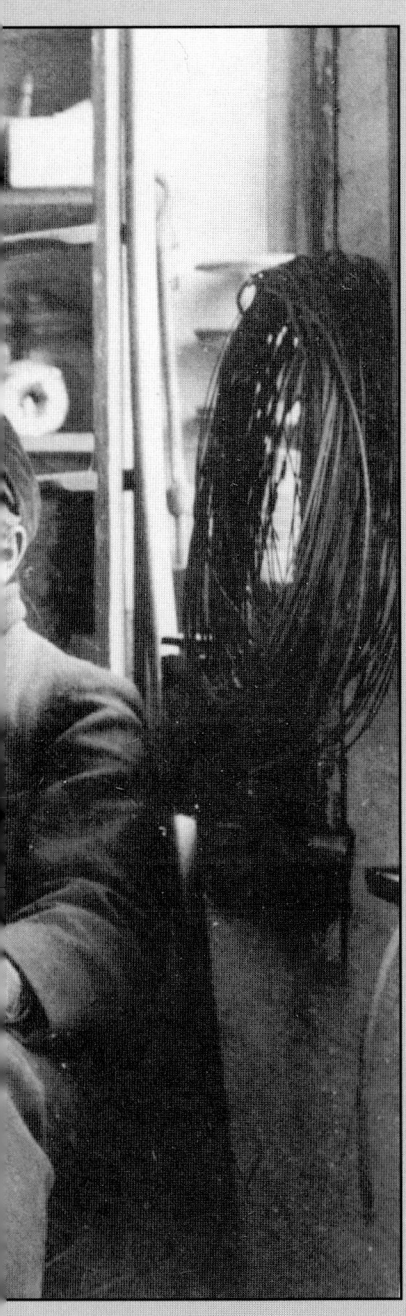

The early 1900s witnessed a country in the midst of celebration as bands marched in parades with the victorious veterans of the recent war. Americans viewed the dawn of the new century as a time of great economic and social promise. In Manitowoc County, the early decades of the twentieth century were years of agricultural and industrial growth. It was also a period when the quality of life, in community development, church and school building, culture, and the conveniences of technology, reached new heights.

It was during the early decades of the twentieth century that the urban areas of Manitowoc County experienced solid growth. The inauguration of rural mail delivery in 1900 helped to bring the outlying areas of the county into closer communication with the three cities, and with the rest of the state and the nation. There was an increase in civic pride, harking back to the historic Indian name for Manitowoc, "Munedoowk," or the "home of the good spirit." The organization of new villages and towns across the county brought ever more amenities to the rural areas, as did the development of larger central shopping districts in the three major cities of Manitowoc, Two Rivers, and Kiel.

## A Tide of Immigrants

In addition to the county's many German and Irish immigrants, most of whom arrived between 1840 and 1900, Manitowoc was enriched by a diversity of other immigrant groups. The Polish community in the county began to make its presence known even before 1900, with the organization of significant churches, including the congregations of St. Luke's in Two Rivers (later separated to form the Sacred Heart Parish), St. Casimir Parish in Northeim (Newton), and St. Boniface and St. Mary's in Manitowoc (dedicated in 1899). Just after the turn of the century, in 1906, the growing parish of St. Mary's organized its own Catholic school in a new brick building. This parish also established the county's first Polish Catholic social service agency, the Felician Sisters' Orphan Asylum, in 1888.[1]

At first many of the Polish settlers moved to county farms, but by the 1890s a large number also occupied an area just outside the city of Manitowoc that came to be called "Polish Hill." In 1891 the hill was taken into the city itself, by a revision of the charter, and later became the Seventh Ward. Many of the settlers found work in the booming shipbuilding industry, or worked on the docks or on the many lake steamers. As laborers, they became the backbone of the Democratic Party, endorsing Woodrow Wilson in both 1912 and 1916. The population of this Seventh Ward in 1910 was 3,700, increasing to 4,500 by 1920. By the early 1920s one in six people in the city of Manitowoc was of Polish descent.[2]

While still residing in a distinct enclave within the city, and in several rural communities, the Polish settlers at first spoke only in their native tongue and maintained close ties to their families back in the old country, or in Milwaukee or Chicago. However, after the turn of the century, the second generation began to value formal education and to learn the English language. The ethnic census of graduates from Manitowoc's high school indicates this growing emphasis on advanced education within the Polish community. Although only one or two of the school's graduates were Polish in each class prior to 1915, the number increased thereafter until it began to average a dozen or more by the 1920s.[3]

Similarly, the immigration of Bohemian and Czech settlers to the county concentrated at first in rural areas, particularly near Kossuth, Cooperstown, Franklin, Francis Creek, Gibson, Mishicot, and Kellnersville. Before 1900 there were only 50 to 60 members of this ethnic group living in the two major cities, out of 2,377 in the entire county. Among the earliest churches established by this immigrant group were Virgin Mary Catholic Church in

Tisch Mills, St. Wenceslaus Catholic Church in Greenstreet, and St. Mary Catholic Church in Reedsville. A sectarian community center, where many of the early Bohemians gathered to socialize, was the Stastny Hotel in Francis Creek. Many dances and weddings were held there at the turn of the century and Bohemian music and food abounded.[4]

Another immigrant religious group, the Jewish settlers, followed a similar pattern. The county's earliest Jewish families had come from Germany in the 1860s. One of these, the Joseph Mann family, settled in Two Rivers and operated a mercantile store and a sawmill. Joseph Mann became mayor of Two Rivers in 1886 and the family later bequeathed money for the city's public library, the Joseph Mann Library.[5]

Other Jewish families followed, particularly in the years around 1900, when the persecution of Jews in Russia and Eastern Europe became severe. Many settled in Manitowoc and worked at the various factories growing

*Members of the Polish community gained recognition as they established churches in the county. One of those churches, St. Mary's in Manitowoc, founded the county's first Polish Catholic social service agency—an orphan asylum, shown in this 1907 photo. The Felician Sisters, who operated the orphanage, farmed the surrounding land and occasionally were compelled to beg door to door to help make ends meet. Courtesy, Manitowoc County Historical Society*

there. Several newcomers who could not secure employment became peddlers, buying up scrap metal, fabric, or rags and driving around the county in horse-drawn wagons to sell trinkets, cookware, or cloth in return. In the process, they met residents from many immigrant groups, all of whom were perfecting their English-speaking skills. It became a form of education in itself. By 1900 there were 30 Jewish families in Manitowoc and several others in Two Rivers.

The first Jewish religious services were held on Saturdays in the Saenger Hall, leased for that purpose. Early weddings were often conducted at Turner Hall, but the settlers wanted a religious home of their own. In February 1900 members of the Jewish community gathered at a private home and organized the first congregation, the Anshe Poele Zedek, and hired a rabbi for six dollars a week, with promises of more money if he could offer classes to the children.[6]

Soon the congregation purchased an old Norwegian schoolhouse and moved it to 1221 South 13th Street. There it was remodeled into the Anshe Poele Zedek Synagogue, complete with a new Ark for the Torah, created by two men who were skilled carpenters with the Manitowoc Seating Company. The congregation worshipped there until a new brick synagogue was constructed in 1925.[7]

As even more Jewish refugees were forced out of Europe, they needed aid and shelter, which the community provided. The Golden family of Manitowoc used their spacious home as a stopover for immigrants until they could secure jobs and housing. The synagogue congregation provided food, clothing, and medicine when needed. Individuals in the congregation also sponsored several families, helping to pay for their passage and promising their support to assist with the immigration restrictions against "paupers."

The congregation prospered and kept strict rules for religious observances. At least 10 people were required in order for a service to be held at the synagogue. Each family was asked to pay 25 cents a month and members who missed Saturday services were fined 25 cents a week. All members were forbidden to work on the Sabbath, and the peddlers were expressly asked not to travel the county and sell their wares on Saturdays.[8]

Benevolence to the community at large remained a hallmark of the Jewish families. Simon Schwartz bequeathed money for a community counseling center and established a $6,000 fund to provide two college scholarships for Lincoln High School graduates. In 1927 the first B'nai B'rith Lodge (#1071) was organized in Manitowoc as a social and fraternal fellowship. The lodge's first 33 members comprised 95 percent of the Jewish men in the area. One of the lodge's first service projects was the sponsorship of a Boy Scout Troop.[9]

Jewish families from both Two Rivers and Manitowoc could gather in the lodge or synagogue easily because of the new streetcar line that connected the two cities. However, one family remembered the great blizzard of 1924, when the streetcar line was halted and many people could not return home and had to stay for two days with friends before the storm abated.

The community's Jewish women also organized a social and service society, part of the National Council of Jewish Women. This group studied history and current politics, and sponsored Hebrew classes for the synagogue's children. They also held card parties and rummage sales to raise

*ABOVE: Joseph Mann and his wife, among the county's earliest Jewish settlers, contributed to the growth and development of the city of Two Rivers. Mann operated two businesses and became mayor of Two Rivers in 1866. After his death in 1886, his family donated the funding to help build the city's first public library in 1892. It was christened the Joseph Mann Public Library. Courtesy, Lester Public Library, Two Rivers*

*LEFT: Another prominent Jewish family that brought growth and leadership to the community of Two Rivers was the Sigman family. Iman Sigman, pictured here, grew up in Two Rivers and later opened clothing stores in Manitowoc and Two Rivers. Sigman was one of the founders of the B'nai B'rith Lodge Manitowoc Chapter and was well known for contributing his time to the chamber of commerce and other local organizations. He retired in 1967 and died in 1976. Courtesy, Manitowoc County Historical Society*

the necessary money for their community work. While some of this money assisted programs in the community, some was sent overseas to aid schools in Palestine, where Jewish refugees were migrating from Europe. Later the council, the lodge, and the synagogue congregation sponsored six German Jewish families, who were refugees fleeing from Hitler's persecutions.[10]

In addition to the Schwartz and Mann families, another Jewish family that provided community leadership was the Sigman family. Iman Sigman was the oldest child in the large family that came to Two Rivers from Poland in the early 1900s. His father worked as a rag peddler or found odd jobs at the Two Rivers docks and breakwater. Sigman helped the family earn money, having to leave school after sixth grade. However, he later was able to attend Marquette University and returned to Two Rivers to play a leading role in the establishment of two clothing stores, one in Manitowoc and another in Two Rivers. Like others in his congregation, Sigman was active in the chamber of commerce and in many local charitable organizations.[11]

## Politics and Public Utilities

While Manitowoc County had remained strongly Democratic throughout most of the nineteenth century, the issues of the new century brought other forces to the forefront. After 1900 a spirit of reform was in the air as Wisconsin led the country in adopting progressive political changes under the leadership of Governor Robert M. LaFollette. In Milwaukee, the new spirit was spearheaded by the German Socialists who captured the mayoral race and the city council for many years. Manitowoc, too, had its reformers and its own group of Socialists who urged a variety of changes in the new century.[12]

Leading the way in the city of Manitowoc was industrialist Henry Stolze, Jr., the son of German immigrants to the county who had settled on a nearby farm in the 1860s. Instead of farming, Stolze turned to inventing and patented a candle holder for Christmas trees that led to the creation of his own company in 1888, soon known as the National Tinsel Company. Stolze was 46 years old when he won the post of city mayor as a Socialist candidate in the 1905 election. He argued in favor of municipal ownership of the water and electric utilities, but could not succeed in persuading the city council to follow suit.[13]

Failing to get reelected in either 1907 or 1909, Stolze began to build a local Socialist organization. In this effort, he worked closely with a young Socialist from Galesburg, Illinois, Carl Sandburg, a paid organizer for the Socialists, who would later win great fame as a poet. He also built up a following through editorials in the Socialist newspaper, the *Manitowoc Daily Tribune*.

Their work produced results as the county's three cities, Manitowoc, Two Rivers, and Kiel, all sent delegates to the state Socialist convention in 1908. While some people viewed the Socialists as akin to dangerous Marxists, the calm and steady successes of the Milwaukee Socialists went a long way to assuage their fears. Socialist leaders from Two Rivers were able to provide a model for the Manitowoc leaders to follow, since they had accomplished the municipal takeover of their public utilities in 1902. Representatives from Kiel learned from Manitowoc's example, coming to the same conclusion to have the city operate their water and light companies during the 1920s.[14]

In 1908 Socialist leader and presidential candidate Eugene Debs visited Manitowoc and received an enthusiastic reception at the Turner Opera House. As one newspaper reported the event,

**In the evening the Turner Opera House was packed with an enthusiastic audience to hear Comrade Debs' magnificent address. Special cars had been run to Manitowoc from Two Rivers, and Comrades had come to the meeting from as far south as Kiel, east across the lake from Ludington, and north as far as Michicott [sic].[15]**

However, Debs did not fare well in Manitowoc during the presidential race of 1908, running well behind the Democrat William Jennings Bryan and even behind Republican (and victor) William Howard Taft. As one commentator put it, "The people of Manitowoc had already placed their trust in Henry Stolze to run the city, but [they would never] trust Eugene Debs to run the country."[16]

By the spring of 1911 many citizens had begun to agree with the concept of municipal ownership of utilities and Henry Stolze was returned to the mayor's office. At his victory celebration, Stolze noted that his election showed "that the people of Manitowoc are losing their prejudices against the name of socialism." This time, the city council began to work toward municipal ownership by purchasing the waterworks with a $230,000 bond issue, which took effect in October 1911.[17]

The result was enormously popular as city water rates decreased by 20 percent, wages for the workers rose substantially, and the city still earned a slight profit on the waterworks operation. As one politician commented,

No. 630,423. Patented Aug. 8, 1899.
H. STOLZE, JR.
Candle Holder for Christmas Trees
(Application Rec'd May 19 (Aug.)
(No Model.)

Witnesses
John Maupin
By His Attorneys.

Henry Stolze Jr. Inventor.

"If this was the first step along the road to socialism, few Manitowoc citizens complained!"[18]

Stolze was reelected in 1913 and succeeded in bringing the electric utility under

*ABOVE: With his strong Socialist principles to guide him, Henry Stolze, Jr., became a prominent leader in the city of Manitowoc during the early 1900s. He served four terms as Manitowoc's mayor and originally proposed the idea that municipalities take ownership of public utilities. In 1911 Mayor Stolze saw his dreams come true when the city agreed to purchase the waterworks. After his reelection in 1913, Stolze helped the city establish municipal ownership of the electric utility the following year. Courtesy, Manitowoc Public Utilities*

*LEFT: Before he became mayor of Manitowoc, Stolze founded the Stolze Manufacturing Company, later known as National Tinsel, which produced Christmas tree ornaments and tinsel. Considered a pioneer in the industry, Stolze also received a patent in 1899 for inventing a Christmas tree candleholder. Courtesy, Manitowoc County Historical Society*

municipal ownership in the next two years at a cost of only $146,000. In selling the electric utility to the city, owner John Schuette gave a farewell address on January 2, 1914, in which he argued that he and his company had served the city well since its founding in 1889. "From the very beginning," he noted, "we recognized the prejudice existent against a monopoly and knew that customers served by it must be more delicately treated than those served by a competitive industry..." He added that he believed that the company had always offered fair rates for electricity and closed by stating, "Now then, farewell, with the hope that the city's guardianship...will prove a success and satisfactory to all our citizens."[19]

Just as with the water utility purchase, the new public electric utility was able to both expand its output, with the purchase of new Allis generating machines, and to lower its rates. From 12 cents per kilowatt hour in 1914, the rate was reduced 30 percent to only 8 cents three years later. By 1916

*Prominent businessman John Schuette was operating a flour and grist mill on Quay Street when he proposed to open an electric plant in the city of Manitowoc. Schuette established the Electric Light Company in 1889 and furnished the city with electricity for the next quarter-century. Courtesy, Manitowoc Public Utilities*

the utility had discontinued the production of direct current and only the safer alternating current was supplied to homes and businesses.[20]

Stolze was reelected in 1915, but retired two years later. By that time the water and electric utilities, christened the Manitowoc Public Utilities, were thriving, although the telephone and gas companies remained private. Stolze had served four terms as mayor, and was the only Socialist ever to hold a major office in the county. Reflecting on his association with Stolze, Republican alderman and historian Ralph G. Plumb wrote: "I never believed he was more at heart than a municipal socialist, in other words a man who believed a community the size of our town was happier and better satisfied when they owned and operated those utilities that were serving the people."[21]

After Stolze's departure from office the Manitowoc Public Utilities, which he had created, became the state's largest municipally owned utility. Operated by a commission with five members of the city council, the mayor, and its own chairman, the utility built a new facility at Quay Street on the lakefront for both its water and electrical plants. From that location, it could readily supply not only pure water and electricity to the city's homes and factories, it also piped steam heat to several businesses.[22]

Soon, underwater cribs were built about two miles out into Lake Michigan from which pumps brought in the fresh water and purified it. Within the next two decades the city's main streets were well illuminated by modern streetlights that had underground wiring to avoid the visual clutter of poles and wires.

Using the company's pure water supply, the malting industry grew rapidly with plants also locating near the lakeshore for access to the utilities' water, as well as to the shipping docks. Both the very successful Rahr and Zinn malting companies were leaders in this field. The local brewing industry also benefited from the low cost of this pure water, including Kunz, Bleser & Co. (later the Kingsbury Brewery) and the Rahr Brewery. The increased capacity of the public utilities became an important component in the growth of Manitowoc's industrial base during the next decade.[23]

### Business Enterprise in the New Century

In addition to the growing success of Stolze's National Tinsel Company, the county witnessed the start-up and growth of a number of other enterprises after the turn of the century. The completion of a $946,000 federal improvement project at the harbor provided a great stimulus to both trade and shipbuilding in the area. Moreover, in 1911, Wisconsin's Vocational School Law

*Kingsbury Brewery (formerly Kunz, Bleser & Co.) was yet another well-known brewery that prospered in Manitowoc County. Located in Manitowoc on the corner of Ninth and Marshall, the brewery was eventually purchased by Heileman Brewing Co. Frederick Kunz, the last master brewer of the Kunz family, stands in front of the brewery building which was eventually razed in 1963. Courtesy, Mrs. Frederic Kunz*

stipulated that all cities of 5,000 or more should provide a vocational school to train students over the age of 14. The popularity of this program resulted in the development of a larger skilled workers' pool in Manitowoc and a resultant growth of industry to make use of these well-trained workers.[24]

In aluminum manufacture, the Aluminum Specialty Company grew rapidly after 1915, when it began to make aluminum cookware and automobile hubcaps. With the development of the automobile industry in nearby Michigan, and with carferry service across the lake, orders for hundreds of thousands of these hubcaps began to pour in from Studebaker, Buick, and Dodge. Under the leadership of George Vits, the company also pioneered in creating an employee insurance plan, which provided security for all of its employees.[25]

Another enterprise that had already created numerous jobs for area workers was the Hamilton Manufacturing Company. In 1912 the firm began an entirely new venture with the beginning of its steel furniture production unit. The new product line soon took off and Hamilton continued to innovate, developing cabinets for the new technology of radio in the 1920s and "Child Craft" furniture such as playpens, cribs, and potty chairs in the 1930s.[26]

In addition to bringing jobs and prosperity to the area, the company served the community of Two Rivers through its contributions to local civic institutions. Beginning in 1920 it sponsored one day of the county fair, which became known as "Hamilton Day." Moreover, it paid for the creation, uniforms, and training of a new community band, which soon became the most popular feature of the fair and of numerous local parades, marching to such favorites as "A Hot Time in the Old Town Tonight," and "Hail, Hail, the Gang's All Here."[27]

However, what has been described as the "company's greatest gift" was the donation of a $250,000 structure to be used as a community house and town center. James E. Hamilton had already conducted extensive research into the facilities used by other communities and wanted Two Rivers to have the best possible hall. His other benevolences included donations to several local churches, the Two Rivers' Hospital, YMCA, and a swimming pool for the local Washington High School.[28]

Also in Two Rivers, the Paragon Electric Company, founded in 1905, sold porcelain insulators, battery boxes, ground cones, and lamps as a wholesale operation. The manufacturing portion of the firm began several years later when owner Edward M. Platt secured a contract to build hand-wound time switches, and began business in a large garage. Soon Platt added the production of poultry lighting time switches, ventilation controls, and automated cattle and hog feeders to serve the Wisconsin agricultural market.

The company also began to manufacture insulated wire and cable for the growing electrical and telephone market of the early twentieth century. It innovated with the creation of more sophisticated industrial timers for stokers and even thermostat controls for residential use. However, the timer that made Paragon most of its profits was the patented linotype clock that turned on linotype (printers') machines two hours before the typesetters reported to work in the morning, so that they were heated to the necessary temperature for typesetting.[29]

After World War I and the depression that followed, Paragon moved its manufacturing plant from Manitowoc to Two Rivers. This 1941 relocation allowed for a significant expansion in its facilities.[30]

The Portland Cement Company, which began operations in Manitowoc in 1922, produced the special gray cement that had been created a century before in England and was named after the fine building stone on the Isle of Portland. With its cheap water transportation and good harbor, Manitowoc was an ideal location for the new plant which could ship its product across the Upper Midwest. At that time more than 90 percent of the cement used for new buildings in the United States was of the Portland quality, manufac-

*In this 1920s photo, Two Rivers commercial fishing tugs* Sunrise, *owned by Henry La Fond, and the* Clara S., *owned by Fred Wilke, break ice on the East Twin River on their way out to Lake Michigan. Courtesy, Rogers Street Fishing Village*

*Boats from Two Rivers' commercial fishing fleet gather in the harbor in this image from 1934. The U.S. Coast Guard Station and the North Pier Lighthouse are in the background. Courtesy, Rogers Street Fishing Village*

tured by mixing finely ground limestone and clay, which was then burned at a very high temperature. The Manitowoc production plant later merged with several other such facilities in Michigan and Ohio.[31]

Also in the construction trades, the new Eggers Plywood Company of Two Rivers was established before the turn of the century and grew rapidly in the building boom after 1900. Eggers produced plywood for wall paneling, desktops, bowling alley gutters, and doors for shipment across the United States.[32]

In 1914 the Eastman Company, founded by J. Peter Eastman, opened its doors in Manitowoc with the production of a flexible rubber hose for use in industry. Soon the firm pioneered in the creation of wire-reinforced hoses, which provided greater strength, and also in coupling assemblies, which allowed for the safe joining of high-pressure hoses. After its first two decades in business, Eastman was producing several thousand different kinds of hoses and couplings for the national market. It later merged with the Imperial Brass Company of Chicago to form Imperial-Eastman, a leading producer of fluidic devices and components.[33]

Food processing took a step forward in 1907 with the organization of the Lakeside Packing Company of Manitowoc. The business specialized in the processing and canning of locally grown vegetables, including corn, peas, beans, beets, and carrots. At the turn of the century, before the technology of preserving goods by freezing had come into its own, most housewives were doing less of their own food preservation. With the growth of cities, many families no longer had gardens, and grocery chain stores looked to commercial canneries for supplies to stock their shelves. Up to 80 percent of Lakeside Packing's canned vegetables were sold on the East Coast of the United States to meet this growing urban demand.[34]

A second food-processing venture, the A.M. Richter Sons Company, produced high-grade vinegar for supermarket chains. Although it had been founded in 1875 the firm experienced its most significant growth after 1900 due to the diversification of its products and the ability to reach a national market. Through the purchase of a competitor, the Milwaukee Vinegar Company, A.M. Richter was able to enjoy an expanded portion of the market for its white, cider, malt, and Creole vinegar products by the 1930s.[35]

Another enterprise, the Consumer's Steel Company, Inc., was established in 1922 as a coal plant, and much later converted to steel production. The coal production facility, on Spring Street, produced an abundant fuel supply for use in the nearby utility plant, as well as for shipping to industrial users around Lake Michigan.[36]

Another heavy industry, Manitowoc Dry Dock Company, opened its doors in 1902 with the acquisition of the Burger & Burger Shipyard in Manitowoc for the production of all-steel ships. Founded by Charles C. West and Elias Gunnell, both of whom were trained in shipbuilding and engineering in Chicago and Buffalo, respectively, and worked together at the Chicago Ship Building Company, Manitowoc Dry Dock benefited from the trained labor force in Manitowoc, as well as from the ready access to the Wisconsin Central Railroad and the 337-foot graving dock at Burger. In its first 15 years, Manitowoc Dry Dock continued to build wooden vessels while it began the conversion to steel ship production and repair.[37] Beginning with small boats, such as scows, tugs, and small passenger vessels, the company later expanded its scope to produce the large, steel-hulled Great Lakes freighters. Its first all-steel vessel, the *Maywood*, was launched in 1905. Soon it was producing cement carriers, lighthouse tenders, dredges, tankers, and related equipment. In 1908 Manitowoc Dry Dock purchased Manitowoc Steam Boiler Works in order to produce its own marine boilers for the steam ships. In a similar move the following year, the firm acquired Gunnell Machine Company to incorporate its own equipment division as part of the enterprise. In 1910 the company changed its name to Manitowoc Shipbuilding and Dry Dock (later The Manitowoc Company), with a number of subsidiaries.

In its first 14 years of operation between 1902 and 1916, the busy enterprise built 70 ships, including two with the first turbo-electric drive capability, the *Joseph Medill* and the *Graeme Stewart*, both in 1907. The huge steel freighter, the *Nevada* (1915), was later sold by the Goodrich line to the Russian Imperial Navy. Just before the entry of the United States into World War I, the company constructed its first ocean-going vessel, the *Surveyor*, built for the U.S. Coastal and Geodetic Survey.[38]

### The First World War

When Europe entered the "Great War" in early August 1914, orders for war

*Born in 1839, Henry Burger (Sr.) was a native German who began to build small sailing craft in 1863. Just a few years later, Burger established a firm in Manitowoc with his nephew George. Burger & Burger would become not only one of Manitowoc's prominent shipbuilders, but a principal shipbuilder in the United States. Courtesy, Burger Boat Company*

materiel, supplies, and food from European countries began to pour in to the United States. Many companies in Manitowoc County, as well as its farmers, would soon become suppliers to both the British and German war effort. This was perfectly legal until America joined the war. With the entry of the United States into the war on April 6, 1917, the need for ships and war materiel increased even more dramatically.

Three months after war was declared, the National Guard unit of Manitowoc received orders on July 14 to spend six hours daily drilling. On August 6 the unit left town to report to Camp Douglas for active duty training. This Manitowoc unit became part of Company H, joining the 127th Regiment, 32nd Division (the famous Red Arrow Division), and reporting next to Waco, Texas.[39]

After more training, the Red Arrow Division was sent to France in February 1918, just in time to turn back the massive German offensive on the Western Front at Chateau-Thierry. The French commander who witnessed their heroism dubbed them "Les Terribles," and the nickname proudly stuck. By late summer the division was transferred to the Meuse-Argonne front where it held off further offensives until the official armistice was declared on November 11, 1918. Members of the division were highly decorated, receiving more than 800 medals from the American, Belgian, and French governments.[40]

*In 1938 Burger & Burger made an unprecedented move in the shipbuilding industry by building a vessel with a steel—rather than wood—hull. The company had constructed the country's first all-welded-steel auxiliary ketch—a type of sailing vessel—and named it the* TAMARIS. *Competitors, who dubbed the steel-hulled boats "tin cans," were soon proved wrong when the new hulls proved to be much stronger than the wooden hulls. Courtesy, Burger Boat Company*

*Charles C. West (top) and Elias Gunnell (above) founded Manitowoc Dry Dock Company after purchasing the Burger & Burger Shipyard in Manitowoc in 1902. West, a marine engineer and naval architect, became the company's general manager. Gunnell, an experienced shipbuilder, designer, and mechanic, became president. The business expanded and diversified through the years to become the Manitowoc Shipbuilding Company and eventually The Manitowoc Company, Inc. Courtesy, The Manitowoc Company, Inc.*

Waiting on the homefront, citizens in Manitowoc County celebrated the armistice and then celebrated again when news reached them that the 32nd Division was due to sail for home from France on February 19, 1919. Finally, on May 19, the local units arrived in Manitowoc to be greeted with a massive parade and reception and praised by their local commander, Major Walter Abel.[41]

In addition to the service of its soldiers, Manitowoc County contributed to the war effort through the skills of its local industries. The Manitowoc Aluminum Specialty Company began to produce aluminum canteens and mess kits for shipment to Europe in 1914, a process that accelerated with America's entry into the conflict. During the war the firm manufactured several million canteens, born of its special knowledge of the durability of aluminum cookware. At the war's end Manitowoc Aluminum Specialty created a new national advertising campaign, promoting "Mirro, the finest aluminum."[42]

Also affected by wartime orders, the Hamilton Manufacturing Company turned to the production of airplane fuselages, bringing military and government inspectors to Two Rivers to perfect the specifications. By the end of the war the plant had converted to round-the-clock shifts on an assembly line, manufacturing more than 40 fuselages per day. Further diversification followed the war, with the creation of all-steel laboratory equipment and new designs in medical furniture and equipment. During the 1930s the company also innovated with the creation of the all-steel automatic clothes dryer. Soon both electric washers and dryers were rolling off the assembly line as fast as had the wartime fuselages.[43]

A third significant local enterprise that joined the war effort, Paragon Electric, was able to utilize its expertise in industrial timers to create the vital time controls for explosive devices. The military orders for timers to detonate land mines and anti-aircraft explosives helped to offset the company's reduced orders for other industrial and consumer timers due to the required wartime electrical "brown-outs."[44]

Another key enterprise in Manitowoc that supported the war effort was Manitowoc Shipbuilding Company, which began to build all-steel ships for the U.S. Navy—particularly those used by the U.S. Shipping Board Emergency Fleet Corporation to counteract the disastrous loss of Allied shipping to German submarines. Orders also came from Norway and from the Cunard line of Great Britain. Because these countries agreed to prepayment, Manitowoc Shipbuilding was able to dramatically increase the scope of its operation to meet the demands of these new contracts with the expansion of its yards and the construction of a new erection building. Before the war's end the company had constructed more than 30 vessels of 3,500 tons each. One of these ships, the *Coquina*, was the first cargo vessel sunk by the Japanese in the Pacific during World War II.[45]

To produce this massive number of vessels, Manitowoc Shipbuilding employed a work force of more than 2,000 men and women. Workers flocked to the area since wartime wages at the shipyard ranged from $10 to $20 per day. Because local housing was not sufficient for this huge number of employees, a subsidiary of the company began to construct more than 100 homes in the area for workers' housing. It also established a dormitory, the Riverview Inn, with 200 rooms and a dining hall capable of feeding 600 men. In addition, an old Goodrich steamer, the *Chicago*, was converted into a floating hotel with facilities for another several hundred employees.[46]

When the war ended, a slump in shipbuilding followed and the company turned to repair work on both ships and railroad cars to keep its work force intact for several years. Charles West also traveled to Michigan, where he worked as a consultant for the U.S. Naval Bureau of Construction at the new Ford Motor Company shipbuilding plant near Detroit.[47]

After a corporate reorganization in 1920, which brought West into sole control, the company pioneered in the creation of the first self-unloading

freighters. In the early 1920s the *John A. Kling* and the *Charles C. West* were launched. Other contracts followed, which returned prosperity to the business. In the next decade the company built several large carferries, including the *Pere Marquette* (1924) and the largest suction dredge boat in the world, the *New Jersey* (1927).[48]

One aspect of the county's business and culture that did not prosper during the war were the German-language newspapers. In the strong passion against all things German, Wisconsinites rechristened sauerkraut "Liberty cabbage" and rejected German language and culture as somehow unpatriotic, since our enemy was the Kaiser. During the war years Manitowoc's two German newspapers, the *Nordwestern* and the *Die Wahrheit*, had difficulty selling papers and went out of business by 1918.[49]

*A new age of shipbuilding had begun in Manitowoc when Manitowoc Dry Dock Company launched its first steel vessel— the passenger steamer* Maywood—*in 1905. Courtesy, The Manitowoc Company, Inc.*

ABOVE: *When the United States entered the war in April 1917, men from the county left for training and active duty by August. This image shows men leaving Two Rivers in May 1918, just six months before the signing of the armistice that ended World War I. Courtesy, Manitowoc County Historical Society*

RIGHT: *The Manitowoc Shipbuilding Company rapidly expanded during World War I, when numerous contracts were negotiated for the firm to begin building 3,500-ton freighters for the war effort. By the end of the war in 1918, the company had constructed more than 30 freighters. Courtesy, The Manitowoc Company, Inc.*

## Culture and the 1920s

During the postwar period, Americans wanted a "return to normalcy" and the pleasures of civilian life rather than the sacrifices of war. This was the decade when the automobile began to play a key role in American life, when the movies achieved great popularity, the "talkies" began, and radio came of age.

Although the Department of the Navy relinquished its control of the shipping radio station after World War I, Manitowoc did not have a commercial station until several years later. In 1925 a temporary station broadcast from the Mikado Theater in honor of its 10th anniversary. Using the call letters "WHBL," which stood for "Wisconsin has beautiful lakes," the station only lasted for several weeks. However, the local interest in radio had begun.[50]

In 1926 two Manitowoc men built station WOMT and began a local broadcast on November 8. Although the part-time job as an announcer and disc jockey at WOMT was exciting, one of the founders, W.H. Biesemeyer, did not like the static noise of the crude equipment, nor the disagreeable electric ozone odor it gave off. A native of Kansas, Biesemeyer had worked on ship's radios on the Great Lakes for several years before coming to Manitowoc in 1911. When two of his ships went through severe storms in Lake Superior, Biesemeyer decided to change to a job on land instead.[51]

Employed by the Marconi Wireless Telegraph Company, Biesemeyer began to operate the radio-telegraphic unit (ship-to-shore radio) that had its unit on top of the tall Rahr Malting Building near the lakeshore. There were only two men employed at this communication to all ships within range, and each had to work eight-hour rotating shifts, seven days a week.[52]

When the chance presented itself to open his own small commercial station, WOMT, Biesemeyer seized it. Even with its low wattage and its static,

*Still reeling from a decline in contracts after World War I ended, Manitowoc Shipbuilding began to reemerge as a prosperous company in the 1920s with the advent of self-unloading freighters and carferries. The* Pere Marquette 21, *built by the firm in 1924, was the first of several carferries constructed for the Pere Marquette line. The* Pere Marquette *carried railroad cars, passengers, and vehicles across Lake Michigan. Courtesy, Mason County Historical Society, Ludington, Michigan*

the station quickly caught on. Less than a month after it first began broadcasts, by Christmas of 1926, its organ music reached into many homes during its 50-watt, four-hour broadcast day. Francis Kadow, a local newspaperman, soon joined Biesemeyer and became one of the most popular announcers at the station.

Three years later, in 1929, Kadow and the station applied for an affiliation with the United Press wire service so that they could bring national and international headlines to their radio broadcasts. Through this hook-up, the radio station could announce important events, such as the stock market crash later that year, and residents could learn the latest news almost instantaneously.[53]

Even more popular than early radio were the movies shown in Manitowoc's three motion picture theaters—the Mikado (1915), the old Crystal (which burned down just before the war), and the Vaudette. Occasionally, movies were also shown at the old Turner Hall, but the film industry kept a tight rein on the release of their movies and even controlled the projection equipment patents. When the new Capitol Theatre was built

*WOMT became Manitowoc's first commercial station after W.H. Biesemeyer and Francis Kadow joined forces in 1926. WOMT, which stood for "World's Only Mikado Theater" was named after the local theater operated by the Kadows. Students in this 1940s photo were involved in a youth program at the WOMT studio. The station came under new ownership in the 1970s and still broadcasts to Manitowoc County today. Courtesy, Manitowoc County Historical Society*

in Manitowoc in 1920, it had all of the modern motion picture equipment, including Edison's updated projector.

The Capitol Theatre was also the first in town to have the capability of sound projection and was thus the first to show the talking movies, beginning with the big hit, *The Jazz Singer* starring Al Jolson. As the theater manager remembered, "None of us believed there was that much money in the world that this picture started to bring in."[54]

In response, other theaters in town installed sound equipment and worked on the quality of their acoustics by covering their walls with "celotex" to bring the sound reverberation in the back to the same 12-second standard as the front for a uniform transmission of sound.[55]

Another aspect of the 1920s was Prohibition, which came out of the 18th Amendment to the Constitution. The attempt to "dry out" the country lasted 14 years, until Franklin D. Roosevelt helped to end it in 1933. However, for the decade of the 1920s, breweries, malt factories, taverns, and beer halls had to seek other avenues to make money. Most of the taverns in Manitowoc converted to become "soft drink parlors," although a number of them also had a secret back entrance where a person could buy illegal "hootch." Others had basement rooms, with special peekholes in the door and a password for entry. These "speakeasies" relied on illegal liquor, much of it coming through Canada. As a thriving port city, Manitowoc sold its share of this contraband.[56]

## Growth and Progress in Kiel

The third-largest settlement in the county, Kiel, became an agricultural center even before the turn of the century, incorporating as a village in June 1892. With growth and development during the first two decades of the twentieth century, the village was large enough to become a city just before Christmas, on December 15, 1920. Like the county's other two cities, Manitowoc and Two Rivers, Kiel soon developed its own civic institutions, including its own public library housed in the city hall building.

Soon the settlement launched its own newspaper, the *Zeitung*, published in German for the many readers in this strong German enclave. However, with the onslaught on so much anti-German sentiment during World War I, the paper was sold to another publisher in 1918 and became the *Tri-County Record*, printed only in English.[57]

One of the community centers in Kiel was the first Catholic Church, Peter and Paul, which dated back to the 1850s. Closely tied to the heart of German community life, this church founded its own parochial school in 1903 and built a new church structure in 1907, followed by the construction of a home for its order of Sisters eight years later. Enrollment in the church's school grew so rapidly that by 1918 the size of the school building was doubled.[58]

## Famous Sons of Manitowoc County

One notable problem of the "Roaring Twenties," which did not touch Manitowoc directly, was the national scandal known as Teapot Dome. Named for the oil wells in Wyoming at Teapot Dome, the trouble rested with bribes accepted by various government officials to let private oil companies, notably Sinclair, drill for oil on government land. Two Rivers native Thomas J. Walsh was one of the U.S. senators who investigated and exposed the scandal, which resulted in Secretary of the Interior Albert Fall going to jail.[59]

Born near Two Rivers in 1859, Walsh was part of a family that had immigrated to Wisconsin nine years earlier from Ireland. His father, Felix, had served as village president of Two Rivers. Although devout Roman Catholics,

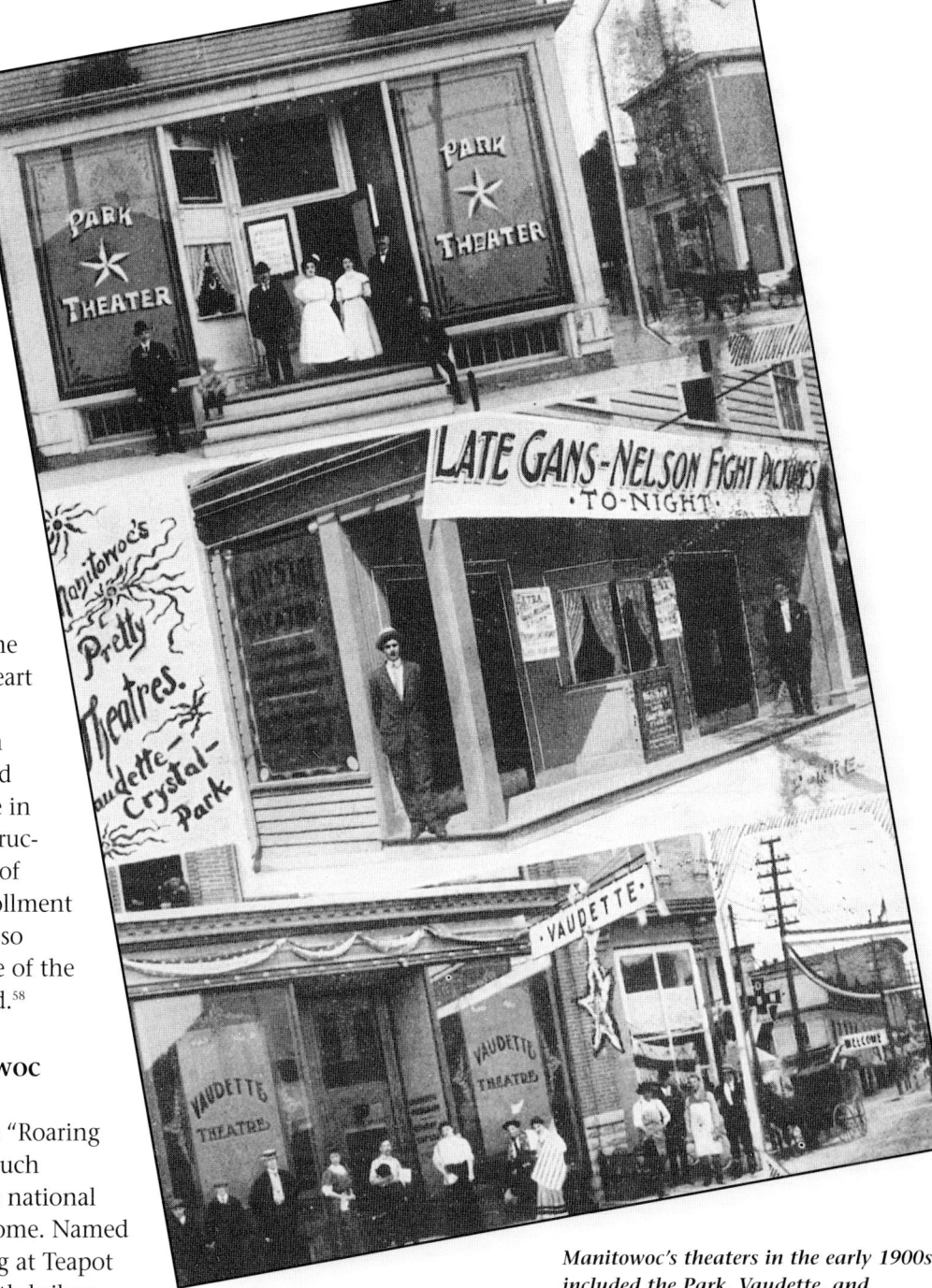

*Manitowoc's theaters in the early 1900s included the Park, Vaudette, and Crystal. Manitowoc's newest theater, the Aschers Capitol, didn't open until 1921, but it provided its audiences with the latest movie equipment available to show motion pictures. Courtesy, Manitowoc County Historical Society*

*At the turn of the century downtown Kiel had a rapidly expanding shopping district. This photograph shows the buildings that housed some of the city's popular businesses at the time. From left to right are the Ammann Cigar Shop, the State Bank of Kiel, C.T. Schroeder's Grocery, P.E. Kabel Drug Store, Hollensteiner General Store, and the Commercial Hotel. Courtesy, Kiel Historical Society*

*Born to Norwegian parents in 1857, Thorstein Veblen spent his early years in Manitowoc County before moving with his family to Minnesota. An important American economist and social critic, Veblen gained international attention with the 1899 publication of his most notable work,* The Theory of the Leisure Class. *He went on to publish two more books before his death in 1929. Courtesy, Manitowoc County Historical Society*

the Walsh family had sent their son to the public school in Two Rivers where he graduated at age 16 and immediately took a post as a schoolteacher in one of the county's rural districts at Meeme, an Irish stronghold. Walsh later recalled one of his earliest boyhood jobs, that of working as a lamplighter in downtown Two Rivers for a "few pennies a day."[60]

Before attending the university, Walsh served as a district school principal, then moved west to Montana after receiving his degree. His doggedness in the cause of justice became a claim to fame. "Acting virtually alone for the first year and a half of the oil lease investigation..., Walsh, like a bloodhound, early caught the scent of corruption and pursued it through briar patch after briar patch until his quarry was treed," reported the local newspaper. Before the investigation made a public splash, Walsh was an unknown member of the Senate (where he served from his adopted state of Montana), who yet possessed "one of the body's keenest legal minds and a...reputation as one of its driest."[61]

Another famous son, who also later moved west, was Manitowoc County native Thorstein Veblen, one of the most influential intellectuals and writers of the early twentieth century. Veblen was the fifth of six children born to Thomas and Caroline Anderson Veblen on a farm just north of Valders in 1857. As a boy, Veblen was described as gangly and awkward. His shy and self-conscious nature chafed when other boys taunted him as "Norskie," the common epithet thrown at Norwegians. His family remained in the area for the first 11 years of his life, later relocating to Minnesota where Veblen graduated from college before attending Yale University for his Ph.D. degree in 1884.[62]

As a social critic and economist, Veblen became nationally and internationally famous for his book, *The Theory of the Leisure Class*, published in 1899, which was a biting social criticism of the American style of society and politics. A university professor, Veblen attracted a number of adherents to his extreme views and left behind a body of social criticism that has been labeled "the most considerable and creative body of social thought that America has produced."[63]

When Veblen died in 1929, the Roaring Twenties were coming to a close. His death came the same year as the stock market crash on Wall Street, which brought in the Great Depression. He died just two years after the great transatlantic flight of a new American hero, Colonel Charles A. Lindbergh, whose solo trip to Paris in the *Spirit of St. Louis* galvanized the attention of the world on a new phenomenon, the airplane.

Although airplanes were new at the beginning of the century with the flight at Kitty Hawk, North Carolina, in 1903, their use for passenger flights, cargo, and mail did not begin for several more years. During the 1920s rural "barnstormers" brought their single-engine planes to many rural areas for aerial shows. By the mid-1920s citizens of Manitowoc saw the need for a local air field, particularly since the Invincible Metal Furniture Company was contemplating building airplanes. The first field was developed on Menasha Avenue but was replaced in 1928, when the city bought 134 acres of land and built air strips and a new hangar for up to 14 planes.[64]

Founded in 1913, Invincible Metal quickly found a market in the United States and in Asia for its strong safety deposit boxes. After a large addition to its factory was completed in 1923, the company began to experiment with the development of single-engine airplanes, finally getting two of its designs licensed by the Department of Commerce. One of its advertisements hailed "The New Master of the Air," and featured a drawing of its "Invincible Center-Wing, Monoplane." However, before Invincible Metal could go into full-scale production of these models, the Depression struck and the airplane was eliminated from its plans.[65]

For local youths who were not watching the new airplanes or attending barnstorming shows, the City of Two Rivers organized one of the state's earliest public recreation programs. Sponsored in part by philanthropist James E.

*The village of Kiel was experiencing its own growth at the turn of the century, including the development of its schools. The community's first Catholic church soon opened the Saints Peter & Paul Catholic School in 1903 and eventually had to expand its facility to accommodate the increasing enrollment. The brick grade school in this 1906 photo was constructed in three stages before 1900, and soon became Kiel's first high school. Courtesy, Kiel Historical Society*

*Recreational activities became a sought-after form of entertainment in the early 1900s as sports such as baseball, basketball, football, tennis, and golf gained in popularity. The county's first country club—the Lakeside Club—opened in 1910. The clubhouse, as seen in this photo, was located between the Little Manitowoc River and Waldo Boulevard. Courtesy, Manitowoc County Historical Society*

Hamilton, the city used its community building as the centerpiece of this program because it provided a sizable gymnasium, bowling alleys, billiard rooms, showers, handball courts, an auditorium, and even banquet rooms. The first program grew out of the local Boys' Club in the summer of 1921, when a director was hired to set up organized sports and activities for area youngsters. Several years later the city itself assumed control and fiscal responsibility for the program and enlarged its scope with year-round offerings, adding volleyball and basketball teams in the winter months.[66]

The City of Manitowoc provided a variety of opportunities for culture and recreation through its strong schools, its growing public library, and its outstanding program of games for youths. In the summer of 1924 the City of Manitowoc followed the example of Two Rivers and established its own municipal recreation program, utilizing vacant lots around the city for baseball games and other organized activities. Funded by the public schools, the program employed a director and other workers to set up neighborhood teams and keep the city's youngsters happily occupied throughout the summer months. It was the start of a long-standing commitment by the city to area youths.[67]

Due in part to this sponsorship, local interest in baseball grew rapidly during the 1920s—the decade that saw the creation of the sport's earliest stars, notably Babe Ruth. Similarly, football teams throughout the county developed local rivalries during the 1920s, as did basketball teams in every location that had an indoor hall for games. The American Legion also sponsored a regional, semi-professional football team in the early 1920s, which played the new squad from just north, the Green Bay Packers, in an early skirmish.[68]

*When the city purchased land for an expanded airfield in 1928, Manitowoc Air Service, Inc., was born. Shares of stock sold for $100 each. Courtesy, Manitowoc County Historical Society*

Ice hockey, too, began as a "regulation" sport in the county in 1926, with the area's first team, the Buccaneers, challenging teams from as far away as Appleton and Menasha.[69]

The games of golf and tennis also found a following during the 1920s. In 1910 the county's first country club, the Lakeside Club, was established between the Little Manitowoc River and Waldo Boulevard. In 1929 another course, the Lincoln Fields Golf Course, was built on Reed Avenue and others soon followed. Tennis became popular as courts were constructed near the area's high schools.[70]

With a total county population of 44,978 by 1910, Manitowoc could support this growing variety of sports teams, entertainment activities, and recreation programs. During the next decade, before 1920, the population would grow again, this time by another 16 percent to more than 51,000.[71]

## The End of the Jazz Age

As the Jazz Age came to a close by 1929, residents of Manitowoc County could look back on an era of growth and prosperity since the war's end. The decade had brought hundreds of new jobs to the county, as well as the new technology of radio and talking movies. The area's rich traditions in music and bands continued throughout the decade as local and traveling orchestras and jazz groups filled the town halls and theaters with the rich sounds of early swing and New Orleans jazz. Many of the dances were held on weekends, even on Sundays, as one local orchestra advertised "last dance before Advent" on its posters.[72]

Even with the popularity of this modern music, many local residents who attended these dances still requested their old-time favorites, particularly the polka. One local group, Duke Janda's Orchestra, played both polkas and the tunes of Glenn Miller, Tommy Dorsey, and Duke Ellington. The group's moment of glory came when they cut their first record at the studios of WOMT Radio.[73]

Whether dancing to polkas or playing the newly popular game of golf, the citizens of Manitowoc County looked forward to years of prosperity in the 1930s, little knowing what lay ahead. The county's agricultural, shipbuilding, and industrial enterprises had established a strong footing during the century's first three decades. It was a foundation upon which the survival of the Great Depression ahead would rest.

*The Duke Janda Orchestra was one of Manitowoc County's so-called "modern" bands that mimicked the sounds of Tommy Dorsey and Glenn Miller. Janda and his "Modernaires" also played polka music—a popular request at events such as weddings. Janda and his orchestra tasted a bit of fame when they cut a record at WOMT to help audition a young singer for Lawrence Welk. Courtesy, Manitowoc County Historical Society*

## CHAPTER SIX

# Decades of Change

*On April 30, 1942, Manitowoc Shipbuilding launched the USS PETO, the first submarine built on the Great Lakes for the U.S. Navy. The submarine had to be launched sideways because the Manitowoc River lacked the width and the depth to accommodate a standard "end first" launch. Courtesy, The Manitowoc Company, Inc.*

T he Great Depression brought an end to Prohibition and the gaiety of the Jazz Age. It also brought many hardships to the residents of Manitowoc County, including unemployment and reduced farm prices. Workers and farmers struggled to survive the economic crisis, and federal assistance in the form of relief, jobs, and conservation programs was crucial. With the onset of World War II, orders for shipping and industrial goods soared and prosperity returned to the county's farms as well.

Wartime production changed the shape of the county's economy in the postwar period, and the 1950s and 1960s brought a boom in housing and education. The communications revolution, particularly the arrival of television, brought county residents into closer contact with the rest of the country in a new way. The era of space travel, nuclear power, and tourism had begun.

## The Turmoil of the Great Depression

After the stock market crash of October 1929, the American economy began a decline into the Great Depression that brought the closing of banks, job layoffs, and resulting bankruptcies. The value of industrial products in Wisconsin declined from $800 million in 1929 to only $320 million in 1933.[1]

In Manitowoc, the decreasing orders for ships and for industrial goods resulted in layoffs at the shipyards, the aluminum factories, and at other industries. Throughout Wisconsin there was a decrease in farm income from $440 million to $200 million between 1929 and 1933. As prices declined, dairy farmers edged close to despair when it began to cost more to produce their milk than they could earn from selling it.

Across the state, the increase in farm bankruptcies in 1933 brought desperate measures. Linking together into the Wisconsin Cooperative Milk Pool, many farmers hoped that by acting in concert they could demand higher prices from dairies. On several occasions in 1933, this cooperative, sometimes joined by the Farmers' Holiday Association of the Midwest, staged "milk strikes," during which they surrounded dairies to prevent milk being taken in or dumped it rather than sell it. While not entirely successful, these strikes did draw both public and government attention to the plight of the farmers.[2]

While not unanimous in their support of these drastic tactics of dumping milk, many farmers in Manitowoc County supported the strike, joining with nearby farmers from the Fox River Valley where the Milk Pool had its strongest following. The creation of the Agricultural Adjustment Act, or AAA, by Roosevelt's New Deal in 1933 began to bring federal attention to farm problems and the promise of price supports and other programs of assistance. Although it did not solve all of the farmers' debt problems, the AAA was welcomed as a positive beginning and allowed many farmers in Manitowoc to survive the Depression.[3]

Other New Deal programs brought relief to county residents as well. Offering jobs and constructive federal projects, the Public Works Administration, or PWA, hired men in Manitowoc County who were on the relief rolls to construct public buildings or roads. One of these projects was the three-story addition to the Washington Street School, completed in 1937. A similar PWA project that hired local men was the construction in 1938 of the sewage disposal plant in Manitowoc, which was jointly financed by the federal government and by a local bond issue.[4]

Federal programs also helped to keep Manitowoc Shipbuilding alive. By 1932 sales at the shipyards had dropped by 75 percent from a 1931 high of $4 million. The next year, 1933, another 50 percent drop brought sales to only $500,000. All dividends were suspended and employees took wage cuts of 10 to 20 percent, followed by another 35 percent just six months later.

*Finding the need to diversify after World War I, Manitowoc Shipbuilding Company ventured into the business of constructing cranes. Its crane-building division became a crucial element of the company's sales and growth after the Depression struck in 1929. In the 1930s Manitowoc cranes were purchased and used in Washington, D.C., to help restore the U.S. Capitol and to construct the Senate Office building, the National Gallery of Art, the Jefferson Memorial, and the National Archives. Courtesy, The Manitowoc Company, Inc.*

Finally, massive layoffs began and by 1933 only a skeletal work force of 350 men remained of the 2,000 or more at the peak.[5]

With no orders for new ships coming in, the company turned to its crane-building division, in hopes that an increased business there could sustain the organization. Although orders for new cranes were few, an ingenious program to rent cranes to builders on a "job-by-job" basis was successful. Builders had an option to buy, and many cranes were eventually sold this way. Another boon for the company were orders from the PWA and the Works Progress Administration, or WPA, of the New Deal.[6]

Both of these agencies were engaged throughout the 1930s in construction efforts on public buildings across the country, providing jobs for the unemployed. Cranes from Manitowoc Shipbuilding were purchased and used to erect a number of such facilities in Washington, D.C., including a new Senate Office Building, the National Gallery of Art, the Jefferson Memorial, the National Archives, and restoration to the dome of the National Capitol itself.[7]

At the Aluminum Goods Manufacturing Company, the onset of the Depression brought a 65 percent reduction in sales by 1932. During the darkest days, however, the management was able to keep three-quarters, or 2,500, of its 3,400 workers employed. By 1935 the demand for certain of its products was holding steady and the company was able to begin slowly rehiring its employees. Three years later, as England and France began to rearm to meet the threat of Germany and Hitler, the firm began to roll out sheet aluminum which was sold under the Lend Lease program prior to America's entry into the war. The firm's name changed many times over the years, from Aluminum Goods Manufacturing Company to Aluminum Specialty to today's Mirro Company.[8]

One very successful New Deal program, the Civilian Conservation Corps, or CCC, was created with the dual purpose of conserving parks, forests, and natural resources, and hiring unemployed young men to work in this effort. Throughout Wisconsin, the CCC hired more than 60,000 young men to work in 45 camps across the state. Their effort to replant forests, protect wildlife, and create new preserves was considered by many to be one of the most important of Roosevelt's programs.[9]

Nicknamed "Roosevelt's Forest Army," these boys, including many from Manitowoc, worked to construct more than 500 bridges, as well as 4,000 miles of fire lanes, roads, and telephone lines across Wisconsin. They also put their efforts into fish and game management and took a census of Wisconsin's deer population. In Manitowoc County, efforts of the CCC, joined by the Manitowoc Fish and Game Association (organized in 1907) carried out several successful programs, including the repopulation of pheasants in the area and the construction of pheasant runs in Manitowoc, Kiel, Two Rivers, Valders, Reedsville, Mishicot, and Centerville.[10]

They also restocked trout ponds, beginning in 1933, through the creation of rearing ponds in Two Rivers, and assisted in the construction of the Centerville Dam in 1935. The CCC was active at both Silver Creek Park and at the county's largest forest at Point Beach, near Two Rivers, in planting thousands of new trees, and constructing fire towers and fire lanes.[11]

In spite of the failure of one-third of the banks in Wisconsin, one local banker commented that none of the local banks in Manitowoc County suffered that fate. Perhaps this was due to the fact that the toll of the Panic of 1893 had been severe on local banks, or because there were very few banks established in the county during the 1920s, when there was such a rash of new bank openings elsewhere. Although closed during the five-day bank holiday mandated by Roosevelt in March 1933, the county's leading financial institutions reopened for business immediately thereafter, having been judged sound by the bank examiners.[12]

By the end of the Depression Manitowoc's two key institutions, the Manitowoc Savings Bank (founded in 1884) and the First National Bank (founded in 1894), were strong—as were the Bank of Two Rivers (1891), and the Two Rivers Savings Bank (1902). Across the county, other key financial institutions kept their doors open, including the State Bank of Kiel (1898), the Reedsville State Bank (1906), the Cleveland State Bank (1907), the St. Nazianz State Bank (1909), the Valders State Bank (1911), the Maribel State Bank (1912), the Collins State Bank (1914), the Citizens State Bank of Kiel (1914), the State Bank of Francis Creek (1916), and the Newton State Bank (1921).[13]

Another threat to many banks during the Depression was the increasing incidence of robberies, as notorious criminal gangs swept through rural

*Modeled after the Eiffel Tower in Paris, Rawley Point Lighthouse is located at Point Beach State Forest, north of Two Rivers. The lighthouse was part of a French display at the Columbia Exposition before the U.S. government obtained the structure. It was later moved to Rawley's Point, considered to be one of the most dangerous areas on Lake Michigan. Courtesy, Two Rivers Historical Society*

areas hitting smaller banks at random. The St. Nazianz State Bank experienced two such incidents, the first in 1930 as the Depression was deepening. The robbers made their way into the bank by using a torch to cut the vault door and took $485,000 in silver. They also left a note on one of the smoky windows saying, "Will be back!" True to their word, they returned the next year in October, but this time took only $20,000 in currency and bonds. They were never caught. The Newton State Bank, now preserved at Pinecrest Historical Village, was robbed only once during its 21 years of operation, on April 6, 1937.[14]

Although most local industries in Manitowoc County suffered severe cutbacks, there were several bright spots on the economic horizon during the Depression. In 1935 the Heresite and Chemical Company opened its doors for production in Manitowoc, making synthetic plastics, synthetic resins, rubber, and industrial coatings. Four years later a new paper-manufacturing plant, the Eddy Paper Company, began operations, producing paper-board shipping containers for the Kieckhefer Container Company of Milwaukee.[15]

Another encouraging development during the Depression was the fact that Prohibition was officially ended just after Roosevelt's inauguration in 1933. As bands played the theme song, "Happy Days Are Here Again," the county's breweries and malting factories renewed production. Area farmers benefited as well, converting from more traditional crops to growing barley for the malting factories. By 1937 some 52,000 acres in the county were devoted to barley, ranking Manitowoc County third in the state in its production.[16]

## Social Programs During Depression Days

Another government program that began during the Depression was the creation of county homemakers' associations across the state. Organized in November 1938 in Manitowoc County, the program brought together hundreds of farm, as well as urban, women who gathered at four or five meetings each year with their assigned county agent. In Manitowoc County, under the leadership of the first such agent, Ruth Huckstead, the clubs were divided into five regional groups, centered in Kiel, Manitowoc, Two Rivers, Valders, and Whitelaw.[17]

At these five centers, local women were trained in leadership skills and club management. They took these skills back to the clubs in their region of the county and, with the continuing assistance of the home economics and extension agent, offered classes in a variety of homemaking skills, some of which were particularly designed to help families survive the shortages of the Depression. Classes included subjects such as nutrition, household management, community and social problems, housing, and child care. The clubs were so popular that they continued to provide assistance during the war and thereafter, addressing key questions that affected families and home management.[18]

Other women's organizations rose to the occasion during the 1930s, providing whatever relief they could to families who were jobless, or without food or a home. One of the key efforts came from the North and South Side relief agencies, which provided budgetary support for the creation of the Community Chest Fund. Through this community-wide fund, families received clothing, fuel, temporary housing, and food, charity that was later supplemented by federal relief programs. In a similar fashion, the Junior Service League did its best to assist families who were destitute, particularly focusing on the care of children through the creation of clinics for newborn babies and their mothers.[19]

For the county's youth, the Boy and Girl Scouts organizations continued to be strong during the Depression, coordinating camping events and social service projects. The Boy Scouts enjoyed outdoor events and conservation programs at their new Camp Sinawa at Pigeon Lake (first used in 1920 and completed in 1927). Used also by the Girl Scout troops until they established their own separate outdoor facility (funded by the Rahr family) at the war's end, Camp Sinawa provided numerous opportunities for young people to escape to the great outdoors, even during the economy's darkest days.[20]

A testimony to the strength of community support for its youth organizations, even during the worst of the hard times, was the fact that in 1934 the Girl Scouts established its first permanent office in the county and in 1935 hired its first full-time director. Activities for the scouts included the staging of a full-scale operetta, which served as both entertainment and as a fund raiser. The next year, 1936, the senior scouts, who needed these activities as much as their younger sisters, became a local Mariner Troop, receiving their Mariner Ship at the harbor, and holding their meetings at the Yacht Club. In 1938 Girl Scouts across the county held their first cookie sale, to raise funds for other worthwhile scouting projects.[21]

Another youth organization, the 4-H Clubs, had organized in Manitowoc County in 1921 and spread rapidly in all of the farm communities. Ten years

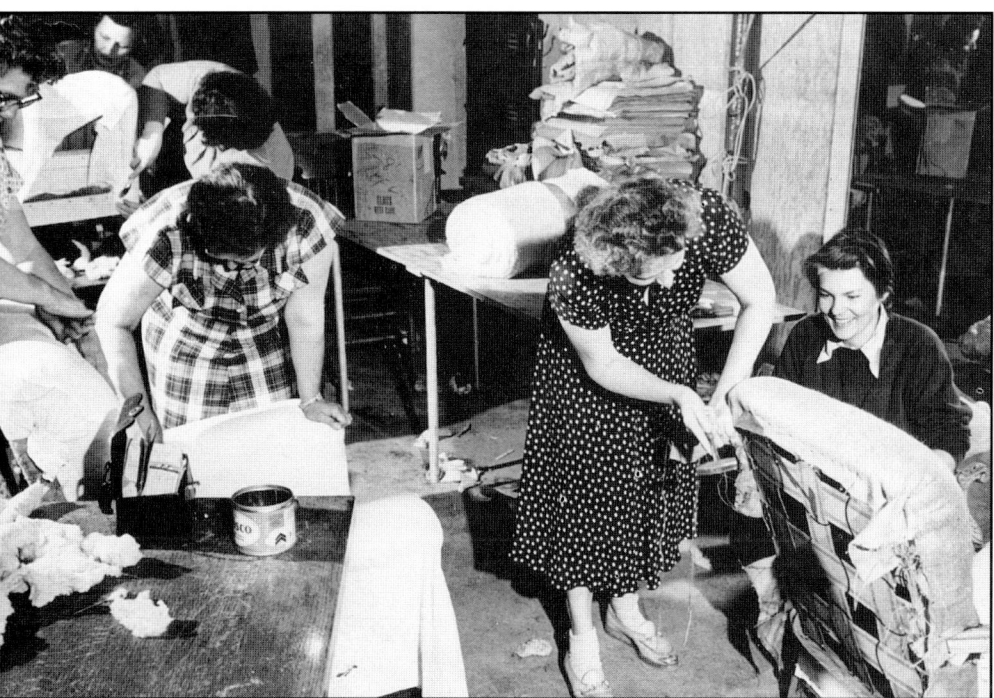

*Members of the Manitowoc County Homemakers' Association, established in 1938, participate in a furniture reupholstering project in this circa 1940 photo. Women from the area participated in a variety of courses that focused on home economics. Courtesy, Manitowoc County Historical Society*

later, as the Depression began, there were more than 350 boys and girls throughout the county involved in agricultural and learning projects through this organization. It also provided a greatly needed social outlet for area youngsters who might otherwise have been isolated.[22]

All of these social clubs brought county men, women, and children together, helping them survive the hard times of the Depression. While many farmers held on and survived the decade's troubles, many were forced to sell out and move to cities to find work. In 1940, as the Depression came to an end, more than 60 percent of the county's population of 61,617 lived in its three largest cities. Manitowoc had more than 24,000 residents, followed by Two Rivers with 10,302, and Kiel with 1,898.[23]

The closer ties between urban and rural areas that had developed during the 1920s and 1930s also helped to build community spirit as county residents worked together toward a variety of goals. As the Depression began to ease, a spirit of renewed optimism was born. With the beginning of Hitler's rise in Germany and with the outbreak of war in 1939, orders for food, ships, and industrial goods began to pour in to local farms and industries. Few Americans believed then that the country would become involved in this second European conflict. They hoped that America could serve, in

*As government contracts created additional work and men were called off to war, many companies added women to their work force during World War II. Women at the Aluminum Goods Manufacturing Company are shown in this 1940s image gauging 20-millimeter brass cartridge cases— one of the many products manufactured locally for wartime efforts. Courtesy, Mirro Company*

Roosevelt's words, as the great "arsenal of democracy" without having to actively join the war.

## A Second World War

World War II in Europe began with the German invasion of Poland in September 1939. America made no pretense of neutrality as it had in the first global conflict. President Franklin D. Roosevelt offered immediate support to allies England and France. Even prior to the United States' declaration of war in December 1941, after the bombing of Pearl Harbor, American industries and farmers began supplying Europe with ships, guns, and food to fight the onslaught of the Axis invasions.

The first call to the Wisconsin National Guard came even before Pearl Harbor, in October 1940. The guard members of Manitowoc County assembled at the new armory building near the fairgrounds and began regular training. Recommissioned as Company E of the 127th Infantry, 78 local men left Manitowoc by train several weeks later for further training in the South. As the train left the station, there were tearful farewells. Americans knew that if the country entered the war, it would be a long and difficult conflict. By October 1940 Hitler's armies had already captured Norway, Belgium, the Netherlands, and France.[24]

By the spring of 1941, in the context of "preparedness," the local Manitowoc unit became part of the army's 32nd Division, continuing its training until Pearl Harbor and America's entry into the war. By early 1942 the division was sent to California, where they boarded transports for Australia and service in the Pacific conflict against the Japanese. By December of that year local men from Company E were sent to New Guinea to attack in the Papuan campaign. There the first local casualty occurred with the death of Private Rudolph Maresh of Manitowoc at Buna.[25]

This first casualty was tragically followed by the deaths of Lieutenant Donald Fury and Paul Whitaker, also from Company E of Manitowoc. John Renak, the next casualty, received the distinguished service cross posthumously for his bravery under fire in the same campaign. Another officer from the county, Roy Wentland, was also killed during this campaign.[26]

After this difficult campaign in New Guinea, the division returned to Australia for amphibious training in preparation for the many island landings that became the mainstay of the American effort in the Pacific theater. Local Manitowoc soldiers, in the "Red Arrow" Division, later took part in the amphibious assaults on the islands of Saidor, Aitape, and Finschhaven, pushing the Japanese back in each encounter. They were also involved in the crucial victory at Leyte Gulf near the Philippines and at Luzon and Villa Verde. In this last battle, the division captured the Japanese general Yamashita, known as the "butcher of Bataan."[27]

This Red Arrow Division, with Company E from Manitowoc, was the first to see action against the Japanese in the Pacific and the first to carry out successful amphibious and airborne assaults. Before its service in the Pacific ended almost four years later, the division had received six congressional medals, 153 distinguished crosses, 845 silver stars, 1,954 bronze stars, and 11,500 purple hearts. It wasn't until after the defeat of the Japanese and the occupation of Japan that the unit was finally deactivated in Fukuoka on February 13, 1946. Several heroes from this division were welcomed back to towns across Manitowoc County that spring.[28]

Other men from the county also fought in other divisions during the war, as the American military established the practice of separating soldiers from the same vicinity so that one horrible battle would not wipe out boys from just one town or county. In addition to service in the Pacific campaign, many local men fought in the battle of North Africa against the German "desert fox," General Rommel, and participated in the amphibious landing in France on D-Day, June 6, 1944. The surrender of the German forces on VE Day, May 8, 1945, and the surrender of the Japanese on VJ Day, August 10, 1945, brought celebrations in every village, city, and farm in the county. The long and costly war was finally over.

*The onset of World War II meant suspended production of cookware for the Aluminum Goods Manufacturing Company. Wartime contracts led the firm to begin manufacturing such products as 20-man mess kits for troops, aircraft fuel tanks, radio and radar equipment, and cartridge cases. Courtesy, Mirro Company*

## The County Supports the War Effort

In addition to sending its native sons to fight, Manitowoc County citizens sent food supplies to soldiers in training and overseas as the first troops left port. Farmers across Manitowoc County responded by increasing their production of hay, oats, wheat, rye, and corn during the war. Local canneries accelerated their production of peas, with 3,780 acres converted to pea growing by 1944. Other farmers followed suit, producing sugar beets, red beets, carrots, and beans for the army's lists, and prices soared accordingly. The

Depression for farmers was over.[29]

Similarly, hog and dairy production increased dramatically in early 1942. While there were some beef cattle in the county, more than 65 percent of the herds were dairy cattle, a number that rose to a height of 82,500 during the war. Egg production also increased dramatically, reaching a wartime peak of 47 million in 1944. Farm families outdid themselves in producing eggs for the war effort, tending a record 393,300 chickens during the early 1940s.[30]

The return of prosperity to local farms brought the creation of new farm organizations. In 1942 the Manitowoc County Farm Bureau was established, buying its own grain storage elevator at Francis Creek and supporting efforts to create a local hatchery and a fuel cooperative. In 1943 the Manitowoc County Dairy Herd Improvement Association was founded with a far happier agenda than the farm groups of the preceding decade. This association organized the area's first milk-testing facility to assure purchasers of the high quality and safety of producers' milk. Similarly, the Manitowoc County Artificial Breeders Association, organized in 1944, provided semen from proven sires to more than 700 farmers for the production of the highest-quality herds.[31]

As local industries geared up to meet the new wartime orders, the area's vocational schools began to offer classes to train workers for critical industries. At the Aluminum Goods Manufacturing Company, wartime production led to the manufacture of coffee filters, meat platters, syrup pitchers, and other utensils for use by the army, in addition to contract parts for airplane fuel tanks, landing gear parts, radar parts, meat cans, cartridge cases, and the same kind of canteens that had been used in World War I.[32]

At Manitowoc Shipbuilding Company, president Charles C. West prepared for orders from the U.S. Navy for destroyers and other surface craft. West realized that it would be necessary to solve the problem of an impassable St. Lawrence River channel, which had a shallow draft for ships prior to the construction of the seaway in the 1950s. Its lock length of only 257 feet (enough to accommodate freighters and some earlier warships) was too short for these new-model submarines, which measured as much as 300 feet. West and his engineers developed an ingenious system of a floating dry dock upon which a larger vessel could be mounted for transportation down the Illinois Ship Canal to the Mississippi, thus avoiding the problems of transporting them out through the St. Lawrence River.

Instrumental in the company's ability to meet the government's orders for these submarines was Charles C. West's son, John D. West, who had come to work at the company in 1932. A graduate of Manitowoc's Lincoln High School, Beloit College, and the School of Engineering at Cornell University, John D. West served from 1934 to 1952 as superintentent of the company's machine shop, before eventually succeeding his father as

*Local industries played an important part in wartime efforts during World War II. Manitowoc Shipbuilding shifted its focus from surface vessels and began the difficult and important task of constructing much-needed submarines. With the help of its newly designed crane—the Model 3900—the company began building the first of 28 submarines. In this photo, two cranes lift a section of the USS PETO. The interior section was blacked out for censorship purposes. Courtesy, The Manitowoc Company, Inc.*

president. He is credited with being instrumental in perfecting the bow plane controls, the propeller drive shafts, the torpedo tube alignment systems, and the periscope hoists on the submarines built in Manitowoc.[33]

When he was summoned to Washington, D.C., in 1940, Charles C. West was asked by the navy to build submarines instead of destroyers, an idea he did not welcome at first. Building surface vessels was a longtime specialty at the shipyards, but the creation of underwater craft presented many difficult challenges. However, West agreed to the navy's request and began an immediate retooling of his plant, with a new fabricating shop measuring 80 by 300 feet. He also went in search of a crane strong and flexible enough to lift 30-ton sections of a submarine onto keel blocks.[34]

Finding no company that produced the desired crane, West turned to his own engineers and crane division with the result that a new, giant model 3900 crane was created with the capability of lifting 60-ton submarine sections. The addition of a torque converter on these cranes allowed for a smoother operation and more precision in the erection process. Not only were these cranes used at Manitowoc for submarine construction, the company received a top-priority order for six of its largest cranes to be shipped to Pearl Harbor (just six days after the bombing on December 7, 1941) to be used in the salvage and rebuilding efforts there.[35]

In addition to the thousands of new jobs created for local men, the firm hired 385 women during the war who worked as welders and in the machine shop. These "Rosie the Riveters" had their own eating area and locker room and enjoyed wartime wages as high as most of their 7,000 male counterparts. As in World War I, local housing was woefully inadequate for this great influx of workers, many of whom received draft deferments because of their special skills. In cooperation with the Division of Defense Housing, the company constructed 600 housing units in a new subdivision named Custerdale, and remodeled several of the old dormitories from the previous war for use by single workers.[36]

As submarine production began, the company had four berths available at one time. New buildings were also constructed for testing facilities and for offices where consultants from the navy worked closely with company designers and engineers. The navy contract called for the firm to build 10 submarines in the next five years, with additional payments for early delivery. As soon as the first submarine was completed, the company had to solve the problem of launching it into the Manitowoc River which was too shallow for a conventional "end first" launch.

The first ship, the *PETO*, was launched sideways into the river (an unorthodox procedure that West had assured the navy would work), and then proceeded under its own power out into Lake Michigan where its equipment was tested and fine tuned. On April 30, 1942, the *PETO* was the first submarine launched in Great Lakes history and became the first of a total of 28 submarines subsequently built at Manitowoc Shipbuilding.[37]

The *PETO* then proceeded down Lake Michigan to Chicago and down the Illinois River to Lockport where the pontoon dry dock awaited it. With its periscope removed for low bridges, the pontoon and submarine were towed south through Illinois and down the Mississippi River, reaching New Orleans on January 11, 1943, some 288 days ahead of schedule. The company's retooling and ingenious design efforts had paid off. The original 10 submarines were delivered almost two years ahead of schedule, and more orders from the navy came in.[38]

With the completion of its 28th submarine, Manitowoc Shipbuilding was awarded its fifth navy "E" medal for excellence. Its submarines sank 488,737 tons of enemy shipping during the war, and one of its subs, the *RASHER*, sank more tonnage than any other submarine but one during World War II. However, the company's contribution to America's war effort grew even more.

*John D. West, son of Charles C. West, joined Manitowoc Shipbuilding in 1932 following his graduation from Cornell University. During World War II, when the company built 28 submarines for the U.S. Navy, John was credited with making numerous design and scheduling improvements that cut building timetables and construction costs. John succeeded his father as president of Manitowoc Shipbuilding in 1957. Upon his death in 1989 at the age of 83, John had maintained a 56-year association with The Manitowoc Company, Inc., while serving his community through philanthropy and volunteerism. Courtesy, The Manitowoc Company, Inc.*

With the great success of the submarine program, West was again called to a conference in Washington, D.C., in 1942, where the navy asked him to build landing craft for amphibious operations. West agreed and another berth was created for this project. Although the navy estimated that each landing craft would cost at least $100,000 to build, the shipyards at Manitowoc delivered 36 such vessels at an average cost of only $65,000 each.[39]

Two designs of these landing craft were created, the LCT5s and the LCT6s, a heavier model. Each model was launched and tested on beaches north of Manitowoc before being loaded on railcars or trucks for shipment to the navy depots. The LCT5s from Manitowoc received a presidential citation for their "outstanding performance" at the D-Day landing on June 6, 1944, at Normandy.[40]

### Postwar Recovery

As the war drew to a close in early 1945, the shipyards and other local companies looked to the production of consumer goods for their survival. Manitowoc Shipbuilding had been commissioned by the army to construct ammunition boxes prior to the war's end and this project lent itself to conversion of the plant to the production of consumer goods such as ice machines, refrigerators, freezers, and even dry-cleaning machines.[41]

Similarly, at Aluminum Goods Manufacturing Company, soon renamed Mirro Aluminum, household goods, pots, pans, and pressure cookers became the postwar basis for prosperity. In Kiel, the H.G. Weber Company converted to the production of paper bags, and in 1946 the Jagemann Stamping Company of Manitowoc was established as a producer of finished metal goods.[42]

The returning soldiers found brides and the postwar baby boom began. Local merchants experienced a dramatic upsurge in the demand for consumer goods. At Two Rivers' Schroeder Bros. Department Store, the late 1940s and the 1950s brought great expansion in the flooring and drapery departments. The appliance area also grew, offering customers new washers and dryers, refrigerators, and stoves. Sales in the grocery area boomed, as a new self-service layout was instituted. In the late 1950s the store opened a new adjacent one-story building that sold clothing, called the Sport Casual Shop.[43]

With postwar prosperity, new industries came to town. One of the most successful of these, Lube Devices, Inc., opened its doors in 1962 on Nagle Avenue in Manitowoc, the site of an old chicken farm. Holding several

*Before landing crafts—known as LCTs—stormed the beaches at Normandy, many were undergoing testing on the beaches along Lake Michigan just north of Manitowoc. This landing craft was built by Manitowoc Shipbuilding during the war. Courtesy, The Manitowoc Company, Inc.*

patents on new ways to produce lubricating equipment, the company manufactured a variety of components for hydraulic and lubricating systems, shipped across the country.[44]

Another local firm experienced dramatic expansion in the postwar period, when convenience in food preparation was in great demand. Founded in 1928 as the Chermake Meat Market, a local sausage production facility expanded into The Cher-Make Sausage Company with a new production plant in 1948. Three years later extra smokehouses were added, and other additions followed in 1955, 1962, and 1966. Making a variety of popular sausage products and shipping them throughout the country, the company rode the great boom in packaged food sales brought by the postwar period.[45]

With the growing demand for ready-made clothing and textiles, other local enterprises also prospered. The Two Rivers Knitting Company (founded in 1901), the Zula Hosiery Company (1904), and the Wisconsin Knitting Mill (1904) grew during and after the war. In Kiel, the county's third-largest city, the Hanson Glove Company hired more workers and increased its output. Similar businesses included the Crescent Woolen Mills Company, of Two Rivers, makers of wool and merino sheep yarn, and the Wesco Manufacturing Company, which produced industrial wool packing. Combining expertise in its old skill of making fishing nets with changing consumer demand, the Gagnon Net and the Carron Net companies manufactured both fishing and basketball nets.[46]

*H.G. Weber & Co., established in the 1920s by Herman Gustav Weber, specialized in the production of paper bag machines and paper converting equipment. The firm eventually moved its headquarters and factory from Sheboygan to Kiel in the 1930s. Like many companies after World War II, H.G. Weber turned to the manufacture of consumer goods by producing paper bags. Courtesy, Kiel Historical Society*

Another company that experienced tremendous postwar expansion was the Metal Ware Corporation of Two Rivers, located on the site of the old Mann Brothers Pail Company. Founded in 1932, the firm experienced growth during the war and added on to its production plant eight times between 1944 and 1964. The postwar consumer boom was particularly profitable for Metal Ware because it had purchased the rights for the production of the electric elements for hair dryers, coffee makers, popcorn poppers, egg cookers and poachers, hot cups, camping cookware, and party urns. The growth of hair salons, and the increased demand for cooking conveniences, brought Metal Ware's product into the national market by the early 1950s and great expansions followed.[47]

## Growth of Schools, Libraries, and Local Entertainment
Throughout the decades after World War II, the county's commitment to superior public education continued with the substantial increases in students due to the postwar baby boom. Having united all of the schools in the City of Manitowoc into one district in 1905, the school board could better centralize its planning for this increased postwar enrollment. On Saturday, January 16, 1924, the new Lincoln High School had opened with its beautiful auditorium and new gymnasium which was immediately christened by a basketball game against the team from Sheboygan. More than 1,400 fans attended the game with standing room only. The following Monday, 925 students attended classes at the new high school for the first time.[48]

Saluting the quality of the building and the magnificence of its architecture as a testament to the citizens' emphasis on education, one writer noted the "insistence on architectural beauty...[made] the building a model in its rare combination of practical usefulness and aesthetic outline. Perched on the top of the highest prominence overlooking the lake at the southern extremity of the city and visible for miles to the southward and westward."

*The postwar years were a boon to local companies that produced consumer goods. Companies such as the Metal Ware Corporation of Two Rivers grew by leaps and bounds as the demand for their goods increased dramatically. Courtesy, Lester Public Library*

The structure also featured a great tower, like a beacon light for education, which shone forth "like a lighthouse over land and lake." Former Wisconsin Governor Francis E. McGovern, in his commencement address, said that the tower stood out "like the tower of the cathedral at Antwerp."[49]

Throughout the next several decades, including federally aided programs during the Depression, the Manitowoc school system enlarged several grade schools and added a new natatorium to Lincoln High School. Bond issues during the 1930s provided funding for the construction of two junior high schools, Woodrow Wilson School, on the north side of the city, and Washington Junior High School, on the south side. Even with this extensive commitment to the city's schoolchildren, the board of education did not forget the task of offering vocational education classes, both during the Depression and during the war that followed.[50]

During the 1950s and 1960s Lincoln High School was updated with additions for home economics, art, a new library, and a million-dollar gymnasium, christened the John F. Kennedy Physical Education unit. Further classroom additions followed as the city's emphasis on educational excellence continued into the most recent decades. In the spring of 1970 the Vits family contributed funding to upgrade the swimming pool (the old natatorium) at Lincoln High School, which had long served as an important facility for students and the community at large. One estimate stated that more than 19,000 students and adults had learned to swim there, a vital skill for residents of a lakeshore community.[51]

In the rural schools of the county, supervision of instruction fell to the elected county superintendents, among whom were several dedicated and talented individuals, including publisher John Nagle and C.E. Patzer, who later took a leadership position at Milwaukee Normal School. Communities across the county maintained a strong commitment to the education of their children.

In Mishicot, voters approved a $575,000 bond issue in 1958 to construct a brand-new community high school, with a gymnasium and 24 teaching centers. Similarly, the Valders District, which included the communities of St. Nazianz, Valders, Whitelaw, Cato, Eaton, Liberty, Newton, Manitowoc Rapids, and Rockland, dedicated a new $650,000 district high school in 1964, which also had a modern gymnasium, a state-of-the-art library, and a swimming pool, added in 1965. Two years later voters approved another bond issue for a new junior high building, completed in 1968.[52]

In Reedsville, a similar pattern of strong support was evidenced as the community replaced all of its antiquated school buildings in 1962 with brand-new high school, junior high, and grade schools. Residents of Kiel followed with the construction of new elementary schools in Kiel and Meeme during the 1960s and a new unified public high school in 1970 at a cost of $2.1 million. Through an earlier reorganization of the district, the Kiel Unified School District brought in students from 14 rural areas around the county. Unified schools, made possible through busing, could provide a far

greater range of educational offerings and opportunities for students in all subjects, from the arts and music to scholastics and sports.[53]

As the local teacher training school began to graduate more qualified teachers, standards rose throughout the county. At first, in 1901, the teacher-training classes were held on the third floor of the old Garfield School in Manitowoc. By 1904 they were moved above the city library on North Eighth Street, later the location of the Manitowoc Maritime Museum. In 1922 the construction of a County Teachers' College on North 18th Street and Michigan Avenue in Manitowoc provided a permanent home and a lasting commitment to better preparation for teachers. The building, recently renovated, now houses the Manitowoc County Heritage Center.[54]

For the next several decades, graduates of the school could enter the teaching field with a two-year certificate, but by the 1950s a college degree was customarily required. From the early 1950s until 1971, graduates of this normal school program began to transfer to one of the four-year programs within the state, often at Milwaukee or Oshkosh, where they received further preparation and a baccalaureate degree. In 1971, with the rise of the unified University of Wisconsin System, state support for the older state teachers' colleges, such as Manitowoc's, was phased out.[55]

Higher education within the county had long been represented by two normal schools—the publicly supported County Normal School, established in 1901, and Holy Family Normal School, forerunner to Silver Lake College, established in 1885 by the Franciscan Sisters of Christian Charity at Holy Family Convent on Alverno Road in Manitowoc. The standard two-year program prepared the members of the Franciscan Community to teach in parochial schools staffed by the Franciscan Sisters across the country.

As requirements for teacher certification became increasingly stringent after World War I, there was a need for a four-year college to prepare the Sisters as teachers. In 1935 construction began on a college wing added to Holy Family Convent. Named Holy Family College, it was a four-year liberal arts college approved by the University of Wisconsin for preparing elementary teachers and later accredited by the North Central Association of Colleges and Secondary Schools. The first degrees were conferred in 1939.[56]

Another major change to its mission occurred in 1957, when the college admitted its first lay women students who took degrees in a variety of fields, but with no commitment to join the order or work within the church community. Three years later the college undertook its first major fund drive and constructed a new campus with four convergent wings in a three-story classroom building, a library, art and music studios, and new scientific laboratories. Other features included a new chapel, an administration wing, cafeteria, and residence center. With these new facilities, student enrollment at the campus doubled during the 1960s. In 1969 another landmark change made the cam-

*John Nagle, a well-known educator and publisher in Manitowoc County, began his teaching career in Maple Grove at the age of 17. He later served as superintendent of schools in the county from 1880 to 1881. His strong interest in journalism led him to become editor and eventually publisher of the* Manitowoc Pilot. *He served as editor until his death in 1900. Courtesy, Manitowoc County Historical Society*

*Lincoln High School as it looked in 1929, five years after it opened. The building itself was praised by many for the beauty of its prominent tower, architecture, and location. The school expanded its facility through the years to include a natatorium, and an updated library and gymnasium. Courtesy, Manitowoc County Historical Society*

*Holy Family College was founded as a two-year school in 1885 and later changed to a four-year institution. In this 1959 photo, Sisters of the convent are seen leaving a cornerstone dedication ceremony that was held in conjunction with a commencement for one lay woman and 28 nuns. Just two years before, policy was changed to begin admitting lay women to the college. Photo by* The Herald Times; *courtesy, Silver Lake College*

pus co-educational with the admission of male students for the first time. At that time, the college officially changed its name to Silver Lake College.[57]

During the subsequent decades the college further broadened its curriculum to offer more than 20 programs of study, including areas such as business and health-related fields. It also began a program to admit older, nontraditional, adult students, many of whom were seeking retraining for different employment opportunities. As the diversity of its offerings grew, the college became a more important presence in the community, bringing in many cultural offerings, fine arts and theater programs, and widely known lecturers. Conservatively figured, the college noted that its economic impact on the community was at least $32 million annually by the celebration of its centennial in 1985.[58]

The other institution of higher education in the county, which became the two-year University of Wisconsin Center, began during the mid-1930s as part of the public university in Green Bay. During the early 1960s the University of Wisconsin Board of Regents mandated that a two-year center system be established that would rely upon each home county to support its physical plant, but would be part of the larger university budget for all other financial support. The citizens of Manitowoc responded and raised the money to construct a new university campus in 1967, which welcomed 500 students who could attend either for a two-year university associate degree or could transfer to one of Wisconsin's four-year campuses for a baccalaureate degree. In 1971, when the University of Wisconsin merged all of its component parts, the University of Wisconsin Center at Manitowoc became an integral part of the University of Wisconsin System. In 1998 the name was changed to the University of Wisconsin-Manitowoc.[59]

Along with its schools and colleges, the county's libraries experienced strong citizen support throughout the postwar decades. By the 1950s the old Carnegie Library building in Manitowoc was badly in need of repair and expansion. Finally, in 1967, the community celebrated the opening of a brand-new facility, at 808 Hamilton Street near the lakeshore, on the site of the former Roosevelt Elementary School. Thirty-one years later, in 1998, the city opened a splendid new library facility, with windows looking out to the

lakeshore and riverfront. Located just five blocks north, the $6.2-million edifice houses a state-of-the-art computer network, as well as a local history reference room and a widely diversified general collection.[60]

Similarly, the public libraries in both Kiel and Two Rivers received strong community support. A modern library in Kiel was dedicated in 1971, and the City of Two Rivers completed its new Lester Public Library in 1997, located on Memorial Drive just across from the lakeshore. With its collection of more than 60,000 books, the library could partner with the county's other strong collections to offer citizens a great variety of resources for research and reading.[61]

The years of the Great Depression, World War II, and decades of postwar recovery and prosperity brought modern communications, television, freeways, school growth, and university development to Manitowoc County. By the 1970s the county looked ahead to the last quarter of the twentieth century when its status in business, industry, farming, education, and maritime facilities would grow even more rapidly. With continued expansion on the horizon through the construction of new roads and freeways, the position of Manitowoc County as a leading port, a site for business growth and development, and a thriving linkage of interwoven cities and communities made its title, the "Beacon on the Lakeshore," a valid one.

*By 1969 male students no longer had to leave the county to obtain their four-year degree. That year Holy Family College became Silver Lake College and the school became a co-ed institution. Courtesy, Silver Lake College*

*The Manitowoc County Courthouse is an outstanding example of turn-of-the-century beaux arts neoclassical architecture. Listed on the National Register of Historic Buildings, the courthouse was designed by Christian H. Tegan, whose works include public and commercial buildings, schools, churches, and a number of residences in Manitowoc and Two Rivers. The exterior of native limestone houses a central marble-columned staircase directly under the dome. Once glass covered, the dome suffered severe damage in a hailstorm early in the century and was recovered in aluminum. A proposal to restore the dome to its original appearance is presently being considered. Courtesy, Manitowoc County Historical Society*

## CHAPTER SEVEN

# The Progress of Recent Decades

1970 – 1999

*The S.S.* Badger, *largest carferry on the Great Lakes, sails each summer between Manitowoc and Ludington, Michigan, carrying tourists, cars, and recreational vehicles. Equipped with state-rooms, two restaurants, a gift shop, and museum, the* Badger *makes the 55-mile trip between Manitowoc and Ludington in four hours, cutting 370 miles off the distance by land. Courtesy, Lake Michigan Carferry Service*

*I*n the past three decades Manitowoc County has enjoyed continued prosperity based on the strength of its industries and the successes of its many farms. As the new century approaches, the commitment of county residents to celebrating the past decades of achievement has increased. Along with new buildings, such as schools and libraries, the county has engaged in valuable projects of historic preservation, keeping the legacy of the past alive while planning for the century to come.

## Population and Economic Trends

The county's population, which increased by almost 20 percent between 1950 and 1990, held steady at around 80,000 just before the turn of the century, making Manitowoc the third most populous county of the "Bay-Lake District" in northeastern Wisconsin. Only Brown County, with the city of Green Bay to the northwest, and Sheboygan County, just south, had larger populations, followed by Marinette, Oconto, Door, Kewaunee, and Florence counties.

Moreover, the population distribution of Manitowoc County has continued to be roughly 60 percent urban and 40 percent rural. More than 48,000 of the 80,000 people reside in the county's three largest cities—Manitowoc, Two Rivers, and Kiel—with another 7,458 living in its nine incorporated villages. The remaining 24,879 citizens live in one of the 18 towns, from Maple Grove and Cooperstown in the northwest corner of the county to Meeme and Centerville in the southeast. The county's many industries and its agricultural, educational, governmental, and service-sector employers hired more than 45,000 county residents in 1995, keeping the unemployment rate around 5 percent, well below the national average.[1] Both the population trends and the growth of industry bode well for continued prosperity in Manitowoc County in the twenty-first century.

## Advances in Health Care

What is now Holy Family Memorial Medical Center began in 1899 in response to a call from the community. Growth and change have made Holy Family Memorial what it is today, a comprehensive health care provider whose doors are always open to anyone needing health care. Holy Family Memorial's commitment to serve has been motivated by the Franciscan Sisters of Christian Charity and the spirit and leadership of those who founded Manitowoc Memorial Hospital. The merger of Holy Family and Memorial in 1991 secured a long-term commitment to Manitowoc County.[2]

Development of the Holy Family Memorial health network began in 1993 when physicians Jim and Mike Hoftiezer and Internal Medicine Associates affiliated with Holy Family Memorial. By mid-1999 the network had evolved to include 10 physician clinics that encompassed individual practices and multi-physician clinics. Other network members included outpatient diagnostic and therapeutic centers, retail pharmacies, home medical services, and a Physician Hospital Organization.

In July 1998 Holy Family Memorial began construction of a Cancer Care Center at its Western Avenue campus. The center, affiliated with the University of Wisconsin Comprehensive Cancer Center in Madison, is part of an $8-million Centennial Building project. The project includes two new oversize operating room suites and expansion of the Short Stay Surgery Centre. It will benefit Manitowoc County residents for decades to come.[3]

The Two Rivers Community Hospital has also served Manitowoc County residents as a major medical center since 1927. To keep pace with the growing health care needs of the community, and to remain technologically advanced, an addition was completed in 1962 and in 1993 the hospital affiliated with the not-for-profit Aurora Health Care system.

Aurora is continuing that tradition of service with the recent construction

*The historic Schroeder Bros. Department Store is seen in this 1990s photo. The building was completed in 1899 by Peter Schroeder (1831-1917) who, with the help of his father, opened a small dry goods store in Two Rivers in 1891. The store occupied the first floor of the B. Mayer building on the northwest corner of Washington and Cedar (now 18th) streets. By 1896 his three brothers had joined him. Today the store is operated by John and Tim Schroeder, the founder's grandsons, continuing the family tradition of service to the community. Courtesy, Schroeder's Department Store*

*The new Aurora Medical Center is scheduled to open in mid-2000. The 180,000-square-foot facility is centrally located between Manitowoc and Two Rivers. Courtesy, Aurora Health Care*

of the Aurora Medical Center on Memorial Drive between Manitowoc and Two Rivers, centrally located to serve its satellite clinics in those communities. The new 180,000-square-foot facility provides state-of-the-art computerized registration and diagnostic services and a rehabilitation center to facilitate the return of injured patients to work and normal life. In addition to a beautiful view of the lakeshore, upper floors contain modern surgical and laboratory services, a pediatrics unit, and maternity suites.[4]

Aurora's planned "Next Generation of Quality Health Care" includes continuing use of the Two Rivers Community Hospital for a variety of non-acute care services. The Hamilton Memorial Home, a long-term care facility adjacent to the hospital, may expand into the building. The Visiting Nurse Association of Wisconsin also has offices in the Two Rivers building and, along with other health care support services, is expected to remain there with room for future expansion.[5]

With both Holy Family Memorial Medical Center and Aurora Medical Center, residents of Manitowoc County can look forward to ever-improving health care quality in the next century.[6]

## New Technology, New Enterprises

Many of the county's most enduring enterprises have demonstrated a steady commitment to better technology and better service in the past three decades. The historic Schroeder's Department Store has kept abreast of the times with expansions in 1974 and 1986, and extensive remodeling in recent years. Still operated by the grandsons of the founders, the store has blended tradition with marketing skills to supply the community with its many retail needs.[7]

Nearby in Two Rivers, the area's other successful department store, Evans, boasts of a world-class toy department that offers thousands of toys for all ages on one of its floors, as well as crafts, apparel, garden supplies, and housewares on other levels.[8]

The Hamilton Manufacturing Company is known today as Fisher Hamilton Inc., a wholly owned subsidiary of Fisher Scientific International, a worldwide distributor of supplies and equipment for science. Fisher Hamilton is the world's largest manufacturer of laboratory furniture and fume hoods. Markets served include health care, industrial, and education. Subsidiaries of Fisher Hamilton include Epoxyn Products of Mountain Home, Arkansas, a producer of epoxy resin laboratory work surfaces, and Systems Manufacturing Corporation of Conklin, New York, a leading manufacturer of computer furniture systems.[9]

The Mirro Company, which celebrated its centennial in 1997, has kept abreast of the many developments in aluminum, with the construction of two additions to its main manufacturing facility in the early 1990s. Acquired by Newell Rubbermaid in 1983, Mirro has undergone the "Newellization" process of improved manufacturing efficiency, pruning nonproductive product lines, reducing inventories, and trimming excess costs. Since the acquisition the company has focused on its core business of aluminum cookware and bakeware manufacture with great success.[10]

At The Manitowoc Company, the historic ship repair business has been outdistanced during recent decades by the growth of its diversified operations, including food-service equipment and crane sales which together comprised more than 93 percent of its sales in 1998. Replacing retiring CEO Frederick Butler in July 1998, Terry Growcock looked to acquisitions as part of the firm's growth strategy for the new century. Along with continued diversification, The Manitowoc Company also planned to increase its international presence in the new century by expanding its production of crane and food-service equipment to three continents by targeting select foreign market opportunities.

A recent enterprise in the county, the Spancrete Plant at Valders, brought the technology of pre-stressed, hollowcore concrete production to Manitowoc and the surrounding area. Construction on the plant actually began in 1956, when Henry Nagy of the Spancrete Corporation of West Allis purchased land near Valders to expand his operation. The newly patented extruder machine could pour hundreds of feet of hollowcore concrete every hour onto long beds through which steel rods had been

*This 1972 photo of the Spancrete plant in Valders shows an operation that produces one of many pre-stressed concrete structural forms manufactured there. Courtesy, Spancrete*

stretched. When the concrete was cured, the rods were cut, creating the pre-stressing that gave the hollowcore beams their great strength.[11]

The Valders location meant that Spancrete could take advantage of its proximity to Green Bay, the Fox Valley cities, and also the Sheboygan area where a new Kohler plant was being constructed using Spancrete. The new plant had a 600,000-square-foot-capacity and required a crew of skilled workers who could run the rabbit machine, which stretched the steel rods, as well as the highly sophisticated concrete extruder, which actually poured and shaped the hollowcore beams.[12]

Also keeping abreast of new technology, Manitowoc Public Utilities installed a new 20-megawatt bed boiler in 1990 to meet the demands of clean air standards and the energy needs of its 15,000 customers. Still a successful, municipally owned utility, the company continues to contribute about $2 million each year to the city treasury out of its more than $25 million in revenues.[13]

A new technological development, nuclear energy, came to the county in 1966 with the construction of the Point Beach Nuclear Power Plant. The first

of two 500-megawatt units to be located on the lakeshore north of Two Rivers, in the town of Two Creeks, was completed in 1970. The plant was built by Westinghouse for Wisconsin Electric Power Company to serve the eastern half of the state and Upper Michigan. With the addition of a second unit in 1972, the plant has stood as a symbol of the latest technology in energy production, and as a reminder of the energy needs of the growing economy on the eastern shore of Wisconsin.[14]

The Point Beach plant has experienced more than three decades of clean, safe, and efficient operation. In recent years an additional 24 megawatts of capacity has been added to the plant with the installation of newly designed turbines to both units.

*Manitowoc Public Utilities' first waterworks and electric plant were constructed at the intersection of South Seventh and Columbus streets in 1914. While the two streets no longer intersect, the landmark has grown in the same location to include a modern power plant, state-of-the-art microfiltration water treatment plant, and business office. Courtesy, Manitowoc Public Utilities*

Wisconsin Electric Power, along with other utilities in Minnesota and Wisconsin, announced early in 1999 the formation of a nuclear management company to sustain long-term safety, optimize reliability, and improve the operational performance of the Point Beach plant.

An Energy Center located adjacent to the plant has hosted more than 700,000 visitors since it opened in 1969. An energy nature trail captures the beauty of the outdoors around the plant, complementing the Point Beach State Forest and campgrounds located a short distance south of the plant site. A new Energy Center opened in 1999, adding to other new construction at the plant including engineering and training buildings.[15]

The energy-producing capacity of the Point Beach plant, which employs more than 700 staff, has operated to the benefit of residents both within and outside of Manitowoc County.

### Enlightenment and Culture

The appreciation of the county's residents for libraries has resulted in an outstanding commitment to their growth and development during the past three decades. In fact, in 1997 and 1998 both of the county's two largest cities have undertaken successful projects to build new libraries. Two Rivers'

new $3-million Lester Public Library was completed in 1997, and the Manitowoc Public Library moved into its $6.2-million building by the lakeshore in 1998.

The county's commemoration of its cultural past has also enhanced opportunities for learning and entertainment during the 1980s and 1990s. Beginning in the 1980s, a local citizens' group made plans to renovate and revitalize the old Capitol Theatre, which had staged its original opening night gala in Manitowoc on June 16, 1921. For more than 30 years the theater had offered exciting vaudeville acts and then movie entertainment to area residents until it fell into disuse in the 1960s and was scheduled for demolition.[16]

The Masquers, a community theater group that worked to save the Capitol, donated $50,000 toward its purchase and restoration, a sum that was generously matched by Mrs. Helen Schuette. The Society to Preserve the Capitol was formed and began a community fund drive that resulted in the 1987 purchase of the building, with the help of its former owners, the Marcus Corporation. Realizing its heritage as the "Jewel on the Lakeshore," the building was restored to its historic elegance after a successful $1.17-million fund drive.[17]

To make the Capitol Civic Centre complex more versatile, two adjacent properties were purchased, providing for a large meeting and reception area. As completed, the Capitol has become the performing home of 14 community arts, music, and theater groups. It also houses the Lillian and Francis Kadow Movie Museum, with its unique collection of photographs autographed by Hollywood stars.

With its bright marquis entrance and sizable seating capacity, the Capitol has been able to host national touring companies, traveling Broadway

*Completed in 1998, the 52,000-square-foot Manitowoc Public Library was designed to provide a spectacular view of the Manitowoc River and harbor. An entire city block was razed to provide the needed space when the library outgrew the Hamilton Street facility, which was built in 1966 to replace the smaller Carnegie Library on North Eighth Street (now the site of First National Bank). Situated in the heart of historic downtown Manitowoc, the new building features data cabling to accommodate tomorrow's information technology. The interior contains shelving space for an estimated 10 to 15 years of collection growth. The City of Manitowoc, the Manitowoc Public Library Foundation, a special capital campaign committee, and a number of gifts and donations combined to raise the $6.2 million required to complete the project. The building stands as an excellent example of Manitowoc County's commitment to its citizens, and as a monument to the generosity of its residents. Courtesy, Manitowoc Public Library*

shows, concerts by the Milwaukee Symphony Orchestra, and the Glenn Miller Orchestra. It is also the performing home for children's theater productions and all of the Masquers' plays. Local choirs use the facility for seasonal productions, and the theater hosted the April 11, 1999, Peter, Paul and Mary show. With more than a dozen top-quality productions each season, the Capitol exemplifies the virtues of historic preservation as well as serving as a cultural mecca for the entire region.[18]

### Bringing History into the Present

The success of the campaign to save the Capitol Theatre is only one of many ways in which the citizens of Manitowoc County have shown their respect for the past through the efforts of historic preservation. The county is replete with museums and reminders of the area's rich heritage. One ethnic center, Valders, celebrates its Norwegian heritage with a parade featuring floats, one of which is a Viking ship.[19]

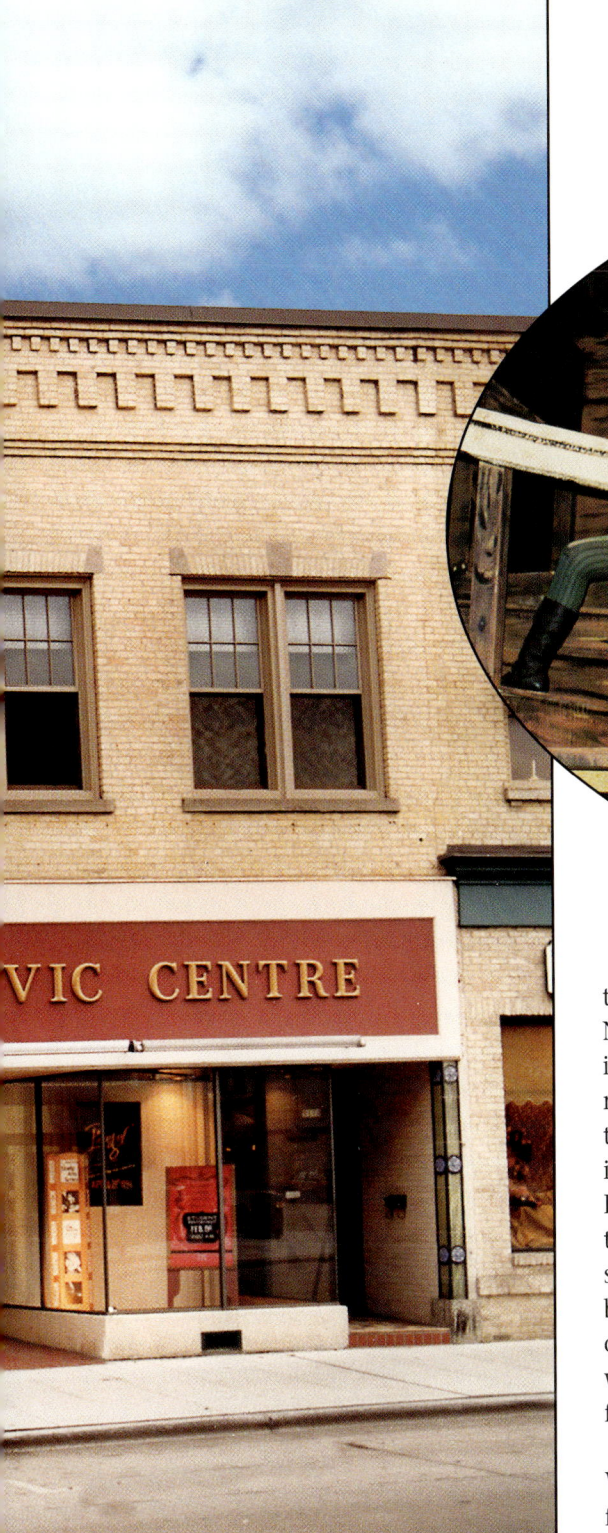

In Two Rivers, the nomination of the old fishing village to the National Register of Historic Places in the late 1980s brought an awareness that even the most humble cottages can provide lessons about this important part of the lakeshore's French Canadian heritage. Called the Rogers Street Fishing Village, the site features two commercial fishing boats, an 1886 lighthouse, and four original fishermen's shanties, all of which serve to recreate the historic fishing culture of the 1800s.

Also in Two Rivers, the Washington House, an old hotel from the 1800s, has been restored as a museum and ice cream parlor by the Two Rivers Historical Society, so that the ambience of life in an old hostelry won't be lost forever. Across the street, another Historical Society museum called the Hamilton Wood Type & Printing Museum is located in space provided by Fisher Hamilton Inc. This museum displays all equipment needed in the manufacture of wood type, and printing presses to show how wood type was used to form the backbone of the country's printing industry many decades ago.[20]

To celebrate its maritime history, Two Rivers has opened the U.S. Coast Guard Exhibit at the Rogers Street Fishing Village Museum near the harbor. The exhibit depicts the story of many daring rescues by the men of the Coast Guard who risked their lives to save others. It also chronicles the area's worst storms and the toll of shipwreck disasters in Lake Michigan.

Similarly, in Manitowoc, the Wisconsin Maritime Museum features many exhibits about the history of shipping on the Great Lakes. Wisconsin's largest maritime collection, it also hosts a World War II submarine, the U.S.S. *Cobia*, an international submariner's memorial and a National Historic

*LEFT: The Capitol Civic Centre complex, the "Jewel on the Lakeshore," has been restored to its historic elegance through the efforts of the Society to Preserve the Capitol. Opened in 1921 for the showing of silent movies, the theater also hosted a number of notable vaudeville performers who traveled north from Chicago on the famous Loew entertainment circuit, before being leased and operated as a movie theater by Marcus Industries of Milwaukee. That lease expired in 1982 and the Marcus Company chose not to purchase the building, providing the opportunity for local citizens to organize the preservation movement. The "Jewel" opened its doors to the public in 1987 and has since provided the area a steady schedule of big-name and local entertainment. (The double doors to the right of the marquee lead to an adjoining museum of local entertainment history.) © Michael Thomas, PhotoTechnics.*

*ABOVE: The revitalized Capitol Theatre, the cornerstone of the Capitol Civic Centre complex, is the performing home of 14 community arts, music and theater groups. These include The Masquers, Lakeshore Wind Ensemble, Manitowoc Symphony Orchestra, Peter Quince Performing Company, Jean Wolfmeyer School of Dance, Kristine's Dance Studio, TRACTS, and fine arts performing groups from area schools and colleges. This production of "Peter Pan" was performed in 1998. Courtesy, Capitol Civic Centre*

*Visitors to the Wisconsin Maritime Museum enjoy a recreation of some of Manitowoc's waterfront buildings as they appeared in the late 1800s. The cargo and passenger carrying packets and "whalebacks" of the Goodrich Transportation Company (replicated office at right in the picture) dominated Lake Michigan steamship traffic into the early decades of the twentieth century Courtesy, Wisconsin Maritime Museum*

Landmark. The *Cobia* was not built in Manitowoc but is similar to the 28 submarines that were built there during World War II. The submarine provides a valuable educational tool, since tours include discussions of how men actually lived and survived on board. Moreover, school, adult, or scout groups can arrange to spend the night on the sub, to make the reality even more vivid.[21]

Another special exhibit at the Wisconsin Maritime Museum illustrates the history of shipping on the Great Lakes, and the saga of Manitowoc's own record of shipbuilding through the years. The exhibit features scale model ships showing the special designs of ships from many eras.[22]

In addition to the history of shipping, the gracious homes of the past have been preserved by local efforts. The restoration of one of Manitowoc's finest old homes, the Vilas mansion, has resulted in the creation of the area's first art museum. Listed on the National Register, the museum displays a fine collection of American paintings, and exhibits of arts and crafts in the setting of a restored and elegant Victorian home. The collection also includes antique dolls, Chinese ivory carvings, and an annual exhibition of the "Art of Tablesettings" as well as "Christmas in the Mansion."

ABOVE: The USS Cobia, a World War II submarine, is one of many exhibits in the Wisconsin Maritime Museum, the state's largest, in Manitowoc. The Cobia is a National Historic Landmark of the same class of submarine as 28 similar ones constructed during WWII in Manitowoc shipyards. Photo by Ron Hoerth

LEFT: A modern replica two-masted schooner of the Gloucester type makes its way through the Two Rivers harbor. A three-masted schooner similar to the Gloucester model was produced by the Burger Boat Company in the mid-1800s, beginning Manitowoc's tradition of shipbuilding. Photo by Ron Hoerth

*ABOVE: The L-shaped John West Gallery of the Rahr-West Art Museum was designed and built in 1986 to provide additional space for rotating exhibitions and work from the museum's permanent collection of American Art. Courtesy, Rahr-West Art Museum*

*RIGHT: The Victorian mansion that houses the Rahr-West Art Museum was originally the home of Joseph and Mary Vilas, a pioneer Manitowoc family. Built between 1891 and 1893 at a cost of $35,000, the 13-bedroom house was designed by Milwaukee architects George Ferry and Alfred Clas. Courtesy, Rahr-West Art Museum*

*FACING PAGE, TOP: These farm buildings, constructed in 1859, today house the Natural Ovens Food and Farm Museum. The museum and bakery are located just south of the Manitowoc city limits. Visitors are welcome and public tours are available. Courtesy, Natural Ovens Food and Farm Museum*

*FACING PAGE, BOTTOM: A demonstration of hay baling as it was done in the early 1900s makes use of vintage farm machinery restored to operating condition at Pinecrest Historical Village. Owned and operated by the Manitowoc County Historical Society, Pinecrest Village is located seven miles from downtown Manitowoc. Photo by Ron Hoerth*

Both the creation of the Wisconsin Maritime Museum and the renovation of the Rahr-West Art Museum would not have been possible without the outstanding patronage of one of Manitowoc's leading citizens, John D. West (son of Charles C. West), who served as chairman, chief executive officer, and vice president of The Manitowoc Company until his retirement in 1988. West and his wife, Ruth St. John West (formerly of Ithaca, New York), had long served the community they loved through philanthropy and volunteerism. In addition to the two museums, West had led the Manitowoc/Two Rivers Area Chamber of Commerce, the City Recreation Board, the Community Fund (today's United Way) Board, the Rotary Club, the Manitowoc-Two Rivers YMCA, and the Manitowoc Vocational Board.

The county's most ambitious effort at historic preservation is the outdoor museum owned and operated by the Manitowoc County Historical Society, called Pinecrest Historical Village, which has 25 historic buildings preserved in a natural setting. Among the structures are original log homes from the

ABOVE: Kurtz's Restaurant in Two Rivers continues its tradition of serving traditional German fare. Courtesy, Kurtz's Restaurant

RIGHT: Manitowoc's Beerntsen's Candies, a Manitowoc institution, still has its original soda fountain and black walnut candy cases. Courtesy, Beerntsen Confectionary, Inc.

ABOVE: Housed in the village's oldest schoolhouse, the Norman Rockwell Center in Mishicot contains an extensive collection of the artist's work. Courtesy, the Norman Rockwell Center

LEFT: A historic reenactment of a wagon train makes its way through Manitowoc County to Cleveland during Wisconsin's sesquicentennial celebration in 1998. Photo by Ron Hoerth

FACING PAGE, BOTTOM: An overview of Lincoln High School in Manitowoc. The high school has been recently revitalized with attention given to adding needed space and to historic preservation of its architecture and landscape. Courtesy, Manitowoc Public School District

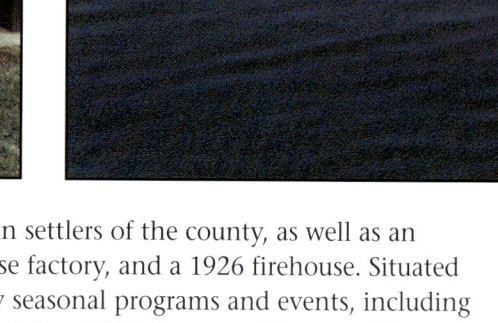

*TOP: The colorful Dragon boat races take place each year in Manitowoc Harbor. Photo by Ron Hoerth*

*ABOVE: In addition to sponsoring Fish Derby Days (a winning crew is pictured), the lakeshore's only full-service marina provides comprehensive marine services and storage, a ship's store, charter fishing, a six-lane launch ramp, 250 wet slips, new and used yacht sales, sailing instruction, and charters. Owned by the City of Manitowoc, the marina is operated by Sailboats, Inc. Photo by Ron Hoerth*

Norwegian, Bohemian, and German settlers of the county, as well as an 1870s general store, an 1890s cheese factory, and a 1926 firehouse. Situated on 60 acres, the village hosts many seasonal programs and events, including "German Fest," "Fall Harvest Festival," and "Christmas at Pinecrest."[23]

The Manitowoc County Historical Society has a large and active membership of more than 1,700 citizens who volunteer at the many events held by the Society each year. In addition to the seasonal festivities at Pinecrest Historical Village listed above, the Society sponsors annual Mother's and Father's Day celebrations at Pinecrest each May and June, as well as a children's program every August.

In October 1999, the Society held a Peshtigo Fire commemoration that presented the story of the great 1871 conflagration and discussed its effects in Manitowoc County. Moved to its new headquarters at the Manitowoc County Heritage Center, the former County Teachers' College on Michigan Avenue, the Society publishes quarterly newsletters and preserves an extensive archive and research collection of county history and artifacts.

Another museum with an interesting historic collection is Zunker's Antique Car Museum in Manitowoc, which displays more than 40 old cars, an old gas station, antique motor bikes, and old bicycles, as well as lunch buckets and children's dolls. Just south of the city is the Natural Ovens Food and Farm Museum, which provides a view of the history of the area's farming and of the art of bread making and baking over the decades.[24]

*ABOVE: Commercial fishing boats shown moored in Two Rivers' East Twin River in the neighborhood known as the Rogers Street Fishing Village. The building with the mottled roof, built in the early 1900s, is used to store fishing nets and equipment. The area extends left to the Rogers Street Fishing Village Museum whose exhibits highlight the importance of the lakeshore's French Canadian heritage. Photo by Ron Hoerth*

*RIGHT: A windsurfer takes advantage of the breeze in Manitowoc's harbor. The area inside the breakwaters annually hosts a number of aquatic events including boat races and sailboat lessons given by the Manitowoc-Two Rivers YMCA situated on the shore nearby. Photo by Ron Hoerth*

Manitowoc's vintage candy shop, Beerntsen's Candies on North Eighth Street, has been preserved with its original soda fountain and black walnut candy cases, where homemade confections are displayed. In Two Rivers another historic business, Kurtz's Restaurant, founded in 1904, still serves some of the same German recipes enjoyed by patrons at the turn of the century. Nearby, the Two Rivers History Museum is housed in the former convent home of the Sisters of Saint Agnes, dating from 1903. The museum features many exhibits about the religious, ethnic, and cultural history of the area, as well as a collection of antique sheet music in the music room.[25]

In Mishicot, the village's oldest schoolhouse has been restored and converted into the Norman Rockwell Center and collection of shops. A 1907 tavern and restaurant in Valders has been preserved as a historic dining facility known as Sam's.

Another school-based historic preservation effort has renewed the interior of Manitowoc's 76-year-old Lincoln High School while preserving its impression of history and tradition. The cosmetic facelift has been augmented by infrastructure upgrades, telecommunications wiring, new multimedia and science facilities, and other innovations to meet present-day educational needs. One of Manitowoc's most beloved landmarks, Lincoln carries a sense of history for generations of citizens. Built in 1923 on scenic Roeff's Hill on the shore of Lake Michigan, the school's original garden setting was designed by noted Prairie School landscape architect Jens Jensen, a student of Frank Lloyd Wright.[26] Jensen's lavish scheme for Lincoln—sugar maples, native plants and

wildflowers, curving flagstone walkways, and his trademark council ring—was never completely realized. Today the only vestiges of his design are several towering maples, a grassy bowl (which Jensen called a "play meadow"), and the circle drive in front of the school's main entrance. A later addition, the statue of Abraham Lincoln in the center of the circle drive, was donated by the Class of 1961.[27]

Among the favorite pieces of local history that have been preserved is the ferry the S.S. *Badger*, which began a new sailing season in 1992 between Manitowoc and Ludington, Michigan, across Lake Michigan. Although the carferries once represented the heyday of Manitowoc's lakeshore maritime success, the service had been discontinued during the 1980s and several of the ferries had been scrapped or turned into barges. However, the *Badger* survived and sailed again when a new season of ferrying began. The ship offers staterooms, a gift shop, and dining, and ably symbolizes the spirit of lake travel that has been rediscovered during the 1990s. It sails to Ludington, Michigan, carrying tourists and cars, but no longer rail freight.[28]

## Tourism and Revitalization

The Manitowoc/Two Rivers Area Chamber of Commerce has worked to attract new industries and businesses, as well as to celebrate the area's many tourist attractions.

During the 1980s Manitowoc County experienced a growth in tourism, as well as businesses, due to the construction of both new roadways and marine facilities. In 1983 the completion of the north-south Interstate Highway 43, connecting Milwaukee, Chicago, and Green Bay, brought interstate travelers into the county in ever-greater numbers.

In 1990 the City of Manitowoc created and began developing the I-43

*ABOVE: Cyclists from all over the United States come to Manitowoc once each year for the annual Bike Invitational race sponsored by the First National Bank. Several northside downtown streets are blocked off to give the cyclists the right-of-way on a race course reputed to be one of the most challenging in the nation. A festival atmosphere prevails as spectators and families crowd the sidewalks to cheer the riders and enjoy side-street entertainment. Photo by Ron Hoerth*

*FACING PAGE: Sunrise over the tranquil waters of the Manitowoc Marina announces another day of health and recreational opportunities along the lakeshore. The parklike shoreline hosts runners and joggers daily. Turnouts and parking spaces beckon motorists on Maritime Drive to pull off for a moment to enjoy the vista of sparkling waters. Pleasantly scattered benches and picnic tables provide resting places for walkers and workers on their lunch break. Photo by Ron Hoerth*

Industrial Park at the northwest corner of Interstate 43 and US Highway 151. The park is over 240 acres in area, and is the home to several major industries including Kaysun Corporation, Zenith Sintered Products, Northern Laboratories, Dayco Eastman, and Jagemann Stamping Company. The city purchased 218 acres in 1998 to further expand the park in the future. The I-43 Industrial Park was the city's second such industrial park, the first located east of South Rapids Road between South 41st Street and Custer Street.[29]

In addition to the interstate highway, the harbor at Manitowoc has benefited from continued improvements in recent decades. In addition to federally funded dredging projects, the construction of a new $7-million Manitowoc Marina in 1985 resulted in a state-of-the art facility that attracts recreational boaters to the area. With 250 deep-water slips, the marina also provides 24-hour dockage attendants and luxurious showers and lounges for boaters, as well as a ship's store and gift shop. Near the Marina is the Inn on Maritime Bay, with a lakefront restaurant and accommodations. The new facility has put Manitowoc on the list of desirable destinations for Lake Michigan boaters from Chicago to Mackinaw.[30]

Boaters can also enjoy docking along the waterfront in Two Rivers, close to the Rogers Street Fishing Village and the historic lighthouse and Coast Guard Station. Sport fishermen, particularly, often frequent area marinas offering fish-cleaning facilities and slips for boats of all sizes. Few reminders of the old net-making days exist around the harbor, and only a handful of commercial fishing tugs still operate.

Boaters have been joined by bikers, backpackers, and campers who have come in greater numbers to the county in recent decades. In addition to the Point Beach State Forest with its six miles of Lake Michigan shoreline, the Woodland Dunes Nature Center has become a popular destination for both hikers and nature lovers. At the Dunes Center, hikers and bird watchers can choose from four nature trails including the Cattail Trail, a boardwalk through a marsh and wetland that provides convenience for hikers as well as protection for the natural habitat.

The continuing usage of the area's many beaches and parks is enhanced by facilities such as the Manitowoc County Ice Center, Lincoln Park Zoo, and the county's Exposition and Fairgrounds. The growing popularity of cross-country skiing has brought many more winter visitors to the area to use the trails in various parks and forests. RIVERWALK Festival is Manitowoc's celebration of the waterfront. Held annually on the fourth Sunday in June, this one-day festival features five stages of live entertainment, a variety of delicious food, refreshments, children's activities, and hundreds of arts and crafts vendors. This outdoor festival attracts nearly 30,000 people to the waterfront between the Wisconsin Maritime Museum and the Manitowoc Marina—just east of downtown. In nearby Two Rivers, the annual Ethnic Fest celebrates the area's cultural diversity.

## Into a New Century

With its stable industrial base and an increase in tourism, Manitowoc County continues to be one of Wisconsin's most scenic and viable places to live. The development of its educational facilities, a college and public university, two major new libraries, new health care facilities, new museum facilities, and the Capitol Civic Centre all combine to enrich the quality of life for county residents.

The projected population growth of Manitowoc County for the year 2000 is approximately 6 percent to 85,900 people, and for 2020 is 12 percent to 91,800 (based on 1990 figures), a steady increase.[31] These encouraging projections indicate that the county can look forward to the early decades of the new century, continuing its tradition as a "Beacon on the Lakeshore," a bright location on Lake Michigan's western perimeter.

*FACING PAGE, TOP: A bucolic view along Melnick Road in northern Manitowoc County. The rolling farmland nestles a scenic valley of the West Twin River. This area was originally settled by central European immigrants, many from Bohemia (now the Czech Republic) in the middle 1800s. A number of their descendants have remained in the area of the long-gone Village of Melnick. All that remains of the village is the Presbyterian church and cemetery, which are still in use. Photo by Ron Hoerth*

*FACING PAGE, BOTTOM: The fall season brings families out to rural Manitowoc to take their pick of the county's variety of agricultural products. In addition to pumpkins (shown), strawberries and orchard fruits along with a gourmet's abundance of vegetables are featured in roadside stands and at the Saturday morning Farmers' Market at Lakeview Centre on Memorial Drive. Photo by Ron Hoerth*

# Partners in Progress

*A lone tractor harvests forage for the winter feeding of Manitowoc County's many dairy herds. Agricultural diversity balances with industrial diversity to give the county an unusually stable economy. Livestock feed crops are complemented with truck farm produce. Courtesy, Lakeside Foods, Inc.*

What makes Manitowoc County unique? Certainly the economically well-balanced diversity of business, industry, and agriculture is an important factor, but that also is true of other successful and prosperous Wisconsin communities.

Larger cities still have many of their ethnic neighborhoods—communities within the larger community—and the history of Manitowoc County cannot be understood without reference to the early immigrant groups of Germans, Poles, Bohemians, Irish, French, Dutch, Belgians, Italians, and others. But the old ethnic neighborhoods have all but disappeared except in name. Manitowoc County has become, in general, one coherent neighborhood, and this is a key to its uniqueness as a beacon on the shore of Lake Michigan.

With the immigrant settlement of the lakeshore area came a strong central European work ethic and the religious value of family stability. These immigrants put down firm roots in Manitowoc County soil, started and staffed businesses and industries, and passed on their qualities of hard work and wise management to their sons and daughters, who continue the tradition by passing on those same qualities to their children.

The county has also played a proud role in the stream of national history. Thorstein Veblen, the famous economist who wrote the 1905 bestseller, *The Theory of the Leisure Class*, was born near Valders. The first ice cream sundae was produced in Two Rivers. A young George Armstrong Custer, attached to the Milwaukee Corps of Engineers, was instrumental in the building of Manitowoc harbor's first breakwater, and the present breakwater was built by the corps under the supervision of a young Douglas MacArthur. Each is remembered by streets named for them.

The upheaval of World War II and its resulting technological explosion changed American life to one of rootless mobility, but it has not uprooted the foundations of Manitowoc County. The reputation of its work ethic has attracted out-of-town entrepreneurs who, impressed by the quality of life here, have taken residence in this "good place to raise kids."

Thus the older, established businesses have been augmented by new ventures that have proudly adopted the work and community values upon which the county was founded. Together, both old and new enterprises now band together to solve economic challenges to the area's quality of life, in the very active Manitowoc/Two Rivers Area Chamber of Commerce.

The interdependence of these elements and values is not limited to the private sector. The interdependency of public-sector agencies and community organizations preserves and enhances a high quality of life. Manitowoc County schools and colleges graduate competent workers, managers, and community servants. Emergency personnel, both volunteer and "regular," are well and regularly trained. They are dedicated to, and supported by, a population sensitive to the tragedies and triumphs experienced by neighbors, relatives, friends, and acquaintences regardless of occupation, race, religion, gender, or ethnic origin.

Resources for lifelong learning, appreciation and enjoyment of the fine arts, and exercise and recreation are provided to residents and tourists alike by modern libraries, music and drama groups and the Capitol Civic Centre, one of the finest marinas on the Great Lakes, the Manitowoc-Two Rivers YMCA, and beautifully maintained city and county parks.

Scheduled activities and other services for retired senior citizens abound, and the availability of high-quality health care and leading-edge medical technology for an area of this size is unsurpassed in the state.

Manitowoc County is not paradise on earth. It has its share of social and economic challenges. But there exists in this county a climate of willingness to face and solve community problems collaboratively. Manitowoc County is proud to be American. The cherishing of its ethnic and historic past is a continuing contribution to its uniqueness.

**147**

# Capitol Civic Centre

Who would expect Itzhak Perlman, Bob Hope, Charlton Heston, The Lettermen, The Smothers Brothers, Peter, Paul, and Mary, Marvin Hamlisch, Johnny Cash, Johnny Mathis, Isaac Stern, Kathy Mattea, and many more famous entertainers to appear on the theater stage of a small midwestern city, a thousand miles from the glitter of Hollywood and the bright lights of Broadway?

Restoring and operating a performing arts center, booking popular artists, hosting a dozen local performing arts groups, and doing it "in the black" would seem to be a task possible only in a city the size of Chicago or Atlanta. It is being done in Manitowoc. The Capitol Civic Centre is today one of the finest performing arts centers in Wisconsin.

In 1921 Aschers Capitol Theatre was a northern outpost on the Chicago Loews Vaudeville Circuit. Some of the vaudevillians who visited Manitowoc in those days went on to radio, movie, and television fame, among them a young Waukegan, Illinois, comedian named Benjamin Kubelsky, remembered today as Jack Benny. Between vaudeville and minstrel shows, the Capitol featured movies—silent until "talkies" came out in 1929.

Marcus Theatres of Milwaukee later operated the Capitol but allowed the lease to expire in 1982 without exercising their option to buy the building. In 1986 a new organization, The Society to Preserve the Capitol, saw the potential of the soon-to-be-vacant theater as a performing arts center and, under the leadership of attorney Ron Kaminski, began the initial fund raising to purchase and renovate the building.

The grand opening of the restored Capitol Civic Centre was on October 30, 1987, but there was still much to be done. Continued renovation, equipping, and mainte-

*Aschers Capitol Theatre as it appeared shortly after its opening in 1921. The "Big Feature" advertised on the sign above the marquee was* Is Matrimony a Failure?

nance quickly became a huge undertaking requiring the efforts of literally hundreds of volunteers from all over the county, and necessitated a second fund drive in 1990 with local businessman Tom Beerntsen as chairman. By March 1991 The Society to Preserve the Capitol had exceeded its goal, raising $1.17 million. The final payment on a loan from the city was made on October 30, 1997, the 10th anniversary of the Capitol's opening. Executive director Joseph Ferlo hailed the moment by proudly announcing that: "...our community now owns the Capitol Civic Centre free and clear."

---

**RESIDENT ARTISTS**

*Local Performing Groups at the Capitol Civic Centre*

- Masquers, Inc. (community theater)
- Lakeshore Wind Ensemble
- Manitowoc Symphony Orchestra
- Kidzarts, Inc. (family theater)
- Jean Wolfmeyer School of Dance
- Clipper City Chordsmen
- Peter Quince Performing Company
- Calvary Players
- Kristine Rakos Dance Studio
- Valders High School Choirs
- T.R.A.C.T.S. (community theater)

---

That ownership takes in quite a bit more space than appears at the South Eighth Street marqueed entrance. Consuming a large part of the city block behind the box office is the John and Ruth West Auditorium with its renovated balconies and box seats. Next door is the Lillian and Francis Kadow Movie Museum, and to the east of the auditorium's exit doors on Jay Street is the CCC Annex, the former Schmidtman Building which residents remember as the past home of Carferry School Supplies. The annex now houses the Capitol Civic Centre's loading dock, rehearsal and production facilities, and administrative office.

The CCC hosts performing arts in three dimensions. First, there is the "backbone" of community arts groups (see box below listing resident artists). Second, the Student Adventure Series transforms the Capitol into Manitowoc County's largest classroom. Third, the Lively Arts Series appeals to a mainstream audience, filling the gaps in certain areas where local organizations cannot. This includes such performers as those named in the first paragraph.

All this is accomplished with a paid staff that numbers only six full-time and four part-time employees. The rest of the work is undertaken by more than 150 volunteers directed by a Volunteer Council containing the following divisions: Engineering, Carpentry, House Management/Ushers, Security, Box Office, Receptionists, Special Events, Stage Crew, Maintenance, and Mailings. Volunteers from the community also serve on the board of directors and board committees.

"Thanks in large part to these volunteers," says Ferlo, "the Capitol Civic Centre serves over 60,000 audience members, 500 local artists, and 8,000 schoolchildren each year." As a not-for-profit organization, the

Capitol relies on individual, business, and corporate donations for one-third of its annual operating income. Ferlo continues: "Thanks to our community support, the Capitol Civic Centre, in fact, is financially healthier than most arts organizations in larger cities."

When the wrecking ball smashed the dream of preserving the old opera house on North Eighth Street it was said by some that Milwaukee was close enough to satisfy the "few" devotees of the performing arts in the Manitowoc and Two Rivers area. Now the Milwaukee Symphony, one of the highest-rated symphonies in the nation, comes to the Capitol Civic Centre.

The Capitol Civic Centre, something that "couldn't be done," is now a shining jewel in the proud history of performing arts in the lakeshore area.

*The Smothers Brothers, Kathy Mattea, Itzhak Perlman, and Marvin Hamlisch have all performed at the Capitol Civic Centre.*

*BOTTOM: The interior of Aschers Capitol Theatre as it appeared in 1921. The restored Capitol Civic Centre is remarkably similar.*

# Manitowoc/Two Rivers Area Chamber of Commerce

Ever since the promotion of trade and commerce by ancient Greek, Phoenician, and Roman groups and, later, by the medieval guilds of Europe, merchants, manufacturers, tradesmen, and service providers have found it advantageous to themselves, their customers, and their communities to band together in a "chamber of commerce." That term was first used in Marseilles, France, in 1599. The Manitowoc/ Two Rivers Area Chamber of Commerce is but one in a long history of such associations.

Chambers of commerce promote business unity for economic prosperity, ensuring that both large and small businesses have their concerns carried as a unified voice to elected officials. At the same time, the chamber works for the economic quality and well-being of its community. The life-blood of that activity is the commitment of its volunteers and professional staff members dedicated to the imple-

*The Manitowoc/Two Rivers Area Chamber of Commerce is located at 1515 Memorial Drive, Manitowoc.*

mentation of the chamber's policies and goals.

The first American chamber of commerce was formed by New York City merchants in 1768. By the late 1800s there were 300 active chambers in the United States. The United States National Chamber of

| | Leadership in the Chamber | | | | |
|---|---|---|---|---|---|
| | **Leadership in the Chamber through the years reads like a veritable who's who of Manitowoc County history:** | 1946-47 | Emil J. Kirt | 1976 | John J. Zimmer |
| | | 1948-50 | Richard Schaus | 1977 | Robert E. Horn |
| | | 1951 | Ben F. Fronk | 1978 | Wesley C. Drumm |
| | | 1952-53 | Willot A. Pitz | 1979 | Robert A. Niquette |
| | | 1954 | Edmund A. Napp | 1980 | Jon R. Rex |
| 1916-17 | John G. Johnson | 1955 | Richard E. Cannard | 1981 | Richard H. Wirth |
| 1917 | Harry G. Kelley | 1956 | Lloyd E. Olson | 1982 | Lee Davis |
| 1918-19 | Max H. Richter | 1957 | Robert B. Brown | 1983 | Ronald L. Stangel |
| 1920-22 | Jacob Stangel | 1958 | Lester T. Davis | 1984 | Paul Taddy |
| 1923 | William E. Seibel | 1959 | Jack M. Barenbaum | 1985 | Sister Anne Kennedy |
| 1924-27 | Leland L. Huppert | 1960 | Alois C. Fischl | 1986 | William R. Wettstein |
| 1928 | William Huchthausen | 1961 | Robert A. Peck | 1987 | J. Douglas Quick |
| 1929 | Michael G. Lutz | 1962 | Harry K. Wrench, Jr. | 1988 | James A. Donchek |
| 1930 | William H. Glander | 1963 | Walter G. Huchthausen | 1989 | Theresa R. Burbey |
| 1931-33 | Otto H. Berndt | 1964 | Francis W. Kerscher | 1990 | Karl W. Kahlenberg |
| 1934 | Thomas E. McCormick | 1965-66 | Carl G. Nelson | 1991 | John Dineen |
| 1935 | Wencil C. Urbanek | 1967-68 | John M. Spindler | 1992 | Darrell Olson |
| 1936 | Walter C. Huchthausen | 1969 | Jack Severson | 1993 | Terry Growcock |
| 1937 | Albert J. Kempfert | 1970 | Ray Halvorsen | 1994 | Dean Halvorson |
| 1938-39 | Thomas McKeough | 1971 | Joseph P. Schmitt | 1995 | Jutta Furca |
| 1940-41 | Ernest C. Badger | 1972 | Richard H. Stolz | 1996 | William Schwartz |
| 1942-43 | Frank E. Town | 1973 | Joseph P. Schmitt | 1997 | Curt Drumm |
| 1944 | Thomas E. Reddin | 1974 | D. William Dean | 1998 | Gary Erickson |
| 1945-46 | Clemens A. Reiss | 1975 | Edward C. Fordney | 1999 | Steve Mirecki |

Commerce was organized at the request of President Taft in 1912. Today there are more than 5,000 chambers of commerce in the nation.

The Manitowoc/Two Rivers Area Chamber of Commerce is a voluntary, not-for-profit membership organization, the purpose of which is to promote the interests of businesses in Manitowoc County. It is accredited by the United States Chamber of Commerce. The Manitowoc Chamber was organized in 1916 and the Two Rivers Chamber sometime later. The two were merged to form the present organization in 1970.

The Chamber is governed by a

*ABOVE: The late Joseph P. Schmitt (left) receiving the Manitowoc/Two Rivers Area Chamber of Commerce Speak Up Award in 1984 from board chairman Paul Taddy. In his honor, the award is now called the Joseph P. Schmitt Speak Up Award.*

*RIGHT: Current staff members of the Chamber are (left to right) Jill Cigler, administrative assistant; Jutta Furca, executive director; Trissy Thimmesch, administrative assistant; and Peggy Walkner, office manager.*

board of directors elected by, and from, the membership. Membership investment provides finances with major investors paying a percentage of the Chamber's annual expenses. Other sources of non-dues income

include revenues from such projects as The Franklin Planner Seminar and the Lakeshore Business Expo.

While many laudable words can be spoken about the challenges successfully met by all of the Chamber's past and present leaders, one in particular deserves special mention. The late Joseph P. Schmitt of Two Rivers served two terms as chairman of the board as well as president, and was untiring in his efforts to promote a united chamber of commerce in the lakeshore area. The Chamber's annual Speak Up Award, established in 1967, was renamed the Joseph P. Schmitt Speak Up Award in his memory. This award is given to individuals who consistently and effectively boost the community through their actions, speech, and willingness to promote the Manitowoc/ Two Rivers area as a good place to live.

Among the many community activities the Chamber sponsors, or is closely involved with, are the annual Airport Day at the Manitowoc County Airport, the Career Expo held on the various Chamber

campuses, the Business World workshops annually held on a number of Wisconsin college campuses, and the first (in 1999) School/Community Recognition Banquet held at Silver Lake College. Other Chamber committees are active planning and promoting projects in economic development, tourism, health, small business, and legislation.

According to its mission statement, "The Manitowoc/Two Rivers Area Chamber of Commerce serves its members by providing a forum that fosters and promotes a strong business environment while working to improve the quality of life in the community."

"As in every progressive community," says executive director Jutta Furca, "there are problems and opportunities that are common to all businesses and, as a matter of fact, to all the citizens of our area, about which little can be done unless there is a concerted effort on the part of business and industry. Solving these common problems and capitalizing on the opportunities that arise create a need for a central business-oriented organization—hence the Manitowoc/Two Rivers Area Chamber of Commerce."

# Manitowoc County Historical Society

**"We cannot escape history."**

*Abraham Lincoln*

Most of us do not consciously regard this present moment in our lives as history. To us, history is something that happened in the past. But a hundred years from now people will be looking at our "today" as history, just as we study the "todays" of past lives trying to understand how we came to be the society we have become, in order to enter the future with foreknowledge. As the poet and philosopher George Santayana put it: "Those who cannot remember the past are condemned to repeat it."

Fortunately, there are those who keenly understand that a record of people and events, seemingly insignificant at the moment, will be

extremely important as a source of vital information, education, understanding, and wisdom to future generations. It was just such a group of concerned individuals, led by Judge Emil Baensch, who formed the Manitowoc County Historical Society in 1906 "for the purpose of discovery, collection, preservation, and publication of historical records and data of, and relating to, Manitowoc County."

The MCHS is the sixth-oldest historical society in the state of Wisconsin and one of the earliest to affiliate with the State Historical Society. With only a dozen mem-

bers in its early years, the Society now has more than 1,700 members, is governed by a nine-member board of directors, and is staffed by a full-time executive director, several part-time employees, and dozens of volunteers.

Financial support for the Society comes from membership dues, admission fees at Pinecrest Historical Village and the Manitowoc County Heritage Center, publication and gift shop sales, fund-raising events, and private donations. An endowment fund was created in 1991. The Society receives no federal, state, or local government funds, depending solely on the support of its members and community.

The first public museum sponsored by the Society was opened circa 1925 and housed in the upper floor of the former (Carnegie) public library building (since razed) on Manitowoc's North

*RIGHT: Blacksmithing demonstrations are given at Pinecrest Historical Village, which depicts a typical 1900 rural community in Manitowoc County.*

*BELOW: The Soo Line Depot, built in 1896, and an 1887 steam locomotive are preserved at the village.*

ABOVE: *The Rockwood Fire House, constructed in 1926, is one of more than 25 restored buildings at Pinecrest Historical Village.*

BELOW: *The Thompson log house at Pinecrest Historical Village was built by immigrants who arrived from Norway in the 1850s.*

Eighth Street. The museum was moved in 1941 to the Rahr Civic Center (now the Rahr-West Art Museum) two blocks farther north on Eighth Street.

For many years the Society's administrative office, research library, archives, and map and photograph collection were housed at Evergreen Cemetery Sexton House, built in 1878 by the City of Manitowoc. Funds raised in 1988-1989 were used to renovate the two-story cream city brick building to preserve this important Manitowoc landmark.

In 1996 the Society leased from the county the former Manitowoc County Teachers' Training School at 1701 Michigan Avenue in Manitowoc, a short walk from the Sexton House. A campaign was launched to raise $900,000 to renovate and preserve this historic building, which now houses the Society's administrative office, new exhibits on local history, a research library, educational learning center, auditorium/stage, collection storage, and gift shop. The goal was reached in December 1998.

"The Sexton House has served us well for 10 years," says executive director Bob Fay, "but we've woefully outgrown it. Use of the Michigan Avenue building by the Historical Society will continue and preserve its long history as an educational center."

The "County Normal School," as it was once called, was built in 1922 and graduated its last class of teachers in 1971. The school was converted in 1974 into county government offices. The county board met for many years in the school's assembly room.

In addition to the erection, dedication, and maintenance of historical markers and monuments, the preservation of historical landmarks, setting up exhibits, conducting tours, collecting and providing historical and genealogical research data, and sponsoring centennial and anniversary events, the Society owns, operates, and maintains Pinecrest Historical Village. Located seven miles west of Manitowoc on 40 acres of land donated by Hugo and Eleanor Vetting in 1970, the now-60-acre village is a recreation of a turn-of-the-century community. Historic buildings from all over the county have been, and are being, moved into Pinecrest and restored.

Pinecrest hosts more than 11,000 visitors a year from all over the state, nation, and foreign countries. Audio self-guided and guided tours led by costumed volunteers and staff take visitors into the original buildings of the past, such as the Rank Dressmaker Shop which was built on Franklin Street in Manitowoc in 1894, or the former Presbyterian frame church building once located at the no-longer-extant village of Niles. The church is now frequently used for weddings.

Authentic Norwegian and Bohemian-German log houses show how immigrant settlers lived in Manitowoc County a century and a half ago. Special programs and festivals are held at the village throughout the year, including German Fest, Fall Harvest Festival, and Christmas at Pinecrest.

The Society publishes the *Heritage News* quarterly newsletter to inform members of scheduled events, as well as the award-winning *Monograph* series of articles on agriculture, industry, commerce, government, education, arts, science, religion, ethnic groups, and the experiences of Manitowoc County residents. In all, 70-plus monographs and more than a dozen books and pamphlets have been published by the Society—a wealth of valuable material for local educators, genealogists, and historians.

Interested readers can obtain more information about the Manitowoc County Historical Society from its offices at 1701 Michigan Avenue, Manitowoc, or by writing to the Society at P.O. Box 574, Manitowoc, Wisconsin 54221-0574.

# Mirro Company
## *A Division of Newell Rubbermaid*

There's a bit of Manitowoc in millions of kitchens worldwide, thanks to the Mirro Company, which celebrated its 100th birthday in 1997.

Mirro started with an idea generated at the Columbian Exposition of 1893 in Chicago. There, Joseph Koenig of Two Rivers became intrigued by some displayed German novelties made from a miraculous white metal called aluminum. Two years later Koenig rented a small building in Two Rivers and started the Aluminum Manufacturing Company.

Also intrigued by the "miracle metal," Manitowoc tannery operator Henry Vits, in 1898, retooled his plant to make aluminum articles. In 1909 Koenig's and Vits' companies were combined with the New Jersey Aluminum Company as the Aluminum Goods Manufacturing Company of Manitowoc. The new venture added to its novelty line a double boiler produced for the Quaker Oats Company, thus beginning its rise to become the world's largest manufacturer of aluminum cookware and bakeware and one of Manitowoc's largest employers.

*In the 1930s Mirro workers used giant aluminum presses to make many products including novelty items, bakeware, cookware, and parts for planes and cars.*

By combining the Vits and Koenig names, "VIKO" brand cookware became a household word in America as the firm took a once-luxury metal and, by mass production methods, converted it into high-quality, heavy-gauge pots and pans affordable to the average family. The production of hubcaps for Dodge, Studebaker, and Buick was added in 1915, followed shortly thereafter by millions of mess kits and canteens during World War I.

In 1917, as the war was nearing an end, Aluminum Goods Manufacturing prepared for the postwar boom with a revolution in marketing strategy, placing advertising on a national level in such prestigious magazines as *The Saturday Evening Post, McCall's, Ladies' Home Journal, Good Housekeeping,* and *Better Homes and Gardens.*

The Great Depression brought nationwide unemployment and a 65 percent decline in cookware sales, but the company managed to keep three-fourths of its 3,400 workers on the job through the dark days of 1931 and 1932. As early as 1910, or shortly thereafter, George Vits, then president of Aluminum Goods Manufacturing, had pioneered in labor relations by offering an employee insurance plan that both rewarded and promoted worker loyalty. A dedicated work force, combined with an extensive sales program that rapidly increased chain store and mail-order distribution, enabled the business not only to survive the Depression, but to become a national leader in the aluminum cookware field.

The company's resources were again committed to national defense during World War II. In addition to millions of canteens, aircraft fuel tanks and landing gear parts were produced as well as rolled aluminum for the Lend Lease program.

Showing foresight in anticipating the future, an enduring quality of

*In this 1899 photo workers pose in front of the tannery building converted the year before into an aluminum products factory by Manitowoc businessman and entrepreneur Henry Vits.*

management throughout the firm's history, led to the introduction of the Mirro-Matic pressure pan and electric percolator in 1944 as war-delayed consumer demand began to express itself in the marketplace.

Diversification and growth, however, required expansion. Two new units were constructed on the 104-acre Mirro Drive site between Manitowoc and Two Rivers in 1955 and 1956. A modern rolling mill was added in 1957, and within two years it was achieving an annual production of 60 million pounds of sheet aluminum. Annual capacity today exceeds 84 million pounds.

The rolling mill made it possible to market such new products as aluminum siding, aluminum foil and foilware, and aluminum sport fishing boats. The "year of the rolling mill" (1957) was the year that Aluminum Goods Manufacturing changed its name to Mirro Aluminum Company.

The year 1964 was one of great expansion. Mirro purchased National Metal Coatings, Inc., of Oconomowoc, Wisconsin, for the

Just prior to the Newell acquisition Mirro management had begun the divestment of all non-cookware lines to focus solely on the house-wares business. The boat business was sold and all ties to aluminum siding and electric appliances were severed.

In September 1984 Newell acquired the Foley Company (formerly the Aluminum Specialty Co.) and merged it with Mirro in 1985.

REMA Bakeware in Salina, Kansas, was acquired in 1988, and the WearEver Company of Chillicothe, Ohio, in 1989. The production of both lines has since been

production of aluminim siding. A distribution center was completed on the Mirro Drive property in 1964 and additions to the rolling mill, the boat plant, and Two Rivers Plants One and Four, begun the same year, were completed in 1966. Three years later the Colonial Frocks Company of Gillett, Wisconsin, was purchased and designated for the manufacture of corn poppers and porcelain-coated cookware. A later addition tripled the Gillett plant space.

Major expansion of the Mirro Drive plants, begun in 1981 and

*ABOVE: Workers annealing metal in Mirro's rolling mill, circa 1960.*

*LEFT: Two workers assemble cookware covers, circa 1950. From a small manufacturer of novelty items a century ago, Mirro has grown into a world leader in the cookware and bakeware industry.*

moved to Manitowoc. Although all the products are made by Mirro, the original REMA and WearEver brand names have been retained. From REMA came the "CushionAire Pro" line of insulated bakeware.

Today Mirro can count among its accomplishments not only international leadership in the making of quality aluminum cookware, but also a plus in customer service, boasting 99.0 percent on average.

Mirro's 2,000-plus associates are involved in local charitable and community organizations. Some coach youth baseball teams, answer the phones during a cerebral palsy telethon, or serve as Big Brothers or Big Sisters.

completed four years later, resulted in a highly efficient system that produced cookware from aluminum ingot to fabrication and packaging, in a direct flow from rolling mill to distribution center. A 164,000-square-foot addition to the Mirro Drive complex in 1991 and 1992 increased production by more than 25 percent and provided the means of production for a line of porcelain-coated cookware named "Concentric Aire."

On July 15, 1983, Mirro was acquired by the Newell Company, headquartered in Freeport, Illinois.

Mirro has developed a school-business partnership with Jefferson Elementary School, just blocks from the firm's main headquarters. Mirro has about 80 Associate Involvement Teams and one of them is devoted to

and informative sessions at the main office. Future school projects include a science project on new ideas and inventions for Mirro products, designing a new logo for the Team at Mirro, and Mirro associates giving presentations at the school.

An average of 75 associates are engaged at any given time in continuing education leading to a college degree, in which Mirro reimburses tuition.

## Tomorrow's Cookware Today

Innovation is the key to Mirro's continuing success. This was again illustrated in 1998 at the annual

*ABOVE: At Mirro's centennial celebration in 1997, tours of the main manufacturing complex were given. Associates kept their children safe with wrist-to-wrist connectors.*

*TOP AND TOP RIGHT: Mirro has implemented a school-business partnership with Jefferson Elementary School, located near the company. In 1999 dozens of aluminum sauté pans were painted by art students and some were displayed at the Rahr-West Museum as part of the Youth Art Month exhibit.*

*RIGHT: Items of the "Allegro" cookware line introduced by Mirro in 1998. The revolutionary design is a distinct departure from, and improvement over, traditional cookware.*

the partnership. Dozens of aluminum sauté pans were painted by art students and some were displayed at the Rahr-West Museum in March 1999 for Youth Art Month. Students were invited to Mirro for a tour

housewares exposition in Chicago sponsored by the National Housewares Manufacturers Association, when Mirro unveiled its revolutionary new WearEver "Allegro" line. Allegro was developed after months of research and design stemming from an intensive study of people's cooking habits and their most commonly encountered cookware problems.

Mirro designers point out that traditional cookware is simply not made for pouring. The steam is hard to control and pouring often causes the contents to run down the side of the pot. The unique shape of the Allegro items allows for round-bottom stirring in a vessel with four squared corners for pouring.

When it comes to draining, the new design features a lid with a built-in strainer. Cover handles mesh with vessel handles for easy draining without fear of accidental scalding. The handle locking system is the same used by NASA on the space shuttles.

Boil overs are now a thing of the past. The Allegro recessed lid design allows for liquid to boil up through a steam vent and to be stored in the one-cup capacity lid, where it cools and automatically returns to the vessel.

Mirro teamed with DuPont to give the Allegro line a revolutionary new non-stick surface that is safe for use with metal utensils. And, finally, the new design can be stacked or stored with the covers on, or conveniently nested, one vessel inside another.

## Who Is Newell Rubbermaid Inc.?

The history of the Mirro Company would not be complete without mention of its parent entity, the Newell Company, which was founded in upstate New York in 1902. Corporate leadership and headquarters were established in Freeport, Illinois, from 1921 to 1965.

Since 1965 Newell has transformed itself from a small, single-product company into the multiproduct, multinational, multi-billion-dollar family of businesses that it is today. In 1996 Newell celebrated its 75th anniversary, listing the following associate firms:

Levolor Home Fashions, High Point, North Carolina; Newell Window Furnishings/ Kirsch, Freeport, Illinois; Intercraft/Burnes, Taylor, Texas; Lee Rowan, Fenton, Missouri; Amerock, Rockford, Illinois; Amerock Hardware Systems, Rockford, Illinois; BernzOmatic, Medina, New York; Bulldog Fastener, Memphis, Tennessee; EZ Paintr, Milwaukee, Wisconsin; Sanford, Bellwood, Illinois; Newell Office Products, Madison, Wisconsin; Anchor Hocking

*The company's main manufacturing facility on Mirro Drive.*

Glass, Lancaster, Ohio; Anchor Hocking Specialty Glass, Monaca, Pennsylvania; Mirro Company, Manitowoc, Wisconsin; Goody Products, Peachtree City, Georgia; Calphalon, Toledo, Ohio; Kirsch Window Fashions Europe, Brussels, Belgium; Newell Europe, Slough, England; Newell International, Rockford, Illinois; and Newell Southeast Asia, Liaison Office, Taipei, Taiwan.

Newell completed its largest acquisition, the Rubbermaid Corporation of Wooster, Ohio, in March 1999. Newell Rubbermaid Inc. currently has more than 40,000 employees worldwide, and will enjoy profitable sales of more than $6 billion in 1999. The company is well positioned financially to continue its own corporate growth, and also to invest in the internal growth and success of its proven winners like the Mirro Company of Manitowoc.

**MIRRO.**
A Division of
**Newell Rubbermaid**

# J.J. Stangel Company

> "Under the spreading chestnut tree the village smithy stands..."
>
> *Henry Wadsworth Longfellow*

The blacksmithing era is a fading memory in our nation's history, but supplying the smithy with tools and materials in 1917 brought about one of Manitowoc's oldest continuing businesses, the J.J. Stangel Company, now a subsidiary of Industrial Distributing Group, Inc. (IDG).

Founder Jacob J. Stangel actually began his hardware career as a youthful employee of a local Manitowoc hardware store in 1889, working his way up to manager. Later, in his thirties, he and two partners bought the business and reorganized under the name of Worel, Zeman and Stangel.

The name changed to J.J. Stangel Hardware Company when Stangel set out on his own and built a three-story distribution center on the corner of South Eighth and Quay streets. The newly named firm opened its doors on August 21, 1917, four months after the United States entered World War I. A son, Arthur G. Stangel, joined his father in the business at that time. A second son, Harvey J. Stangel, joined the business a few years later. The company moved to its present location on Custer Street in 1974.

Until the armistice of November 11, 1918, Manitowoc was a major war industry center. The J.J. Stangel Company was kept busy supplying blacksmith and mill supplies, retail and wholesale hardware. The end of the war again turned the company's attention to the civilian market and an automotive supply department was added in 1919, and branches opened in Sheboygan, Plymouth, Algoma, and Sturgeon Bay.

Jacob Stangel died in 1922 as a result of an accidental fall down the elevator shaft of his three-story building. His sons, Arthur and Harvey, carried on. Joseph Zimmer joined the company in 1936 as office manager, as later did his sons, John and Joseph A. Upon the retirement of Harvey Stangel in 1969, John Zimmer became executive vice president and general manager. He remains active as president of the company today.

During World War II the Industrial Supply Division expanded in sales of abrasives and tools to plants and shipbuilders in the area. A Builders Hardware Division operated until 1972. In 1986 the J.J.

*The Stangel distribution center at the corner of Quay and South Eighth streets as it appeared in 1935. A longtime landmark in Manitowoc, the building and entire block was razed in 1996 for the construction of the public library.*

Stangel Company purchased the Mill Supply Division of Schlaefer Supply Company, a major supplier to paper mills throughout Wisconsin and Upper Michigan.

In 1997 Stangel merged with eight leading industrial supply companies to form the Industrial Distribution Group. The merger created a nationwide supplier of cost-effective solutions for manufacturers and other users of MRO (maintenance, repair, and operating) products. J.J. Stangel Company trades on the NYSE under the IDG symbol as a $600-million-plus distributor. IDG now has 54 locations in 46 cities, 3,200 vendors, and 1,700 associates.

From blacksmithing and tools for war production, through automotive supplies (discontinued in 1965),

today's product line, in addition to hand, power, cutting, threading, machine, and precision tools, includes abrasives and brushes, coolants, lubricants, sealants, sorbents, adhesives, tapes, fasteners, MRO supplies, and general hardware. The company stocks 20,000 items with an inventory value of $2 million and has rapid access to the IDG inventory of 700,000 items with a value of $60 million.

Stangel continues to be a leader in providing its customers with electronic ordering and invoicing (EDI) capability. Most of the firm's major vendors are linked via EDI and stock availability systems to help speed delivery of non-stock orders.

In addition to using UPS and other commercial carriers, Stangel maintains a small fleet of trucks for direct deliveries to customers within a 75-mile radius of Manitowoc. Stangel serves customers in Upper Michigan through its spoke operation, Northern Tool of Kingsford, Michigan.

Having pioneered toll-free phone and fax for area customers, the company also works closely with customers to help them lower costs. This is done by providing "user friendly" ordering programs, storeroom management programs ("Bin-Fill"), process improvements, and a 900-page catalog that includes technical information. Mini-catalogs, called "Stangel Solutions," are published monthly and mailed to customers.

The firm is also dedicated to products distributed by Stangel.

The J.J. Stangel Company provides its customers with large-inventory, high-order fill rates, 100 percent on-time shipments, and a commitment to quality. A formal quality-improvement process was put in place in 1984, with ISO 9002 certification in 1998, and the firm is the recipient of several Vendor Partner Awards. An ongoing team approach to continuous improvement involves all Stangel employees in the quality process. Their "Perfect Service Insurance" program assures customers of Stangel's commitment to "Do It Right The First Time, Every Time."

One of the company's continuing strengths has been its ability to anticipate change and to prepare

helping customers with safety and environmental concerns, scheduling by customer request a number of training seminars. These are often presented in cooperation with the manufacturers of the national brand

itself in advance to serve new and emerging markets. As a subsidiary of the Industrial Distribution Group (IDG), Stangel will continue to be a leader of innovative products and procurement solutions for industrial customers throughout Wisconsin and Upper Michigan.

*ABOVE: The J.J. Stangel Company distribution center as it appears today, located in Manitowoc's Custer Street industrial park.*

*LEFT: Stangel maintains a small fleet of delivery vehicles for 100 percent on-time delivery to customers within a 75-mile radius of Manitowoc.*

# Aitken-Reed Inc.

An outstanding ability to change and move rapidly into new and emerging markets is the unique hallmark in the history of Manitowoc's Aitken-Reed Inc. Formed in 1946 by William Aitken and Dewitt Reed, former engineers with Paragon Electric in Two Rivers, the company began by producing mechanical and electric timing devices for the heating and farm lighting markets. In the mid-1950s the partners purchased Lakeshore Industries and began to manufacture and sell ham radio transmitters. Later in the same decade Aitken-Reed began making and selling citizens band ("CB") transceivers.

At about this same time the firm made its initial entry into the countertop appliance market as a supplier of lead wires and ceramic-based heating coils to the Aluminum Goods Manufacturing Company (now Mirro Company). Service to this market was considerably expanded in 1965 when Nicholas B. Jagemann, with 22 years of experience in the appliance industry, purchased the business—which at the time had only seven employees.

It took only a few years for Aitken-Reed to become a major supplier to the Midwest countertop appliance industry. By 1969 the company needed a larger facility, so a 24,000-square-foot plant was built on Manitowoc's south side.

By this time Aitken-Reed employed nearly 30 people. Additional expansion took place in the early 1990s, when the firm purchased and renovated the former Foster Needle building, adding 17,000 square feet on the adjoining property.

By the early 1970s production of timers and radios ceased as concentration shifted to the application of Aitken-Reed's wire-processing technology to a variety of businesses outside the appliance market. In

*Aitken-Reed's Lindbergh Drive facility on Manitowoc's south side houses the corporate offices and the wire products group.*

1973 John M. Jagemann joined the firm. Leadership continuity in the family-owned enterprise was assured when John purchased Aitken-Reed from his father, becoming president in 1981.

During the 1980s and 1990s the product line was expanded to include complex electrical lead assemblies and wiring harnesses, and today this commercial/industrial product line represents over 50 percent of the company's business.

With a staff of 125 full-time and part-time employees, Aitken-Reed today serves customers in a variety

of markets, including countertop appliances, microwave ovens, ice-making and soft-serve machines, commercial washers, food-serving equipment, air and liquid compressors, heat guns, electric motors, lawn and garden equipment, hydraulic cranes, timing devices, lighting fixtures, water-conditioning equipment, and agricultural equipment.

Aitken-Reed's success in the face of competitive pressures can be attributed to outstanding customer service and superb quality. During the past decade the company and its employees received numerous "Supplier of the Year" awards. To maintain this tradition into the twenty-first century, Aitken-Reed is dedicated to constant improvement, not only in cost reduction and product quality, but also the ongoing education and elevation of its personnel.

# Color Craft Graphic Arts, Inc.

**C**ustomer service is the key to any company's success, as Color Craft president and owner Tom Foster has discovered.

Color Craft, a manufacturer of paper board folding cartons and commercial printing, serves a wide variety of customers—from a family-operated county candy maker (Pine River Pre-Pack) to the county's largest employer (the Mirro Company).

"Our service is what sets us apart. We're able to have a quick turn-around, which our customers really

*Color Craft built a 45,000-square-foot facility in the city's I-43 Industrial Park four years ago. The company's distribution, folding, and die cutting are all handled at this facility. Color Craft was the first business to buy land in the new park and was one of the first to open a facility there. In addition to the I-43 plant, Color Craft has a 44,400-square-foot plant in downtown Manitowoc.*

*Color Craft offers a wide variety of design and pre-press services. The company's graphic designers work with customers to help them achieve what they're looking for.*

like," explains Foster, who purchased Color Craft in 1983. "Providing good customer service helps build strong business relationships," Foster continues. "We handle a lot of repeat business and much of our new work comes from word of mouth."

Color Craft uses its ability to complete projects quickly along with its strong design capabilities as a way to attract and retain customers. In addition to serving businesses locally, Color Craft has an established clientele throughout Wisconsin and across the country.

"Our ability to get a job done quickly *and* well is a big plus for us," says Foster, adding that Color Craft specializes in short, immediate product runs.

Keeping up with technology is another way Color Craft serves its customers. By staying on top of all the different kinds of software and the latest upgrades, the firm's employees can work with whatever clients give them.

"Most places just need to keep up with one kind of software. Here, we have to know them all," Foster says. "It's an endless race to keep up

with technology but it's something we need to do to serve our customers better."

Color Craft was founded in 1929 as a commercial printing company. In 1967 Russ Johnson and four partners purchased the business and began the conversion from letterpress to offset printing. From 1972 to 1981 the firm was owned by Association Life Ins. Co., a subsidiary of International Harvester. Russ Johnson repurchased Color Craft in 1981, and two years later he sold it to Foster.

Under Foster's leadership, Color Craft has expanded from a small-town printer to a sophisticated specialty packaging company. Physical expansion has been a key part of that continuing growth. Not only have several additions been built onto the downtown facility, Color Craft also constructed a brand-new plant in the city's I-43 Industrial Park four years ago.

The downtown facility has a pressroom with five four-color presses that are controlled via computer, infrared dryers, and a fully equipped pre-press department. The I-43 building handles the company's die cutting, folding, and distribution.

"Before the I-43 building was completed, we did everything here. The new facility allowed us to expand our operations here (in the downtown facility)," Foster explains.

As business continues to grow, Foster predicts even more physical expansion for the company. "We just keep growing and growing. I think that's a credit to our employees and to the level of service we provide our customers," he says. "Our company is built on service."

# Quality Systems Associates Inc.

Jeff Heinzen saw a need in his business community and he filled it.

While employed at Paragon Electric Company in Two Rivers, Heinzen led the firm's ISO-9001 certification process. Since Paragon was the first business in the area to become certified, other local companies contacted Heinzen and asked him how the process was done.

"There weren't many resources out there for companies going through the process," he says. "I saw a real need and decided I could fill it."

Heinzen established Quality Systems Associates Inc. in June 1993. He quickly received plenty of phone calls. "The year 1993 was a real turning point in the ISO-9000 process. A lot of area companies were just starting to look at it and beginning to get involved," Heinzen explains.

ISO-9000 is an internationally recognized quality management system standard. Its companion, QS-9000, is the standard for the automotive industry. To be certified to ISO/QS-9000, businesses must comply with a rigorous set of requirements. An accredited registrar then performs an on-site audit and thoroughly evaluates the company, covering everything from how incoming orders are taken to the final product shipment.

Manitowoc County's strong and close-knit business community provides Heinzen with tremendous business opportunities. "A lot of my business comes through word of mouth. Executives talk with each other and my name gets out there," he says. Some of the area enterprises Heinzen has helped gain certification include Manitowoc Ice, Jagemann Stamping, Bemis Manufacturing Co., the Kohler Company, Foster Needle, J.J. Stangel, Federal Mogul, Rockwell Lime Company, and Manitowoc

*Jeff Heinzen founded Quality Systems Associates in 1993.*

Tool and Machining.

Manitowoc County's strong industrial base means Heinzen doesn't have to venture far afield to find customers. "I'm very fortunate to be located where I am," Heinzen says. "I know of some consultants who spend half their lives on planes."

Heinzen is a certified quality systems lead auditor by the Registrar Accreditation Board. He is also a certified quality auditor by the American Society for Quality (ASQ). Additionally, he has received numerous honors including mention in *Who's Who Among Rising Young Americans* for his contributions to American Society and Business and the 1995 University of Wisconsin Outstanding Alumni Award.

Quality Systems Associates offers its customers a wide variety of services including comprehensive training programs, customized consulting services, and qualified audit services.

The training and consulting provide the company's employees with hands-on experience. Heinzen says this training facilitates the avoidance of rework and promotes a streamlined, cost-effective approach, which is focused on the continuous quality improvement of the organization.

As competition becomes more fierce among businesses, Heinzen predicts there will be more companies seeking ISO/QS-9000 certification in the future. "If there are two firms competing for the same contract and one is certified, chances are that one will get the job," he believes.

"The whole ISO/QS-9000 process forces companies to improve themselves," Heinzen explains. "There are tremendous internal benefits for businesses that go this route."

In the future, Heinzen plans on offering ISO-14000 services to his clients. ISO-14000 is an environmental management system standard. "There are a lot of opportunities out there, but I want to concentrate in these areas. I want to be able to fully meet all of my clients' needs regarding management systems compliance."

# Silver Lake College

*T*o get to know Silver Lake College, you must reach deeper than the serenity of its environment. You must see beyond the brick and glass. For Silver Lake College has a commitment to the God-given gifts of knowledge and wisdom. So if you really want to know Silver Lake College, you must look into the hearts of students, faculty, and alumni. This is where mind, body, and soul harmonize in a celebration of human growth. This is where Silver Lake College truly comes to life.

Silver Lake College has experienced several evolutionary changes since the Franciscan Sisters of Christian Charity established its forerunner institution in 1885 on the shores of Silver Lake. Its purpose then was to prepare young women for the apostolates of the congregation, in schools, orphanages, hospitals, and other institutions that were served under the auspices of Holy Family Convent.

By 1911 hundreds of young women had graduated from the two-year normal school and taught in dozens of Catholic elementary schools throughout the Midwest. During the 1930s the Sisters expanded their educational mission to include high schools. As more advanced education was required, college administrators redesigned the curriculum and prepared personnel to offer a four-year college program of study. In 1935 the state of Wisconsin granted the college's charter as a senior degree-granting institution then known as Holy Family College.

By 1946 degreed graduates, more than two-thirds of whom were directly involved with education, staffed more than 100 elementary and high schools, conservatories of music and art, and nursing schools.

Though lay women had attended the college by special arrangement with the Holy Family Hospital School of Nursing, in 1957 women

were admitted on a regular basis, and the college again expanded its teacher-education programs.

To accommodate the advances in curriculum, the college constructed an entirely new physical plant in 1960. The modern complex includes an expansive library, classrooms, science laboratories, art and music studios, lecture halls, administrative offices, a special education clinic, cafeteria and faculty residence, and an inspiring chapel walled by stained-glass windows depicting the various academic majors offered.

By the end of the decade the college admitted its first male students. In 1969, with a student body representing all socioeconomic groups in the region, the school officially became known as Silver Lake College.

During the late 1970s and early 1980s spiraling inflation and high unemployment plagued the entire country and region. Silver Lake College responded by repackaging and expanding major programs of study for traditional and non-traditional students alike, along with providing substantially more financial assistance for students. By doing so, the college helped the area weather the economic downturn and recorded steady enrollment gains.

Business and computer science programs became important components in the college's diversification. During the 1990s the college has delivered degree completion programs and professional develop-

*Today's Silver Lake College serves the interests and needs of more than 3,300 learners each year while retaining the highly personalized approach to education that has characterized the institution since its inception.*

ment coursework at various Wisconsin locations for business people, educators, and others who have already begun their careers.

These positive outcomes could not be achieved without exceptional faculty, dedicated staff, and forward-looking administrators who serve in leadership roles in both the public and private sectors. The college has also developed specialized, pre-collegiate experiences for area youth, as well as a Lifelong Learning Program for senior citizens, thus serving learners of all ages.

Silver Lake College clearly preserves the religious traditions and high educational standards of the original Holy Family Convent normal school. At the end of the twentieth century Silver Lake College is also an economic force, its statewide economic impact calculated at more than $150 million annually. With its exemplary religious, educational, and economic contributions, Silver Lake College stands as a testament to the vision of its founderesses and benefactors, as well as a dynamic resource for students and the community at large.

For more information, visit the college's web site at www.sl.edu.

**Silver Lake College**
2406 S. Alverno Road • Manitowoc WI 54220-9319

# Burger Boat Company

*Henry B. Burger, "Jr.," 1863-1914.*

**B**urger yachts, world famous for their elegant design and exquisite workmanship, have been a Manitowoc shipbuilding tradition for more than 136 years.

The Burger Boat Company story begins in 1846 with Simon and Margaretta Brauburger, who left their homeland in Germany and immigrated to the United States with their five children. The youngest, seven-year-old Henry B., was fascinated by ships and their journey across the Atlantic. The family originally settled in New York and later moved to Wisconsin where the region so closely resembled the Old World.

Young Henry followed his passion and began to build small sailing craft in 1863 for commercial fishermen. He joined talents with Greene Rand in 1870 and established Greene, Rand & Burger Shipbuilding Company in 1873.

The partnership lasted until Rand's death in 1885. One year later Henry took his nephew, George B. Burger, into partnership, forming the Burger & Burger Shipyard, and in 1887 they purchased the only dry dock in Manitowoc.

Between 1870 and the turn of the century, the Burger name appeared on almost 100 vessels and became synonymous with quality and craftsmanship. In 1902 Henry B. and George B. sold the Burger & Burger shipyard to the Manitowoc Dry Dock Company, which is now The Manitowoc Company.

The Burger name continued in shipbuilding. In 1892 Henry "Jr.," the nephew of Henry B., formed a company in his own name, Henry B. Burger Shipyard, across the river

from the original yard. It is directly from this firm that the current Burger Boat Company has evolved. Henry "Jr." was very innovative and a true visionary. He quickly recognized the potential advantages of the newly developed gasoline engine, installing the first in an 85-foot wooden pleasure cruiser, *VERNON JR.*, in 1901. Within 10 years the company established a reputation for building the finest custom motor yachts anywhere. When Henry "Jr." died in 1914, his wife and four children assumed ownership and management of the yard and it continued to prosper.

Burger's reputation for expert craftsmanship did not go unnoticed by the United States government. Several wooden minesweepers, subchasers, tugs, and rescue crafts were contracted during World Wars I and II and the Korean Conflict.

The advent of electric arc welding allowed Burger to develop techniques for an all-welded-steel hull for pleasure craft. In 1938 Burger built the country's first all-welded-steel auxiliary ketch, the 81-foot *TAMARIS*. The competition hooted, calling it a "tin can," but the laughter soon died when yachtsmen began praising the massive strength of steel versus wooden hulls.

Burger started another trend in 1940 when it launched the first flush deck cruiser, the 65-foot *PILGRIM*. In the early 1950s the Reynolds Metals Company contact-

*RIGHT: The USS* DOTTERAL, *Korean War minesweeper built in 1953.*

*BELOW: The 1901 launching of* VERNON JR., *an 85-foot wooden pleasure cruiser that was the first to incorporate the gasoline engine.*

ed Burger to work on an experimental hull using a new alloy— aluminum. With the development of MIG and TIG welding, the collaboration produced America's first all-welded-aluminum, 36-foot cruiser, *VIRGINIA*, in 1955.

The company was reorganized in 1959. Henry E. Burger, son of the past president, Henry C. Burger, became president and Elias Gunnell II replaced his father-in-law, George M. Burger, as vice president.

The firm became Burger Boat Company, Inc. The first unanimous decision was to end sailboat construction and in the early 1960s management decided to end all-steel construction and focus solely on building luxury aluminum motor yachts. The heydey of flush decks, cruisers, houseboats, and raised pilothouse motor yachts continued through the 1960s, 1970s, and into the 1980s, but behind the scenes, it was the beginning of the end.

Elias Gunnell II and Henry E. made the decision in 1976 to part company. They decided to draw straws and Henry E. won. He chose to buy out Elias' half of the partnership. In 1983 Henry lost his beloved daughter to leukemia, which contributed to his declining health. Finally, in October 1986, due to continuing union problems and a painful lawsuit with a client, Burger sold the company to John McMillian, a customer.

McMillian attempted to relocate the company to his home state of Florida. He was met with much resistance from the community and the work force. A frustrated McMillian sold Burger Boat in April 1989 to United Shipbuilders of America, a newly created subsidiary of Tacoma Boatbuilding Company. Unfortunately, the unexpected loss of several large naval contracts, the newly instituted luxury tax, and blatant mismanagement caused a struggling Tacoma to abruptly suspend operations.

On Friday, November 30, 1990, the closing of Burger was ordered via fax with a 20-minute notice and all 167 employees were told to leave their jobs. This group of workers banded together to form the Former Burger Workers (FBWs) with the hope that one day Burger would reopen.

Their dream came true. David Ross, a Chicago businessman,

*WINDRUSH, 101-foot raised pilothouse motor yacht launched in 1998.*

heard of Burger's plight and traveled to Manitowoc with a friend and business associate, Jim Ruffolo. The challenge to reopen Burger Boat Company lasted 15 months and included hundreds of hours spent with attorneys, city officials such as Mayor Kevin Crawford and City Attorney Pat Willis, and several FBWs.

On Friday, February 5, 1993, Burger Boat Company reopened with an emotional chain-cutting ceremony.

Burger Boat Company today is reputed within the custom yacht industry as being the most successful turnaround in modern-day history. To further validate this distinction, *WINDRUSH*, a 101-foot raised pilothouse motor yacht launched in 1998, was the recipient of the prestigious 1999 Showboats International award for the best motor yacht in its class. With a growing list of repeat customers and 18 contracts signed since it reopened, Burger Boat Company has successfully re-emerged.

# Shady Lane

*I*n the ever-changing business of long-term health care, Shady Lane has done what it takes to stay competitive for the past 48 years.

Shady Lane began as a retirement home for Manitowoc County citizens in 1951. The building was once used by the county as a mental hospital. After a new county health care center was constructed, local attorney Fred Dicke suggested to the county board that a private nonprofit citizen group take over the home. A volunteer board of directors was formed and the name Shady Lane was given to the newly opened retirement home.

To handle the growing population at Shady Lane, the county opened a nursing home on the facility's grounds. Called Park Lawn, the 60-bed facility opened in 1960.

In 1971 a new four-story facility was constructed for Shady Lane. The building had a total of 120 private and 24 semi-private rooms. Shady Lane now houses 168 residents.

In 1993 Shady Lane bought the entire complex from Manitowoc County. A few years later Park Lawn vacated one building, which paved the way for more growth at Shady Lane.

The complex formerly housing Park Lawn has been converted into an assisted-living complex, according to Shady Lane spokesman Kay Pickar. The new complex, Laurel Grove Assisted Living Center, features 34 studio apartments with their own kitchenette and baths. Residents living in the assisted-care facility will also have housekeeping service and meals provided.

"Basically, any service we offer in Shady Lane itself will be provided to the residents of the assisted-living facility, including therapy and nursing services," Pickar explains.

Shady Lane itself is undergoing physical changes as well. All of the facility's rooms are being remodeled and converted into more private rooms.

The facility's changes over the

years haven't been limited to just physical appearances. As health care for the elderly has evolved, so has Shady Lane. In 1986, for example, Shady Lane's board decided residents needed more nursing care. As a result, the facility sought and received a skilled nursing care license and added therapy services.

The lack of local care for Alzheimer's patients led Shady Lane's board to open Seasons, a 42-bed unit committed to caring for Alzheimer's patients.

Commitment to service and quality sets Shady Lane apart, Pickar believes. "We are dedicated to pro-

viding the best service possible to our residents and to their families."

In 1997 Shady Lane received Joint Commission Accreditation, thereby becoming the first and only nursing home in Manitowoc to be certified. "I think this really shows people that we are dedicated to providing the best-quality service to our residents," Pickar says.

*ABOVE: A new four-story facility was built in 1971 to house Shady Lane. A portion of Shady Lane that once housed Park Lawn has been converted into an assisted-living complex.*

*TOP: The original Shady Lane once housed the Manitowoc County mental hospital. Shady Lane's board of directors took over the facility in 1950, and the first residents moved in the following year.*

# Cher-Make Sausage Company

Green Bay Packers fans may not be aware that the hot dogs they have eaten for over a decade at Lambeau Field are officially supplied by the Cher-Make Sausage Company of Manitowoc. The popular "Old World" flavor of Wisconsin sausages has been a hallmark of Cher-Make since 1928 when Emil Chermak began making hickory wood smoked sausages in his small meat market in downtown Manitowoc.

In 1934 Emil started a meat market and the business grew steadily until World War II when

*ABOVE: Company founder Emil Chermak (left) stuffs natural-casing weiners, circa 1940.*

*LEFT: Cher-Make Sausage's product line has grown to include bratwurst, summer sausage, beef sticks, bologna, and hot dogs.*

many employees were drafted and meat rationing began, forcing the company to "downsize" back to the retail business.

When Emil's son Art returned from military service to rejoin the business, father and son made plans to build a new plant, completed in 1948 on the present site and subsequently enlarged to its present 43,000 square feet. The product line, too, has grown from simple sausages to include kippered beef, summer sausage in a number of ethnic flavors, beef sticks, bologna, and, of course, hot dogs.

Emil passed away in 1954 leaving management to Art, who became president. Art is now chairman of the board and Art's son, Tom, is the current president.

After operating for years under city and state inspection, USDA inspection status was granted in

1968, opening the way to new markets beyond the borders of Wisconsin.

A quality-control lab was set up in 1972. Also in that decade Cher-Make managers worked with other sausage makers to develop national standards for the safe manufacture, storage, display, and consumption of summer sausage. Since it needed no refrigeration, the product had enormous potential in the burgeoning gift market nationwide but had previously been sold only on a limited regional basis. These new standards helped to change all that.

In addition to its own name-brand products, which include the newest "Smoky Valley" brand, Cher-Make supplies a number of private labels such as Hickory Farms, Swiss Colony, Figi's, IGA, and a host of fund-raisers and specialty chains. Private-label summer sausage and

beef sticks now account for nearly 60 percent of the business and are shipped nationwide.

Cher-Make currently employs 85 people and produces an average of 130,000 to 140,000 pounds of sausage weekly. At peak times, weekly production can reach 250,000 pounds. Also, maintaining its family tradition of quality and customer satisfaction, the company still provides quick service on small-batch custom orders.

Cher-Make leadership today is young, energetic, full of good humor, and there is no management "hierarchy." Employees work in teams. Formal education is encouraged and great emphasis is placed on internal training and development.

Cher-Make considers its growth to be due to the major factors of quality commitment and customer service. "State-of-the-art machinery and facilities are essential, of course," says president Tom Chermak, "but above all else, quality employees are the backbone of a successful company."

# Manitowoc Public Utilities

The origins of Manitowoc Public Utilities date back to 1889, when the city's forward-thinking aldermen solicited bids for furnishing electric lighting in the city of Manitowoc. Local businessman John Schuette offered to do so at half the cost of the nearest competitor. He was awarded the contract. In a building adjoining his flour- and gristmill, Schuette installed four 20-kilowatt Edison Bi-Polar type generators driven by belts connected to two Corliss-Allis steam engines. Suddenly, daylight lasted until 9 p.m. throughout the year—with help after dusk from the Electric Light Company.

Manitowoc Waterworks Company was also established in 1889 by brothers Eugene and T.W. Gray. Their water plant was located on the Lake Michigan shore at what was then the southern city limits. While both the Grays' and Schuette's entrepreneurship may be credited with providing valuable community services, the stage was soon set for municipal ownership. Under the direction of Mayor Henry Stolze, Jr., the city purchased both the waterworks and the electric util-

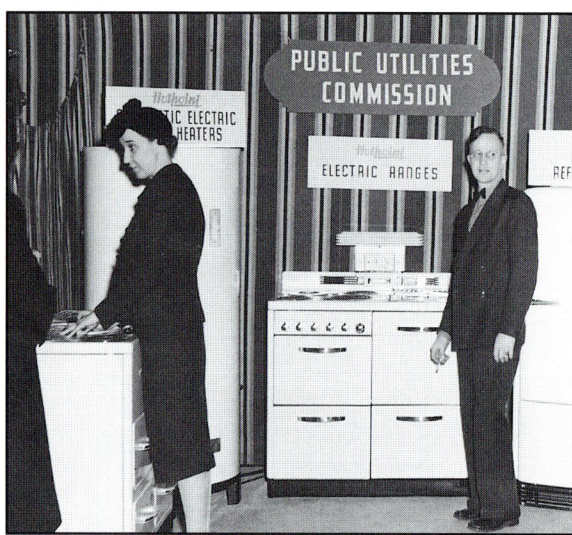

*From the 1930s to the 1950s Manitowoc Public Utilities sold and serviced electrical appliances. At that time few people had electrical appliances, and even fewer local outlets sold them. MPU provided this service to build an infrastructure, making it possible for the public to enjoy the convenience and efficiency offered by electrical appliances.*

ity, in 1911 and 1914, respectively. The waterworks then served 1,811 customers and 211 fire hydrants. The electric plant, with its first steam turbine-generator, had a capacity of 810 kilowatts and served approximately 2,000 customers.

Thus was born Manitowoc Public Utilities, a municipally owned and managed electric and water utility, still headquartered at the original waterworks site, though the southern city limits have moved significantly farther south.

By 1935, with almost 25 years of community ownership, the value of the electric plant and the water works had grown to $2.72 million, a significant return on the original investment of less than $400,000. And MPU was operating completely without bonds or debt.

MPU continually added electricity-producing capabilities to keep pace with growing community demands. By the beginning of World War II, MPU had a capacity of more than 20,000 kilowatts. Still, with industry growth and wartime

*ABOVE: In 1938 MPU constructed a 1.5-million-gallon elevated water reservoir on Reed Avenue at North Eighth Street. The tower, along with high-capacity water mains, helps supply the north side with water at a consistent pressure for consumption and fire protection.*

*LEFT: In the late 1880s electric company workers installed electric lamps and wiring by day, and ran the power plant at night. Here workers service one of four Edison Bi-Polar generators at John Schuette's flour and grist mill.*

*An integral part of MPU's high level of service reliability is the lineman. Called upon to work in all kinds of weather, all hours of the day, MPU line crews maintain the city's electrical distribution system, in addition to street and security lighting. Workers demonstrate here why it is called one of the "highest" professions.*

contracts, there was little question of the need for more power. By the mid-1940s discussion began about the need for power plant expansion.

In cooperation with Rahr Malting Company (now Busch Agricultural Resources), the utility commission approved a plan to supply steam for its large kilns. Steam and hot water sales to nearby customers expanded considerably over time. At the end of the twentieth century, extracted steam heated not only Busch Agricultural Resources, but also Lincoln High School, the Manitowoc County Courthouse and Jail, Bio-Technical Resources, and First German Lutheran Church and School.

By 1950 the plant addition was completed. During that decade two new turbines were added, increasing MPU's capacity to 52 megawatts.

Plant power outages in the late 1950s heightened interest in possible interconnection with the state's electric grid to improve reliability. By the spring of 1961 necessary substations and transmissions lines were completed, and interconnection was achieved with Wisconsin Public Service.

That same year MPU sought additional capacity and the state

Public Service Commission approved the plan to purchase another 22-megawatt generator. As luck would have it, a General Electric turbo generator fitting MPU's exact specifications was in storage, having been slated for delivery to Cuba. When Fidel Castro took over that country's electric utility, the ensuing embargo effectively canceled the order. MPU saved nearly one million dollars.

By the time MPU celebrated its silver anniversary in 1964, the power company supplied electricity to 11,572 customers at just 1.2 cents per kilowatt hour, one of the lowest rates in the state of Wisconsin and, indeed, the nation.

The city's need for safe, fresh water also grew rapidly. In its early years, Manitowoc relied on shallow wells that penetrated the gravel strata beneath the lake bed. With no sewage treatment facility, however, citizens feared the surface lake water. But the wells could not keep up with increasing demand, and the water from them contained such a high iron content that it was often unfit for consumption.

In 1944 two new wells were sunk directly east of the Lincoln High School Tower, and south of Silver Creek Park. These wells utilized a radically different design to augment the capabilities of traditional vertical shafts. Patented by the Ranney Corporation, the wells added horizontal shafts outward like the spokes of a wheel, to increase collection capacities.

The need for water continued to

grow, so MPU turned to Lake Michigan. To make lake water a feasible alternative, a sand filtration system was constructed. It served the community for 30 years, until the completion of a state-of-the-art microfiltration plant in the summer of 1999. With the new plant, the city finally had an absolute barrier to surface water-borne pathogens, with limited use of chlorine and other chemicals.

MPU geared up for the twenty-first century with a 20-megawatt fluidized bed boiler addition in 1991, and a 25-megawatt combustion turbine and transmission lines to reinforce the electrical service to the southwest portion of the city as well as future expansion of the industrial parks west of I-43 in 1999. At the end of the millennium, MPU's capacity stood at 114 megawatts.

Manitowoc Public Utilities' mission is to provide safe and reliable electric and water services for the citizens of Manitowoc, at the lowest possible price, something MPU is able to do because the utility is municipally owned, though managed separately from city government. Unlike strictly private enterprise, MPU is able to focus on the community's needs—the needs of its more than 16,000 customers—without the influence of outside investors. As a result, the families and businesses of Manitowoc benefit directly from some of the lowest utility rates in the nation. Additionally, with assets of more than $100 million, MPU is Manitowoc's largest taxpayer, adding $2 million annually to city coffers.

Because of the vision of early entrepreneurs, dedicated city leaders, and an ongoing team of conscientious, community-minded utility employees, Manitowoc Public Utilities stands poised to continue its mission and to be an integral and essential component in the economic development of the community.

# Associated Bank Lakeshore Region

The life of a banking institution is inextricably entwined
with the life of the community it serves, and none more so
than Associated Bank Lakeshore in
Manitowoc. Founded on April 7,
1884, as the Manitowoc Savings
Bank by German immigrant John
Schuette, this bank continues to
grow, offering an array of services to
meet the growing needs of its community.

Manitowoc Savings Bank opened
for business at the southwest corner
of Eighth and Jay streets, across the

president throughout the Great
Depression and World War II, while
the bank continued to prosper. His
tenure lasted until 1947, when
Henry R. Schuette was named president. Deposits grew steadily, and by
the mid-1960s Manitowoc Savings
Bank again outgrew its facilities. A
new $1.5-million, 32,000-square-
foot, two-story structure was erected
along the Manitowoc River at 10th
and Franklin streets. Everything in
the new bank was designed with
the customer in mind, from the
effortless parking arrangement and

including real estate and investment
brokerage services and insurance
sales, in addition to traditional trust
services, safe deposit and safekeep-
ing services, and mortgage lending
services. Since banks were not then
allowed to engage in the sales of
real estate, investments, or insurance, Manitowoc Savings Bank
divested itself of these services but
added others, including retirement
plan administration and invest-
ment-oriented living trusts. By
December 1982, when East
Wisconsin Trust Company officially
became the trust department of the
bank, assets under management had
grown to more than $160 million.

In 1984, under the direction of
Edward C. Fordney, Manitowoc
Savings Bank changed its name to
Associated Bank Manitowoc, and
the community truly began to ben-
efit from all the larger company had
to offer—without losing any of the
benefits of local banking. With
Gordon J. Weber leading the way,
Associated Bank Manitowoc evolved
into Associated Bank Lakeshore
Region as banks in Valders and
Sheboygan merged with the
Manitowoc office on January 1,
1990, and 1991, respectively.
Recognizing the special needs of the
senior members of the communities
served, the bank established two
retirement community offices, at
Felician Village in Manitowoc and
Pine Haven Christian Home in
Sheboygan Falls, in 1992.

In December 1993 the Calumet
Avenue office was opened on the
city's southwest side. This full-service branch also houses Associated
Bank Lakeshore's training facility.
Two years later the Fond du Lac
office joined the Lakeshore Region,
strengthening Associated's relationship with that market. In 1998
Associated Banc-Corp merged with
First Financial, further increasing
the bank's resources and customer
service opportunities throughout
Wisconsin and Illinois. Associated

*Associated Bank Lakeshore offers a
number of locations in Manitowoc
County.*

street from another Schuette family
venture, Schuette's Department
Store, itself an icon. Less than one
year later John Schuette, president;
C.E. Estabrook, vice president; and
Joseph Staehle, cashier, presided
over a bank with $70,787 in deposits
and capital and surplus of $50,874.

The bank grew each year under
their able management, and in
1920 Louis Schuette was named
president of the bank. Under his
leadership a new building was erected in 1927 on the original site.
Though no longer home to the
bank, this classical building,
adorned with Corinthian columns
and a distinctive four-sided clock,
still stands and serves as a landmark
in downtown Manitowoc.

Edwin Schuette served as bank

centrally located teller windows, to
the easily accessible loan departments and safe deposit boxes.

By 1970 Manitowoc Savings
Bank established the River Heights
branch to serve the growing northwest side of the city, and became a
member of Associated Banc-Corp, a
Green Bay-based bank holding company. In 1973 the bank opened its
first 24-hour automated teller—
commonplace now, but a breakthrough in banking services in the
1970s. A new drive-in facility was
completed on the bank's grounds at
11th and Franklin streets that year,
and two years later a second drive-
in bank was erected on the north
side of the Manitowoc River.

In the interim, Manitowoc
Savings Bank continued to expand
its services. It acquired the assets of
the East Wisconsin Trustee
Company in 1973. This fiduciary
trust company, established in 1908,
provided a variety of services

*Decisions are made locally by the retail, trust, and business banking departments at the community-focused bank.*

Bank Lakeshore alone offers eight locations.

Such prodigious growth, however, in no way changed the local nature of this banking institution. Associated Bank Lakeshore is a community-based bank, with local management. Scott A. Yeoman is the chief executive officer of the bank, taking over for Thomas R. Walsh who moved south to serve as chief executive officer for the newly created Associated Bank Illinois.

"Associated's strength lies in the relationships our banks have with

*Every aspect of Associated Bank's offices has been designed with customer convenience in mind.*

the communities where we do business, and the fact that we give our bankers the power to make decisions at the local level," says H.B. Conlon, chairman and CEO of Associated Banc-Corp.

Associated Bank Lakeshore is community focused. Loan decisions are made locally by both the retail and business banking departments. The trust department administers qualified retirement plans for scores of local businesses, and manages the investments of hundreds of lakeshore area residents.

The bank also sponsors many community events: theatrical productions, high school sports, local United Way campaigns, and signa-

ture events such as the annual "Spirit's Here" Race Festival and Riverwalk.

Such community involvement, however, could not be possible without the banking products and services that keep Associated Bank Lakeshore strong. The bank offers the ever-popular "Packer Checking," as well as a variety of VISA® and MasterCard® accounts. Associated Bank's new HomePower Equity Card may be one of its friendliest and most flexible credit cards yet. The new card, which looks and works like a traditional VISA® card, actually offers homeowners the opportunity to borrow against the equity in their homes, and benefit from any available tax advantages.

It is Associated Bank Lakeshore's commitment to ever-improving products and services, as well as its commitment to the community, that makes this financial institution a partner in the prosperity of Manitowoc County.

# Jagemann Stamping Company

*Founder William P. Jagemann, Sr., initially focused on fulfilling short-run orders.*

*BELOW: A dedicated continuous improvement team combines the talents of toolmakers, press technicians, and engineers.*

**B**usiness analysts measure a firm's progress in terms of sales and profits, equipment and markets. Jagemann Stamping Company has progressed dramatically in terms of those criteria since it was founded by William P. Jagemann, Sr., in 1946. The language of business analysts, however, does not include all the criteria used to measure the success of this world-renowned metal stamping company. At Jagemann Stamping, success is also measured in very human terms.

"We have an exceptional group of people here at Jagemann Stamping Company," says William T. Jagemann, Jr., chairman emeritus and son of the founder. "We can go out and buy machines, but without our people, we wouldn't have a company."

Of course, not everyone is suited to work at this progressive metal stamping company, lauded worldwide as a premier automotive fluid power connector supplier. This is not a place for people comfortable with the status quo. Jagemann Stamping fosters an environment in which teamwork is the norm, creativity is encouraged, and initiative is rewarded. Many of the more than 165 employees started working in the pressroom. Whether they are now team leaders, managers, toolmakers, engineers, or administrative staff, Jagemann Stamping employees know their company's products well, and are eager to help in the pressroom when a few extra hands will help satisfy the customer.

In 1998 Jagemann Stamping Company earned its QS-9000 registration, the coveted international automotive quality standard. The firm earned this distinction not only because of its already high standards, typically manufacturing parts to tighter tolerances than even its customers demand, but also because of its commitment to continuous improvement.

A dedicated continuous improvement team combines the talents of toolmakers, press technicians, and engineers. The team responds to suggestions, tests their feasibility and cost-effectiveness, and ensures the successful implementation of any improvements in both equipment and procedures. In this way manufacturing equipment is modified on site by the press technicians who use it, rather than accepting performance limitations that may be inherent in machinery designed by far-away engineers.

The customized equipment and ever-improving processes enable Jagemann Stamping engineers, toolmakers, and press technicians to manufacture quality automotive ferrules (hose fittings), oil filter cans, and other deep-drawn metal parts. In fact, Jagemann Stamping ferrules are found on virtually every car sold in the United States and many throughout the world, creating reliable, leak-tight seals in fluid power and air-conditioning assemblies.

*Jagemann Stamping's new 175,000-square-foot manufacturing facility is located in the I-43 Industrial Park.*

"We've combined lean manufacturing and progressive thinking," explains Thomas M. Jagemann, the founder's grandson, president and chief executive officer of the firm.

"Our speed and responsiveness set us apart from others in our industry," he says. "It is our ability to respond quickly to both our internal and our external customers that has brought us to where we are today and will take us into the future. In fact, we strive to anticipate what will be hot in the future, and we'll do whatever makes sense to be ready."

Indeed, that is the foundation upon which this business has grown. From 1946 to 1975 Jagemann focused on fulfilling short-run orders manufactured on hand-fed single operation presses. Then, in 1976, recognizing that booming automotive ferrule orders would soon surpass the company's capacity, Jagemann Stamping installed the first of many automated transfer presses, machines that stamp circular blanks from coils of metal, then carry the blanks through progressive dies that form each part to the customer's exacting specifications.

As the century comes to a close, automation is not limited to the transfer presses. The engineering and tooling departments have joined forces to utilize the latest in three-dimensional design software and computer numerical-controlled equipment to engineer and manufacture virtually all of the tooling required in more than two dozen high-speed transfer presses. Automated quality-assurance equipment checks each part for defects and, finding none, sends parts to automated packaging equipment to be carton packed and labeled for destinations both domestic and foreign.

All of these automated processes, however, do not eliminate the role of the press operator. In fact, Jagemann Stamping is striving to increase the skill levels of every

must be done more quickly than ever before. This has prompted our press technicians to design quick-change press tooling and to reduce set-up times between production runs, so the presses run more hours than ever before."

To meet the growing demands of its ever-increasing customer base, Jagemann Stamping is preparing to break ground on a new manufacturing facility, more than double the size of its current 74,000-square-foot plant in a residential neighborhood on Manitowoc's near south side. The new building, to be located in the I-43 Industrial Park, will feature a modular floor plan to accommodate the many, frequently changing functions of the state-of-the-art manufacturing facility.

"We're coming full circle,"

*The company's ferrules are found on virtually every car sold in the United States and many throughout the world.*

press technician. All employees participate in on-site technical, leadership, and team-effectiveness training, and all are eligible for tuition reimbursement at area colleges and universities.

"To stay competitive in the international marketplace, we must do things better than we ever have before," says Thomas Jagemann. "Our production runs are shorter, requiring more press set-ups that

explains Thomas Jagemann. "We're growing to increase our responsiveness to our customers, much as my grandfather did in the late 1940s and early 1950s. Grandpa J. always said, 'Do it right, or don't do it at all.' That's an axiom that served him well, served my father well, and is serving us well as we enter the twenty-first century. We're working diligently to ensure our continued success."

# The Manitowoc Company, Inc.

"Diversification," the economic watchword of the 1990s, is the principle that guided the founders of Manitowoc Dry Dock Company, the forerunner of The Manitowoc Company, Inc. In 1902 Elias Gunnell, an experienced shipbuilder, and Charles C. West, an accomplished marine engineer and naval architect, purchased the assets of a shipyard located in the thriving lakeport of Manitowoc. With the surety of an established wooden ship construction and repair business as their foundation, the two men readied the yard to build and repair steel vessels.

Within Manitowoc Dry Dock's first decade of operation, Gunnell Tool Company and Manitowoc Boiler Works were established. Gunnell Tool manufactured a pneumatic rivet-heating forge and did much of Manitowoc Dry Dock's general machine work. The Boiler Works manufactured marine boilers, dredge dippers, dryers, furnaces, and other heavy metal fabrications. Both firms later merged with Manitowoc Dry Dock to form Manitowoc Shipbuilding Company.

World War I precipitated dramatic growth for the young enterprise. Its work force grew to 2,500, and it swiftly completed 33 Liberty-class freighters for the government. But when the war ended in 1918, additional ship orders were canceled. With its capital tied up in raw materials and an overabundance of manufacturing

*The Manitowoc Company's food-service segment is America's leading producer of ice-cube machines.*

capacity, Manitowoc Shipbuilding was challenged simply to stay afloat during the industry's postwar depression.

To keep its work force intact and the expanded plant busy, Manitowoc converted some of its facilities into a locomotive and railcar repair shop. However, the company never abandoned its Great Lakes heritage and built several types of vessels during this era, including self-unloaders, carferries, tugs, dredges, and even oil tankers.

Charles West also ventured into new arenas. In 1925 Manitowoc Shipbuilding began manufacturing Moore Speedcranes on a subcontract basis. The innovative designs of these early cranes made them ideal for construction, as well as shovel, dragline, or trenching applications. Manitowoc cranes kept the company in the public eye, as they were used throughout the 1930s on such prominent projects as the U.S. Capitol, the Senate Office Building, the National Gallery of Art, the Jefferson Memorial, and the National Archives.

As the United States entered World War II, Manitowoc's shipbuilding and crane expertise coalesced to meet a single need: furthering the war effort. Manitowoc Shipbuilding was called upon to build submarines, the most intricate vessels in the fleet. In addition, it designed and built cranes with the ability to erect submarine hull sections onto the building ways with care and precision. Other Manitowoc cranes were marshaled to aid salvaging operations following

*Manitowoc is the dominant provider of ship-repair, maintenance, conversion, automation, and new-construction services on the Great Lakes.*

the bombing of Pearl Harbor. By the war's end Manitowoc had constructed and delivered some 28 submarines—all ahead of schedule—plus 1,465 landing craft and 284 cranes. Almost 7,000 men and women worked diligently throughout the war to achieve such production.

In spite of the incredible wartime workload, West remained cautious. He had already recreated his company after one war. Following World War II it was time to diversify further. Of Manitowoc's forays into diversification, foodservice proved most successful. In 1945 Manitowoc Equipment Works (the reorganized Boiler Works) produced its first freezer, the Sub-Zero, soon followed by the Two-Zone, a refrigerator/ freezer combination unit. In the early 1960s Manitowoc developed and patented a vertical evaporator, which eventually led to its introduction of commercial ice-cube machines. By 1998 the Foodservice Equipment segment was booming, generating nearly 50 percent of operating earnings of the $695-million corporation.

As the twentieth century ends, Manitowoc's foodservice segment is North America's leading producer of ice-cube machines, walk-in refrigera-

*Known for their versatility, durability, and reliability, Manitowoc's cranes are preferred by leading contractors and equipment rental firms alike.*

tor/freezers, and ice/beverage dispensers. Nine operating companies comprise this $320-million segment, which includes manufacturing facilities in Wisconsin, Indiana, Tennessee, Oregon, California, China, India, and Italy. With more than 80 distributors serving over 70 countries, Manitowoc is well positioned to serve its growing markets both here and abroad. In addition,

the company's acquisition strategy should enable Manitowoc to draw even closer to its goal of becoming a one-stop source for food- and beverage-cooling equipment.

As it approaches its centennial anniversary, Manitowoc's marine operations continue to thrive. Now located in Sturgeon Bay, Wisconsin; Cleveland, Ohio; and Toledo, Ohio, Manitowoc is the dominant provider of ship-repair, maintenance, conversion, automation, and new-construction services on the Great Lakes. Its facilities, which include a 1,154-foot graving dock, a 113,000-square foot fabrication

shop, and a 200-ton gantry crane, are complemented by the most experienced work force of any Great Lakes shipyard.

Manitowoc's third business segment, cranes and related products, is undoubtedly its best known. With an 80 percent market share in the United States and a 50 percent market share worldwide, Manitowoc is the lattice-boom crane of choice by leading contractors and equipment rental firms alike. Driven by new-product development, which has resulted in a series of innovative breakthrough technologies, Manitowoc cranes provide unmatched versatility, durability, and reliability that enable them to command the industry's highest resale values. Complementing its crawler crane business, Manitowoc also holds a significant share of the North American boom-truck and material-handling market with its Manitex and USTC operations.

Looking toward the future, Manitowoc is poised for phenomenal growth. Acquisitions in all business segments, as well as accelerated new-product development, will help Manitowoc achieve $1.3 billion in sales by the conclusion of 2002. Additionally, continuous improvements designed to streamline productivity will help Manitowoc increase profit margins, a boon to the company and its investors alike.

The result of Manitowoc's ongoing innovation and diversity is a dramatic value-added company where quality, like diversification, is not just a watchword but a way of life. The 3,300 employees of The Manitowoc Company live what is both the firm's tradition and its mission: "...to continuously create value for our shareholders, employees, and customers by focusing our talents, energies, and resources to develop innovative, industry-leading products and services that reflect our core strengths and capabilities."

# Wisconsin Fuel & Light Company

Quite a number of Manitowoc residents still remember the huge gas holding tank on the corner of North 10th and Chicago streets, as it snapped, creaked, and groaned in cold weather, slowly rising or lowering in its massive steel frame as the volume within changed. Today that tank is gone—a testimony to changes in the industry and their impact on the Manitowoc and Wausau divisions of Wisconsin Fuel & Light Company as it continues to adapt to new technologies and to the changing demands of its customers.

In the early years the prime responsibility of the utility was providing gas for street lighting.

Established in 1902 as the Manitowoc Gas Light Company, the firm incorporated in 1907 as The Manitowoc Gas Company, manufacturing coal gas in a plant at 11th and Chicago streets.

The coal gas process consisted of baking soft coal in vertical ovens called "retorts." The gas was then pumped through a purification system into the holding tank and the coke that remained in the ovens was sold as a heating fuel. When the company took on its present name in 1923, the "fuel" referred to coke and the "light" referred to gas-fired lighting.

The Manitowoc plant later installed double-ended retorts from which incandescent coke was

pushed by a machine onto a conveyor belt. In Wausau, "stop-end" retorts required workers to draw the charge by hand with long rakes. At both plants the coal was charged into the retorts by hand and the produced coke was conveyed to stock piles by wheelbarrows.

In the early 1930s a "water gas" plant that combined coal, water, and steam to create a carbon monoxide and hydrogen product was added in Manitowoc to supplement the coal gas plant. The water gas was enriched with oil to increase its heating capability.

In 1947 water gas was replaced with 1300 BTU "propane—air gas." At Wausau propane was used to supplement coal gas in the late 1940s with full conversion to propane in 1952 and the discontinuance of coal gas production at that time.

The choice of 1300 BTU propane at Manitowoc coincided with similar choices in many other cities because of its interchangeability with natural gas. The conversion from manufactured gas to propane required redrilling the ports of customers' appliances and changing the orifice size. The inconvenience of conversion, along with customers' fears resulting from several accidental explosions, resulted in a temporary loss of customers in Manitowoc. In part, the explosions were due to the high heat value and specific gravity of propane. For this reason 650 BTU gas was chosen for Wausau, despite the fact that a second conversion would be required when propane was replaced with natural gas. This safety measure was successful, as no explosions occurred at Wausau during the period of propane use.

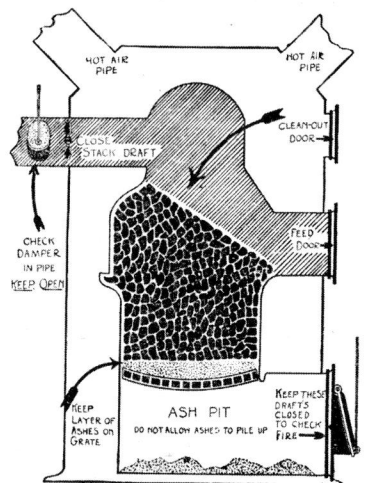
---

*When Wisconsin Fuel & Light Company began its business in Manitowoc in 1903, the "light" in the company's name referred to gaslights. The "fuel" referred to coke, a by-product of the manufactured gas process.*

*Construction of the Michigan-Wisconsin Pipe Line brought Manitowoc access to cheap and plentiful supplies of natural gas beginning in 1950. Prior to that time only manufactured gas was available—an energy source that was far too expensive and limited for extensive industrial uses or home heating the way natural gas is today.*

Natural gas was introduced to most of southern Wisconsin by the Michigan-Wisconsin Pipe Line Company in 1949 but did not reach Manitowoc until late 1950. Most customers were not aware of the changeover since no further conversion was necessary. Rahr Malting Company and Kurth Malting Company were the first customers to receive whole natural gas.

Natural gas represented a nontoxic, clean, safer, and lower-cost replacement for coal gas and propane. Supplying natural gas for industrial, commercial, and residential customers enabled the company to expand rapidly.

In 1944 the common stock of the Manitowoc utility was offered by its parent holding company to the City of Manitowoc. When the city declined to purchase the utility, a group of investors headed by Harry K. Wrench, Sr., of Minneapolis, acquired control. Harry K. Wrench, Jr., came to Manitowoc after the war as company president until 1982, and served on the board of directors until 1994.

The present company resulted from a merger of the separate gas utilities supplying the cities of Manitowoc, on the lakeshore, and Wausau in central Wisconsin. At that time both utilities were about the same size. The names of both, however, have been changed from time to time and both have been affiliated with various holding companies.

The Wausau utility was organized in 1884 as the Wausau Gas Light and Coke Company. In 1950 its assets and liabilities were transferred to Wisconsin Fuel & Light Company and the Wausau company dissolved. The new common stock of Wisconsin Fuel & Light was then offered to the public through the Minneapolis investment banking firm of Kalman and Company. This reduced the stock ownership of the 1944 group to a little more than 50 percent.

Occasional offerings of shares have been made since 1950 but expansion since that time has been financed primarily through retained earnings because of a limited market for the utility's common stock.

Today Wisconsin Fuel & Light Company serves about 48,000 customers through more than 1,060 miles of mains in the Manitowoc and Wausau divisions. Approximately two-thirds of the company's customers, as well as the headquarters functions, are located in Wausau.

Winter heating loads due to the northern climate of the company's service area, and a diversified commercial and industrial market, give the utility an annual throughput of more than 18 million dekatherms. Wisconsin Fuel & Light Company employs approximately 140. Annual revenues now exceed $53 million.

# Manitowoc Custom Molding, Inc.

For many years the manufacturing base of Manitowoc was dominated by three major industries—crane/shipbuilding, brewing/malting, and cookware. This lack of diversity sat hard on the labor market, particularly during the recessions of the 1970s and 1980s, when, at one time, Manitowoc was reported as having the highest unemployment rate in the nation. With those recessions came large corporate mergers and acquisitions, downsizing, and the elimination of many smaller operations within the once-dominant employers. That, in turn, created new need-filling niches for entrepreneurs.

At the dawn of the twenty-first century Manitowoc is booming with business and industrial diversity. Among the entrepreneurs responsible for this prosperous turn of events are James M. LaFond and Philip M. Roll, president and vice-president, respectively, of Manitowoc Custom Molding, Inc.

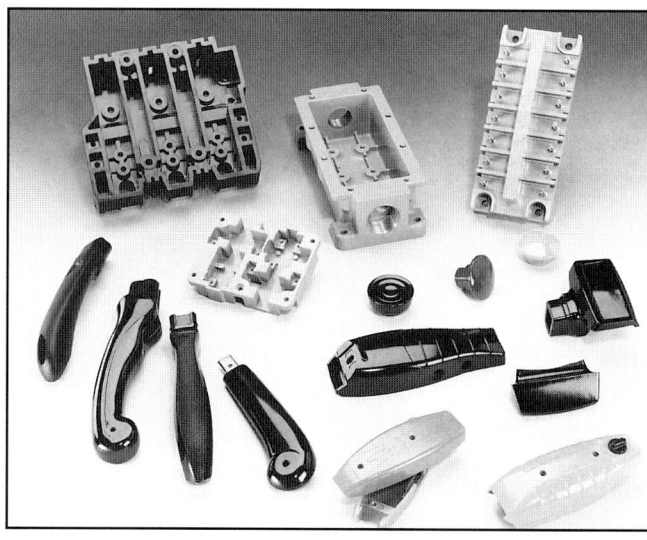

*MCM produces a wide variety of custom-molded thermoset plastic parts for electrical and houseware manufacturers.*

*BELOW: State-of-the-art precision instruments in MCM's quality-control laboratory assure constant compliance with industry standards and customer specifications.*

Jim and Phil found themselves suddenly unemployed in the early 1980s when their employer merged with a larger company and the new management downsized. Undaunted, the two combined their expertise in plastic molding and founded Manitowoc Custom Molding (MCM).

MCM began operations on March 30, 1983. By the end of the year the firm's 16 employees were producing custom-molded thermoset plastic parts for the electrical and houseware industries. Their 14,000-square-foot rented building was rapidly outgrown. Construction began in 1985 on a new 31,000-square-foot facility in the present location. Operations were moved there in February 1986.

In August 1989 MCM received an award presented by Wisconsin Governor Tommy Thompson and *Inc.* magazine publisher Wilson Harrell for ranking 301st on a list of the nation's fastest-growing privately owned companies.

Since then the firm has grown to occupy a modern 65,000-square-foot plant in Manitowoc's southwest side industrial park near the intersection of I-43 and US 151. And MCM has become a leader in thermoset plastic molding, supplying primarily regional customers although its sales territory covers the eastern half of the United States in addition to some export sales to Canada and Mexico.

With an employment level of 130 people and an annual sales volume of $8.5 million, MCM supplies its molded parts to such notable businesses as Rockwell Automation, Eaton Corporation, Deltrol Controls, the Mirro Company, The West Bend Co., Revere Ware Corporation, and Baldwin Piano, among

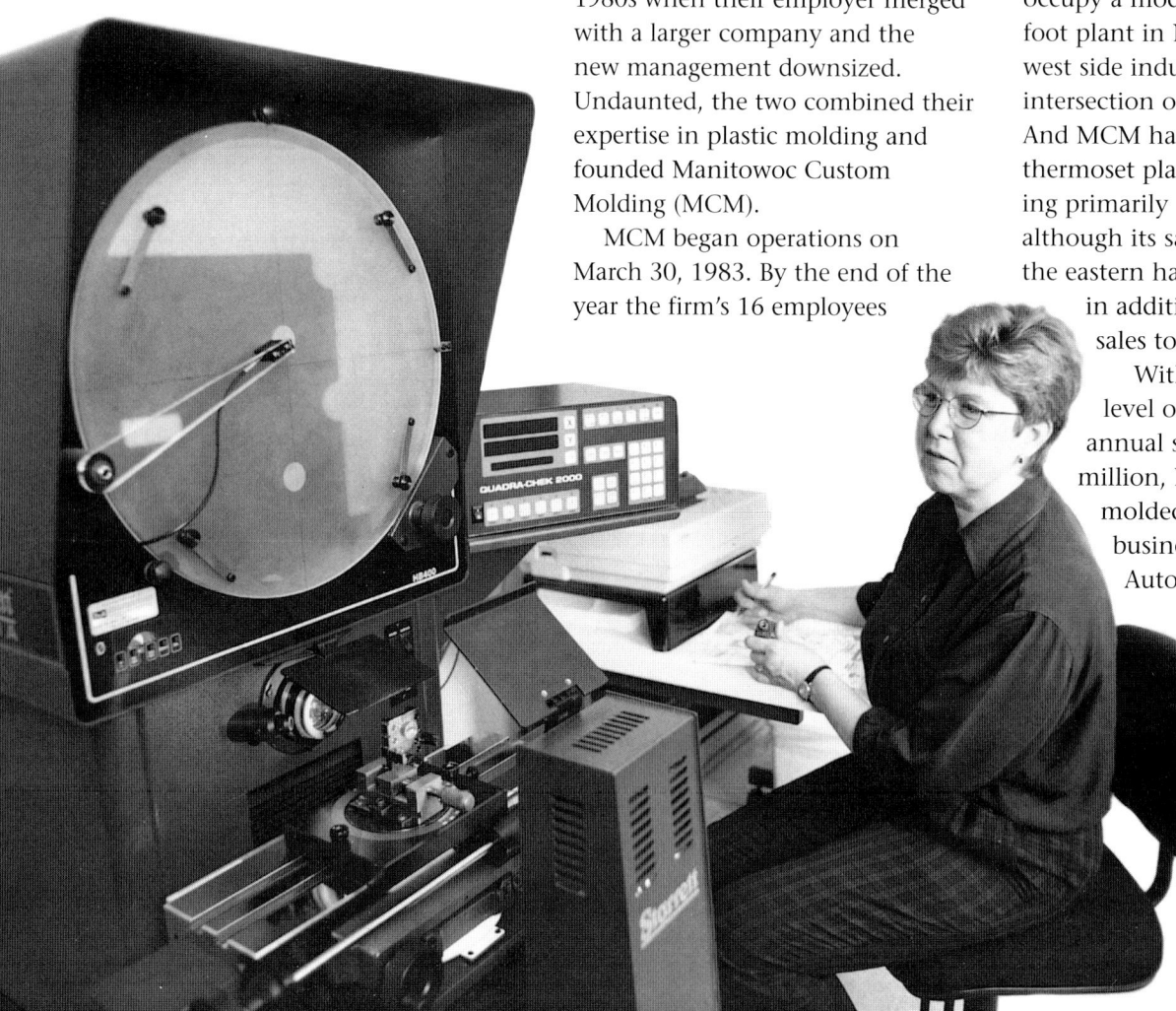

*ABOVE: MCM is equipped to supply a large variety of custom moldings in large or small quantities. Here a worker molds metal inserts into a thermoset plastic part.*

*TOP: Manitowoc Custom Molding's 65,000-square-foot plant is located in the city's southwest industrial park near the junction of I-43 and US 151.*

others. MCM is recognized by Underwriters Laboratory No. B-1277, and is customer certified to Military Standard 45208.

Jim and Phil offer several reasons for the firm's rapid growth. The first is the "initiative of all the people working at MCM." The work force includes a number of minorities "who are good, quality-conscious workers." Despite the fact that some, who do not yet speak English, must take directions through interpreters, "quality parts are produced on time at a competitive price, resulting in increased orders and new customers." Although the workers themselves are responsible for constant quality checks, MCM also maintains a mod-ern quality-control laboratory where state-of-the-art precision instruments are used to verify customer specifications.

A second reason, says Phil Roll, lies in the reduced number of thermoset molders. Thermoset molding of such compounds as phenolics and polyesters requires great precision because that type of material "cures chemically with limited possibilities of reclamation." Produced parts cannot easily be pulverized and reused once the expensive material cures in the molds. "It has to be right the first time."

A third reason, according to Jim LaFond, "is the break-up of companies that used to produce, in-house, all the components for their own manufacturing. Corporate self-sufficiency has given way to 'outsourcing' so companies like MCM are filling a growing need for parts supply."

Finally, high labor intensity, concern about environmental contamination, and the inherent difficulty of working with the material required to produce custom molded parts are other reasons competition has dwindled—once again creating a niche for companies such as MCM. In a given year MCM will produce 1,000 or more different items, in quantities from one to one million. Many of these include metal inserts and MCM maintains a large inventory of inserts in order to meet just-in-time production and maintain its reputation for on-time delivery to customers.

Keeping a close eye on both economic and technological trends, Phil Roll actively served on industry and educational boards and committees. He has served on the advisory board for the Milwaukee section of the Society of Plastic Engineers and has held office in the National Society of Plastics Engineers/Thermoset Division. Lakeshore Technical College has benefited from his involvement on the advisory committee for the Plastics Technician Program, as has the University of Wisconsin planning committee for the Annual Thermoset Molding Conference, which is sponsored by the university's College of Engineering, Department of Engineering Professional Development.

MCM is well equipped to supply the needs of its customers. Major equipment includes compression/transfer presses ranging from 50 to 800 tons, and injection machines from 75 to 475 tons. A complete machine shop is capable of servicing customers' tools and molds.

Jim and Phil are rightfully proud of their company, their workers, and themselves. They show it in their smiles, their friendly conversation, and their eagerness to answer questions in detail as they conduct tours of the plant for existing and prospective customers. Arrangements for such tours are made at the customers' convenience.

# Eck Industries

In the early summer of 1984 a disastrous fire destroyed 50 percent of Eck Industries' foundry. Fortunately the office area and customers' tooling were not destroyed. The 36-year-old business, a mainstay in the manufacturing economy of Manitowoc, appeared ruined. Then something miraculous occurred.

Almost as soon as the last flame had been doused, with twisted steel and debris still too hot to touch, company employees and community volunteers turned out to clean up the mess. A major contractor interrupted its entire summer's contracted work to put its machinery and crews to building a new plant. Several major customers arranged inventory and vacation shut-down weeks to give Eck Industries as much time as they could afford to recover and resume shipments.

In the midst of clean up and new construction, some production was under way in three days. In 10 days orders were being filled and shipped from a plant that did not yet have a completed roof! Fortunately, the summer of 1984 was unusually dry. By the time the annual rains of September came, most operations were covered.

The tremendous response of employees and managers, family members, community, and customers to what otherwise might have been a disaster, speaks volumes about the high demand for the quality products for which Eck Industries is noted. In addition to many other items, Eck supplies cast aluminum cylinder heads for Teledyne Continental aircraft engines. Aviation safety and reliability require a level of quality that few manufacturers are willing to achieve, much less maintain year after year. Because Eck consistently maintains those standards, the firm was able to supply the military with aircraft and missile castings in the 1950s and 1960s, parts for M-60 tanks in the

*A downtown Manitowoc promotional display of Eck Foundries products as they appeared in the mid-1950s.*

1970s, and parts for the Abraham heavy tank and Bradley fighting vehicle in the 1980s and 1990s.

The same is true for the cylinder heads and engine casings Eck produces for Harley-Davidson and Mercury Marine. These types of engines require "fin" cylinder heads for air cooling. The castings are poured into intricately detailed molds made of a sand and chemical mixture that hardens when exposed to air. The mold is destroyed, however, by removal of the aluminum casting so the next casting requires a new mold. Hence, making molds at Eck has been perfected to an industrial art matching the company's equally precise process of casting.

Such was the vision shared by William Eck, Walter Davidson, Robert Davidson, and Andrew Bell when they opened Eck Foundries on June 1, 1948, in the former garage of the Kasper Construction Company on North Eighth Street. Steady growth followed.

Today Philip Eck is president and

*The original home of Eck Foundries, the former garage of the Kasper Construction Company, as it appeared in 1955. Everything behind the small office building in front was destroyed by the 1984 fire, then replaced by the present factory which contains five times the floor space of the old garage.*

Robert Eck is chairman and CEO, and the company supplies more than 100 active accounts including the production of cylinder heads for Winston Cup race cars through contracts with Ford and General Motors. Eck Industries celebrated its 50th anniversary in August 1998 with a dinner and a tour of customer product displays, including the Plymouth Prowler—

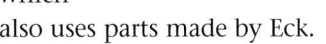

which also uses parts made by Eck.

Eck Foundries officially became Eck Industries in 1981, when an interest in the die casting operation of Scherer Die Casting in Cedarburg was moved from its location in Grafton to Manitowoc. Further diversification came three years later, when Eck Industries purchased the former Consumers Steel Company and changed its name to Consumers, Inc., under the current presidency of David Eck.

Consumers, Inc., carries into steel the same traditions of metallurgical engineering, design, craftsmanship, and quality that have been hallmarks of the Eck family's aluminum casting endeavors. Solar collectors, playground equipment, automated material-handling systems, and postal service collection boxes are but a few of the many custom steel fabrications produced by Consumers. Many of these fabrications are for larger vehicles such as engine bases and fuel tanks for the famous cranes of Manitowoc Engineering Company.

For several years Consumers manufactured hydraulic lifts for Gilbarco, an automotive supplier. In 1991 Gilbarco was purchased and the hydraulic lifts renamed "Manitowoc Lifts." These lifts are now major items in Consumers' production, including its patented "AMS-20" mobile work station. The AMS-20 contains its own hydraulic lift for automotive engine and transaxle assembly removal from beneath the vehicle. The mobile work station is extremely popular with major automotive service buyers as it is designed to be operated safely by one person, considerably reducing the time and labor costs of such operations.

Eck Industries, both the aluminum foundry and Consumers steelworks, are active supporters of continual improvement through education and training as sponsors of the Youth Apprenticeship program at Lakeshore Technical College. In addition, the Eck Family Scholarship program provides stipends each April to students majoring in engineering. Priority is given to the children of Eck Industries and Consumers, Inc., employees, but when scholarships are not assigned to these, consideration is given to high school students residing in Manitowoc County.

Philip Eck gives the employees credit for the continued success of Eck Industries. "Be fair and be truthful to both your employees and customers," he advises. That attitude probably explains why today's vibrant Eck Industries rose again like a phoenix from the ashes of 1984.

---

*LEFT: The engine block and cylinders of the Teledyne Continental aircraft engine are aluminum castings supplied by Eck Industries.*

*BELOW: Eck Industries has been a major supplier of cast aluminum parts for Harley-Davidson motorcycles since 1949.*

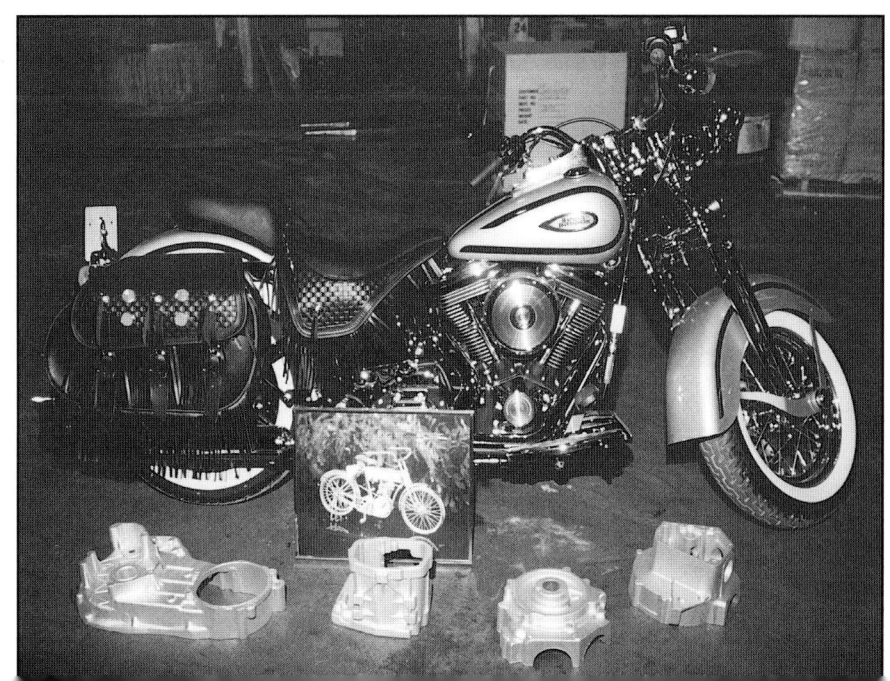

# Insulation and Supply Company, Inc.

Some businesses are named for their founders, others for what they do, and still others have names that are worth exploring. Insulation and Supply Company, Inc., is one such business. Founded in 1948, this firm, still privately owned, is a bit of an enigma. First, it hasn't sold insulation since 1957, when Edward D. and Kathryn Oswald purchased it from Henry M. Wyatt; and second, the supply side of the company is strongly overshadowed by products not even intimated in the name.

Insulation and Supply is one of only two Formica wholesalers in Wisconsin, and it maintains the largest inventory of imported and domestic ceramic tile north of Milwaukee. In fact, if you headed to Insulation and Supply's 48,000-square-foot facility in Manitowoc, or to one of its 10,000-square-foot showrooms and warehouses in Green Bay or Appleton, you'd find more than two million square feet of Formica laminate and 1.5 million square feet of ceramic floor and wall tile.

Insulation and Supply boasts three showrooms that can spark the creativity of any homeowner. The showrooms feature dazzling displays of kitchen counter tops of Formica Surell solid surfaces and plastic lam-inates, Lippert vanity tops, decorative tile installations, and fireplace hearths featuring marble imported from all over the world. Yet, you will leave only with ideas, for Insulation and Supply is strictly in the wholesale business.

When you're ready to buy, any of the company's 1,300 customers in Wisconsin and the Upper Peninsula of Michigan will be happy to accommodate you. The Manitowoc wholesaler creates custom tile sample cards for each retailer, contractor, or installer, offering a glimpse of the more than 75 different lines of ceramic and porcelain tiles. And if that retail establishment doesn't have something you've seen, just ask. Insulation and Supply maintains its own fleet of trucks to deliver to its customers every day.

Yes, every day. This company has a staff that has successfully anticipated home and business owners' desires for decades. The firm annually imports 50 containers of ceramic tile from Italy, Spain, Korea, and Brazil, so Insulation and Supply has what you want—before you know you want it.

Omniscient? Probably not. Experienced? Absolutely. Ed Oswald joined Insulation and Supply in 1949. Warehouse manager Don Marquardt signed on in 1951.

"Most of our 32 employees have been with us 15 or 20 years," says Ed. That's why we're doing as well as we are."

Yes, the company has passed a number of significant milestones since the Oswalds bought the business. Ed remembers when his ambition was to gross $100,000 in a single year. At the close of the twentieth century, annual sales have topped $9 million, and the business continues to grow.

Insulation and Supply experiences such continual growth, at least in part, because Ed is a careful, conscientious businessman. "Pay your bills on time, no matter what," he counsels.

Internally, communication is the key. The offices feature lots of glass, so management, administrative, sales, and customer service personnel are all easily accessible to one another. Additionally, one wall of the warehouse is decorated with the logos of the products the firm sells, to remind everyone at Insulation and Supply of all they offer.

With much smaller profit margins than those of retail establishments, Ed realizes everyone at

*Insulation and Supply's Manitowoc facility spans 48,000 square feet.*

LEFT: *The company has three showrooms—in Manitowoc, Green Bay, and Appleton—displaying a wide variety of kitchen counter tops, vanity tops, and decorative tile installations.*

BELOW: *One of only two Formica wholesalers in Wisconsin, Insulation and Supply maintains an inventory of more than two million square feet of the laminate as well as 1.5 million square feet of ceramic tile.*

the door automatically drops, protecting everyone in the facility from a potentially toxic combination of chemicals.

Insulation and Supply also specializes in boat interiors. The firm supplies major Wisconsin yacht

Insulation and Supply must work hard to enable the business to grow. He and Kathryn are confident that it will, even as they prepare for retirement. Sons Alan, vice president and general manager, and Steven, vice president and sales manager, are prepared to take over management, and son-in-law Scott Huebner, salesman for the Milwaukee-Madison area, works diligently with the rest of the sales force to keep Insulation and Supply a steady supplier for an ever-growing customer base.

The company maintains its enviable position as a leading flooring, counter top, and tile distributor not only because of savvy purchasing decisions, a customer service-oriented sales staff, and quality merchandise, but because of the additional products and services it offers and its willingness to venture into new markets.

Insulation and Supply sells the adhesives that contractors need to affix tiles and laminates to applicable substrates. This end of the business is a specialty unto itself. It's not simply a matter of selling pails of glue or cement. The company's sales staff and customer service rep-

resentatives must know which adhesives work best in a variety of applications. Some adhesives are sold to flooring installers and kitchen and bath remodeling contractors, but others are sold to office furniture manufacturers. It's also a matter of knowing how to store the adhesives. Insulation and Supply stores all adhesives in a room with an automatic door. If any of the substances begin to leak,

builders with tile, solid surface, and laminate counter tops, vanities, and flooring.

True, the name Insulation and Supply does not begin to describe what is sold at 1129 South 41st Street in Manitowoc, but this is a company that does its job so well that when people see the name, they think of creative decorating and design, and the quality products to bring the designs to life.

# HUI

HUI has been a mainstay of Kiel, indeed a cornerstone of southwest Manitowoc County, since it was founded by German immigrant Albert Deibele, Sr., in 1933, but it certainly isn't the same company today. What once was a retail appliance store and later a residential and commercial electric and sheet metal contracting business has evolved into a state-of-the-art contract metal fabricator.

What prompted such change? Certainly, the people involved. Albert Sr. and his eldest son and successor, Albert Jr., focused on the residential and commercial contracting end of the business. When Albert Jr. died unexpectedly in 1989, his younger brother Charles took over the reins. His first task as president was to clarify HUI's direction. Within months the contracting segment was sold to another company, refocusing HUI's attention to contract metal fabricating, a business that Charles believed had great potential.

Since 1990 HUI has experienced significant growth. In eight years HUI revenues have more than tripled, employment more than doubled, and the facility has grown to more than 70,000 square feet.

"Our vision is to be the 'Company of Choice' in all that we do today and tomorrow," explains Charles Deibele.

Of course, that's not an easy task when you do as many different things as HUI does. The firm specializes in complete fabrication from engineered design and prototype development through manufacturing, powder coating, assembly, packaging, and delivery. And HUI does all that and more for a host of diverse original equipment manufacturers (OEMs)—including makers of industrial equipment and institutional seating, lawn tractors and outboard engines.

To become its customers' company of choice, HUI has invested heavily in both people and equipment. Kurt Bell joined the company in 1993, becoming president in 1996. "HUI has always had a great group of people," says Kurt Bell. "The trick has been to focus on what we want to do as a group and for which customers."

HUI invested heavily in state-of-the-art fabrication equipment and the most innovative manufacturing processes. The company is totally aligned to cellular manufacturing throughout, providing the highest levels of overall customer service.

The only shared services with the cells are the environmentally friendly powder coating department and

the just-in-time warehousing facilities based on the Japanese Kanban philosophy.

Powder coating is an electrostatic painting process that is virtually emissions free. Unlike traditional wet painting, there are no dangerous solvents released into the air. With this innovative method, HUI is able to consistently provide superior, long-lasting powder coatings in a variety of standard or custom colors.

HUI's Kanban practices ensure that customers will have their products when they need them. This innovation in the realm of just-in-

time delivery manifests itself in the warehouse portion of a 10,000-square-foot shipping and receiving facility. Parts manufactured to standing orders are carefully staged where they await the customer's request. "We have the part today, so our customer will have it tomorrow," explains Charles.

All this could not happen without incredible internal communications and training. After all, when your manufacturing methods are different than those at most of the companies in the area, you need to carefully train and support your work force. Extensive training programs are conducted on-site for all

*HUI is totally aligned to cellular manufacturing, providing the highest possible levels of customer service.*

*RIGHT: The company specializes in powder coating, an electrostatic painting process that is virtually emissions free.*

employees. Topics include blueprint reading, cellular manufacturing training, and team development.

HUI also supports its employees' educational endeavors at local technical schools and colleges. In fact, it established the Allen Arnold Scholarship in memory of a past HUI team member. This $2,000

*HUI's facility in Kiel has grown to more than 70,000 square feet.*

about our performance," Charles continues. "We share financial information. Everyone has the opportunity to ask questions and participate."

And while the employees are considering the financial health of the company, HUI is considering the physical and emotional well-being of its employees and their families. An on-site fitness center is open to the HUI family around the clock. "We're a very progressive company," explains Charles.

Certainly, HUI is progressive in terms of technology, and in its management and manufacturing philosophies, but it is also progressive in human resources terms. "We have strong, consistent values," Charles says. "We work hard on the soft side of business. Synergy is achieved when the culture is aligned with this vision."

annual scholarship is awarded to a graduating high school senior for further education. The scholarship continues for the student for up to four years.

The company offers a number of other benefits to employees and their families that make HUI an especially desirable place to work. "We run three shifts, five days a week, with voluntary Saturdays," says Charles, "and even in this tight employment environment we have people in reserve. Our regular rates of pay are at market levels, and our incentive variable pay takes us

above market. We have a strong benefits package and a modern, clean facility."

True, many of those benefits are available at other places, and HUI is certainly not the only company to offer all of them. But for HUI, that's only the beginning. "We empower our employees. We shut down the company for our monthly InfoShare meetings. We talk about our customers' requirements, and

# Holiday House of Manitowoc County, Inc.

*I*n the movie *It's a Wonderful Life* Jimmy Stewart is shown by an angel what his town would be like if the hero had never been born. It would be hard to imagine what Manitowoc would be like if Holiday House of Manitowoc County, Inc., did not exist.

More than an enterprise that provides opportunities for people who

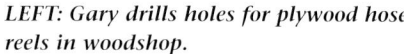

*ABOVE: Holiday House is located at 2818 Meadow Lane in Manitowoc.*

*LEFT: Gary drills holes for plywood hose reels in woodshop.*

experience barriers to employment due to disability or other disadvantages, Holiday House is an indispensable contributor to the economic health of life in Manitowoc County.

The industrious firm creates work opportunities for approximately 200 client-workers and 80 staff personnel by fulfilling the outsourcing needs of about 55 business and manufacturing companies in the lakeshore area.

A tour of Holiday House's main plant on Meadow Lane in Manitowoc or Plant 2 on South 13th Street will find workers involved in light assembly and fabricating, packaging and heat sealing, collating, labeling, and shipping. Others can

be seen working on recycling lines at the MRF (Manitowoc County Recycling Facility). Yet another set of workers can be found assisting tourists and maintaining the building and grounds at the I-43 Rest Areas located between Manitowoc and Green Bay.

Additionally, throughout most of its 42-year history, Holiday House has provided job placement and support services for disabled individuals who have been interested in working in employment situations throughout the community at large.

Holiday House's primary mission is to provide opportunities for disabled or disadvantaged individuals to work and, therein, experience the dignity and sense of accomplish-

ment that comes from earning a paycheck. The multifaceted operation is a bit of tapestry woven with homespun cooperative effort between townsfolk, government, businesses, industry, and people with philanthropic inclinations.

The story of Holiday House is not limited to its industrial operations. The organization recognizes the positive impact of early intervention in the development of infants and young children, both those who show typical growth patterns as well as those who have special needs. Consequently, it provides inclusive child-care services for children ranging in age from four weeks to nine years at the organization's Kueter Child Development Center located on Johnston Drive in Manitowoc.

People in the general public who experience hearing loss can find a variety of resources through Holiday House's Program on Hearing Loss and Deafness. Training is provided in the use of assistive-listening and alerting devices. Other services provided include interpreting and instruction in American Sign Language.

How did Holiday House get its unique name? The answer has everything to do with a wreath, a dream, and a philosophy. Intrigued? Holiday House welcomes visitors.

# Wisconsin Aluminum Foundry

*I*f you have an All-American no-gasket pressure cooker in your kitchen, it was made in Manitowoc by Wisconsin Aluminum Foundry. Established in 1908 by Abraham Schwartz as a small aluminum and brass foundry, WAF is now one of the largest privately owned nonferrous foundries in the United States. Of Abraham and Martha Schwartz's eight children, sons Meyer, Harry, Bernard, and Milton eventually joined their father in the business.

Irwin and Byron, sons of Meyer and Harry Schwartz, respectively, joined WAF in the 1950s. Irwin was president at the time of his death in 1997. Michael Schwartz joined the foundry in 1966 and is the current president. Phil Jacobs, son-in-law of Bernard Schwartz, joined in 1969 and became manager of the Consumer Products Division. David, son of Milton Schwartz, joined in

1983. Milton Schwartz remains active as the company's secretary and treasurer.

The All-American pressure cooker and a small line of "Chef-Way Cookware" were added in 1929 as the family owners began to diversify their company's product line. The WAF cookware line today is known as "Chef's Design," and the pressure cookers are still manufactured as they were in 1929—without a gasket. Also, using the castings from the pressure cooker, the foundry produces a line of electric and non-electric sterilizers.

A series of expansions was begun in 1979 to make the foundry more automated and competitive. That growth greatly increased its capacity and led to

the opening of new markets in sand and permanent mold castings, and brass and bronze sand castings. WAF's base consists of a wide variety of companies throughout the United States, with the major concentration on the production of various types of engine components. The firm's Consumer Products Division exports worldwide.

The unique strength of Wisconsin Aluminum Foundry is found in its versatility and industry-recognized casting know-how. From small-volume custom work to large-volume production runs, WAF is proud to still service some of the same customers it began with more than 90 years ago.

*This unique aluminum casting was made by WAF for the Kissel Car Co. in 1919.*

# Jagemann Plating Company

Joseph C. Jagemann founded Jagemann Plating Company in 1945 with a simple philosophy: Give the best quality and service possible, at a competitive price. That philosophy has stood the test of time for this growing company. When a business provides 100 percent service to industries that demand perfection, that's especially important. As an electroplating company, Jagemann Plating adds the finishing touches to other manufacturers' products.

The process is seemingly straightforward. Metal parts of all sorts, from cookware to computer parts to automotive components, arrive at the receiving dock; are cleaned, dipped in an acid to activate the electrostatic plating, then plated in zinc, nickel, nickel chrome, or copper; rinsed, dried, and packed for return to the manufacturers; or drop shipped to third parties. The plating process changes the molecular structure of the base metal, bonding the corrosion-resistant plating with the metal so it doesn't chip or scratch off.

When you plate items ranging in size from small nuts and bolts to 12-foot parts, however, any notion of straightforwardness is quickly eliminated. Jagemann Plating runs multiple plating lines. Smaller parts are placed in barrels; larger parts are hung individually on rack units, conveyors that carry the parts from tank to tank.

Jagemann Plating also offers baking. This process, used primarily on fasteners (nuts, bolts, and screws), essentially bakes the hydrogen out of the metal. If hydrogen remains in the metal, the parts may become brittle.

Now, more than 50 years and 10 expansions later, the basic processes remain much the same as when Joe ran the plating line, but so much else has changed. The original facility was the size of a two-car garage. Now the modern plant spans 70,000 square feet and is located in a mixed residential and industrial zone with easy access to both local industry and the interstate highway.

Joe died in 1974 and his son Arthur became president and chief executive officer two years later. As the twentieth century draws to a close, Art has turned over the day-to-day operations of the business to his three sons: Scott, president and general manager; Michael, executive vice president; and David, vice president of sales. All of the Jagemanns started their careers on the plating lines and continue to be hands-on managers, working closely with engineers and platers to deliver the best possible service to all of their customers, whatever the product.

*This 1993 photo pictures (from left to right) David Jagemann, vice president of sales; Arthur Jagemann, chief executive officer; Michael Jagemann, executive vice president; Jim Jagemann, production manager; Scott Jagemann, president; and Greg Omernick, vice president, deceased.*

*ABOVE: The company's warehouse is full of customer orders to process.*

*ABOVE RIGHT: Jagemann Plating, located at 1324 South 26th Street in Manitowoc, has a fleet of 10 trucks to pick up and deliver product throughout its territory on a daily basis.*

This third-generation family-owned business is beating the odds by being the best at what it does, offering more value-added services for its customers throughout Wisconsin and Northern Illinois. Jagemann Plating has added a fleet of 10 trucks that pick up and deliver product throughout its territory on a daily basis. It also operates around the clock, seven days a week, and thus has reduced the industry standard of three to four weeks' turnaround to less than one week. Parts arriving in the plant Thursday or Friday typically are delivered back to the manufacturer the following Monday.

Being fast and efficient is not enough for this atypical plating company. Jagemann is quality driven as well. All phases of the process operate under strict statistical process control and all lots plated have thicknesses checked hourly. Salt spray testing, typically for automotive or marine products, is performed as required. Finally, quality-control audit inspections are performed on every job before

it leaves the plant.

Such quality standards demand a comprehensive on-site training program. Initial training programs are individualized for each new plater, and generally range from six months to one year. That is only the beginning. All 180 employees are encouraged to attend monthly supervisor training. And Jagemann Plating encourages and compensates employees seeking additional training at area technical colleges or universities.

Industrial integrity goes beyond issues of quality services, on-time delivery, and competitive prices. At Jagemann Plating integrity

includes environmental steward-ship. The plant is well ventilated and the air is scrubbed before it is released from the plant, dramatically setting this company apart from its competitors.

However, it is the extraordinary wastewater-treatment system that is most noticed outside the plant. The system exceeds local, state, and federal environmental standards, resulting in water that often is cleaner when it leaves the plant than when it arrives. This is especially important since municipal wastewater treatment facilities are not designed to treat for metals.

Jagemann Plating's stewardship extends beyond the community's water and air supplies. The company's test tube logo is emblazoned across many youth basketball and softball jerseys, for Jagemann staunchly supports community sports activities, and cultural events and venues.

Indeed, Jagemann Plating Company has grown based on its ability to develop partnerships with its customers, its employees, and its community, partnerships that will endure far into the future.

*Jagemann's state-of-the-art wastewater-treatment system ensures compliance with today's clean water standards, and shows the firm's commitment to the environment now and in the future.*

# The Cawley Company

Chances are good that the quality name badges you noticed on the lapels of employees around the world were made by The Cawley Company of Manitowoc. More than 90 percent of the firm's business comes from name badges and personalized plates. The remaining 10 percent comes from the gift line, the original founding interest.

In 1946 attorney Mike Cawley established the enterprise in Chicago but soon moved it to Manitowoc. He and his wife imported religious items from Europe to fill a 50-page catalog until 1968, when the company was purchased by James and Warren Kanzelberger. Designer Bill Deau became a part owner and the product line changed from imported religious goods to manufactured social theme items for anniversaries, births, baptisms, weddings, graduations, and the like.

A number of Cawley customers owned hot stamping machines. Others expressed interest in being able to personalize gifts. In response, the company designed and patented the Thermal Engraver and Flex-Plates. Coined metal plates for gift plaques and name badges for retailers were added at that time.

As the name badge and personalizing business grew, additional markets were opened. Ace Hardware, Walgreens, TruServ, trophy dealers, and other customers helped establish The Cawley Company as a gift and personalizing system manufacturer with a network of more than 70 independent sales representatives across the United States and Canada.

In the mid-1980s, under the leadership of James Kanzelberger and James Peterson, the firm shifted its focus to the name badge business. The Cawley Company then targeted the hospitality industry (restaurants, hotels, casinos, resorts, and cruise ships) for sales of the Thermal Engraver, providing the way for customers to produce their own badges.

The Cawley Company became a distributor for Brother International, a manufacturer of labeling machines, in 1991 and introduced a textured plate that enables customers to produce name badges instantly. Additional patents, trademarks, and copyrights followed.

Under its current leadership of Rebel Kanzelberger and James Peterson, Cawley ships its products throughout the United States and to more than 50 foreign countries. The company celebrated its 50th anniversary in 1996, and the following year it was awarded Wisconsin Governor Tommy Thompson's Excellence Award for export shipping.

Among those strengths is an employee-friendly workplace. "Our people are craftsmen and -women," says Peterson. "We are justifiably proud of what we accomplish together, and as individuals. This, no doubt, is the basis for the worldwide reputation for quality and service Cawley products enjoy. We are fortunate that we seldom need to advertise for help, as our employees are our best recruiters."

*These models represent the types of customers served by The Cawley Company. From left to right are a waitress, a golf pro from American Golf, an Avis Rental Car representative, a ski patrolman from the Boreal Ski Area, a nurse from The Forum by Marriott, a blackjack dealer from Rio Casino, a bellman from Hotel Intercontinental, a food server from Burger King, and a wine steward from Royal Caribbean International.*

# Rockwell Lime Company

One of Wisconsin's largest surviving dolomitic lime producers is the Rockwell Lime Company. Its corporate offices, quality-control laboratory, and operations are located on 300 acres in the village of Rockwood just north of Manitowoc.

Founded in 1906 by Michael Brisch, his three brothers, and a group of Chicagoland contractors, Rockwell began with a single kiln that daily produced only a few tons. Four wood-fired shaft kilns were built in 1908 but by 1948 they had been converted to gas, followed shortly by the installation of a gas-fired rotary kiln.

Except for kiln technology, lime production has not changed much over the years. Dynamite blasts still echo in the firm's quarry—one of only a few sources of pure dolomite (calcium/magnesium limestone) in the Midwest, according to Rockwell president James Brisch. Blasted stone is crushed and screened in different size products. A majority of the sized stone is fed into the kiln.

The kiln is a slowly turning cylinder resting on its side at a slight angle. Exhaust fans draw the combustion gases through a dust collector to prevent air pollution. The temperature inside the kiln reaches 2,300 degrees Fahrenheit, burning off carbon dioxide until the limestone is converted into quicklime. The quicklime is mixed with water in a pressure vessel and converted into hydrated lime. Packed in bags or sold in bulk, the company's products are shipped to nearly every part of the United States as well as Canada and offshore islands.

The Allwood Lime Company, adjacent to the present plant, was purchased in 1949. Expansion continued with the installation of a 100-ton-per-day kiln in 1952, and a 300-ton-per-day kiln and pressure hydrator in 1979. A quality-control laboratory was established in 1983, and Rockwell achieved ISO-9002 certification on its quicklime process in 1998.

Lime has many applications. Rockwell's products are used in the smelting and refining of steel, in the making of mortar products, and in the environmental neutralization of certain waste products.

Ownership and management of Rockwell is now entering its third generation. Joseph G. Brisch is chairman of the board, James J. Brisch is the current president, Donald R. Brisch serves as the vice president of operations, and Joseph H. Brisch is the executive vice president. The company employs 48 and uses a network of sales representatives throughout the United States to sell its products.

---

*The lime plant in the village of Rockwood, north of Manitowoc, viewed from in front of Rockwell's corporate headquarters.*

*INSET: After blasting, chunks of limestone were loaded in "drays" and drawn out of the quarry by mules, as seen in this photo taken by* Manitowoc Herald-Times *photographer Lou Fandrick in 1949, just before the changeover to motorized equipment.*

# Dayco Eastman Company

Anyone who has struggled with a leaky garden hose whose swaged coupling has popped off under the minimal 50- to 60-pound pressure of city water supply can certainly appreciate the difficulty of containing hydraulic pressure. The flexible hoses and couplings of so much hydraulic machinery today, from pickup truck bumper-mounted snowplows to huge industrial lifts and cranes, must safely and reliably contain tons of pressure. The employees of Dayco Eastman produce what they believe are the world's most reliable high-pressure couplings and hoses. They may be right, considering the fact that their employer, an industry leader, has outpaced the competition for 100 years.

Dayco Eastman actually had its beginnings in two separate companies. Imperial Brass of Chicago, a

Windiate Building at the diagonal junction of Menasha Avenue and North 11th Street.

The two enterprises merged to form Imperial Eastman in 1961. A period of aggressive growth followed, establishing the company as a technological and market leader in the fluid connector field. Imperial Eastman Canada opened that same year to service the Canadian market with both products of the merged organization.

In 1962 the firm developed the first field hose assembly machine for permanently attached high-pressure hose couplings. This was a revolutionary product as it provided a tool that could be used by cus-

---

*Dayco Eastman's connectors plant is located in Manitowoc on North 24th Street just south of the airport.*

joint ventures were established in the United Kingdom, Japan, Australia, Mexico, Brazil, and Germany, gaining access to international markets.

Imperial Eastman, through a joint venture with Techo-Chemi (a German company), transferred thermoplastic hose and tubing technology to the United States in 1963. The following year the company began producing thermoplastic "Hytron" hose and tubing in limited quantities, and in 1967 a thermoplastic hose plant was constructed at the 24th Street location (now the pneumatics machining area).

In the late 1970s and early 1980s Imperial Eastman again captured industry leadership in the development of a patented "hybrid" hose capable of a tighter radius while operating at higher pressure. The

manufacturer of pneumatic brass valves and fittings, was founded in 1905, and Eastman Manufacturing Company of Manitowoc began producing fluid connectors in 1914. The latter was founded by a small group of investors under Eastman family leadership. An advertisement in a 1930 edition of the *Manitowoc Herald-News* (now the *Herald Times Reporter*) listed J. Peter Eastman as general manager under a picture of the original factory, the still-extant

tomers in the field to make hose assemblies at low cost rather than buying more expensive factory-made assemblies. The concept has been adopted by all major competitors and today is a significant marketing tool throughout the industry.

Many new and advanced tube fitting products such as heavy-duty, flexible, and high-seal fittings were developed and produced at Imperial Eastman's Chicago location during the 1960s. Also during this period

company developed a revolutionary manufacturing process that enhanced machine productivity and efficiency, enabling the hose to be made with a lower labor input, in a smaller manufacturing space, and without the large assets required by conventional processes. A number of new designs emerged from this process, permanently changing high-pressure hose construction in the industry. Hoses with smaller diameters, higher

*Construction of the firm's new hose plant on Dufek Drive in Manitowoc's I-43 Industrial Park was completed in September 1995, although production actually began there in July.*

working pressures, and longer lines could now be produced.

Imperial Eastman merged with I-T-E Circuit Breaker Company in 1971 to form the I-T-E Imperial Corporation. Five years later the business was acquired by Gould, Inc. In 1981 Gould's interest was bought out by management and renamed Imperial Clevite. Imperial Clevite was then taken public in 1986 under the name Clevite Industries. At that time most of the

foreign joint ventures were sold. However, the company continues to supply the export market with metric couplings in British, Japanese, French, and German standards.

Pullman acquired Clevite in 1987, and Pullman was acquired a year later by investor affiliates of Forstmann, Little & Company.

In 1996 Mark IV Industries purchased Imperial Eastman and along with its subsidiary, Dayco Industrial, formed the Fluid Power Business Unit of Dayco Industrial known as Dayco Eastman. The Chicago branch of Imperial Eastman merged with Manitowoc at that time. Dayco Industrial changed Manitowoc's Imperial Eastman's name to Dayco Eastman in 1997, maintaining the

historic memory of the original founding family.

Presently there are two plants in Manitowoc: the connectors plant on North 24th Street (just south of the airport), and the new hose plant on Dufek Drive in Manitowoc's I-43 Industrial Park. Although construction of the hose plant was not finished until September 1995, production there actually began in July.

The hose plant is especially equipped to produce Dayco Eastman's "Eliminator" line of hoses. Here, the company's uniquely developed manufacturing processes come together to make a highly efficient product. In the "Eliminator," for example, an oil-resistant elastomer "core" eliminates the use of a mandrel, resulting in a seamless tube free of material contaminants. Unlike some conventional SAE-standard hoses which contain four layers of spiral-wire reinforcement, Dayco's "Eliminator" has just two layers of super-high interwoven tensile steel reinforcement. This results in lower cost, smaller outside diameter, and considerable weight reduction, while still pressure testing beyond SAE specifications for similar hoses. This is especially attractive to manufacturers of heavy industrial and farm equipment whose designs often leave little room for weightier and less resilient hydraulic lines and connections.

"We will be the dominant power transfer and fluid-handling supplier in targeted industrial markets around the world by the year 2001," expresses the global vision of Dayco Eastman today, whose mission is to "ensure customer satisfaction by providing highly valued engineered systems, products, and services rapidly and profitably." One of Manitowoc's largest employers, Dayco Eastman has earned an international reputation for product quality, safety, and reliability that remains unsurpassed.

# Zenith Sintered Products, Inc.

Would you believe that the crankshaft in your car's engine may be held in place by powder? Just imagine bearings, gears, plates, and a multiplicity of other hard metal parts made from molded powdered metal that, in its raw state, has the consistency and feel of talcum powder.

Traditional parts-making processes start with hard metal castings, then grind, mill, and drill to shape the finished product. Powdered metal parts are molded under tremendous pressure, then "sintered" by the application of extreme heat that literally welds the molecular particles together, producing parts that need little or no additional machining.

That efficient, cost-cutting fact alone may explain the growing demand by major auto and machinery manufacturers for parts made by the sintering process. It was just such a market demand that brought Zenith Sintered Products, Inc., to Manitowoc in 1997. Construction on the 72,000-square-foot-plant, located on Vits Drive in the I-43 Industrial Park, began in July, with production getting under way in March 1998. By that October, 60 employees were working three shifts, six and seven days a week.

The Manitowoc plant represents an expansion of the parent company, Zenith Sintered Products, Inc., of Germantown, established in a Milwaukee foundry in 1962 by the late Tom Tanner. Tod, the founder's son, is corporate president and CEO. He joined the company in 1981 after graduating from Northwestern University and now presides over a complex of four plants in the Germantown area and the new Manitowoc facility. Three of those plants manufacture sintered products. The other two are machine and tool shops.

Zenith is one of only a few manufacturers in Wisconsin that uses the powdered metal sintering process to make industrial parts. "It's very economical to get all the shape and configuration into a part with less machining than you would have with other methods," Tanner points out. "Machining is very expensive, both from a scrap-producing standpoint and the labor and effort that go into it."

The Manitowoc plant is devoted exclusively to the production of bearing caps and clutch plates for use in engines and transmissions in Corvettes, pickup trucks, and sport

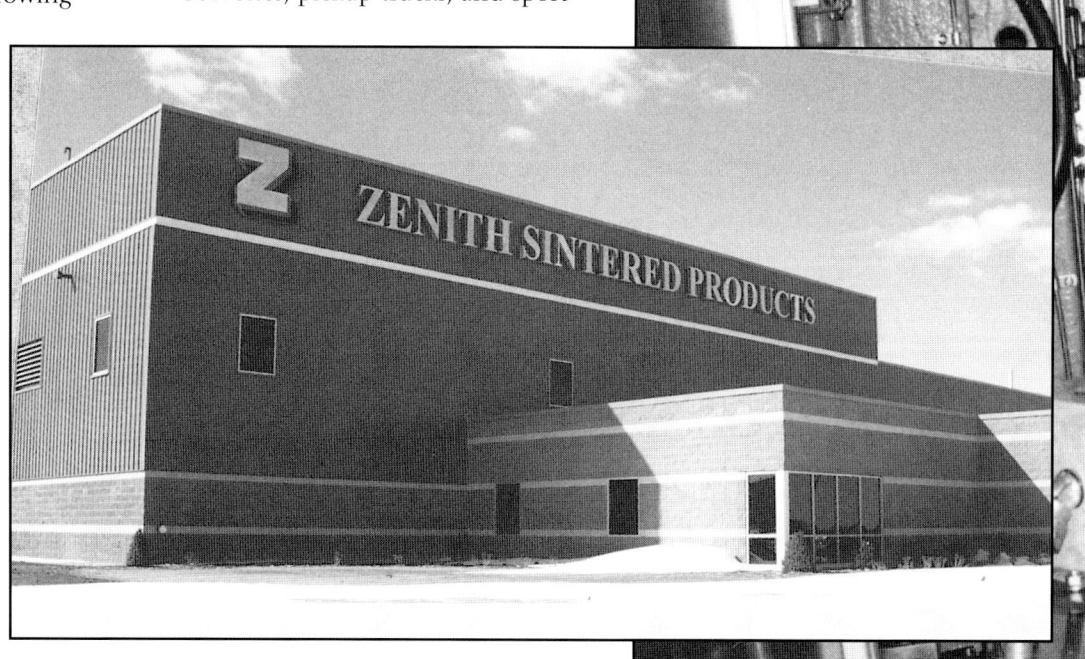

automotive industry.

Powder metal main bearing caps were used for the first time in General Motors' 3100 and 3800 V6 engines beginning in 1993. The product consumed more than 5,000 tons of powder annually, making it the biggest-volume application for powder metal in North America. A few years later Zenith entered into long-term contracts with GM for production and just-in-time delivery of sintered parts, requiring the company to increase its capacity.

*ABOVE: Zenith's new 72,000-square-foot manufacturing facility is located in Manitowoc's I-43 Industrial Park.*

*RIGHT: General Motors' Gen III V8 main bearing caps being processed on one of the lines installed in 1998 at the firm's Manitowoc facility.*

utility vehicles made by General Motors. According to Tanner, about 60 percent of Zenith's annual sales come from supplying parts for the

Designed for high-volume production, the Manitowoc facility consists of production, shipping and warehousing, offices, a quality-assurance and metallurgy lab, and training and conference centers. The plant is designed for future expansion on company-owned land to the west that could double its size.

In addition to the auto parts made in Manitowoc, Zenith makes parts for hand tools, refrigeration equipment, and the lawn and garden industry, including small-

engine maker Briggs & Stratton Corporation of Wauwatosa.

As the company faced the need to expand, Manitowoc was chosen for a number of reasons. When Zenith executives began looking for an acceptable site in mid-1996, they established a "one-hour rule," that is, the most preferable site would be within an hour's drive from the corporate headquarters in Germantown.

"We were looking out west on I-94, south on 94, north on US-45,

and north on I-43," recalls Tanner. "Manitowoc was the most suitable location closest to our 'one-hour rule.'"

Tanner says that Manitowoc city officials were also "very aggressive" in helping Zenith make the decision since factors other than distance had to be considered, such as government incentives, the labor market, and especially competitive electric rates inasmuch as the sintering process uses a large amount of energy.

"There was a good level of interest in the Manitowoc people," explains Tanner, "and it's nice to know you will be welcome. It's much easier then to become a contributing part of the community—not just the economy, but finding ways to provide employees with opportunities for education and community service, as well."

The company is especially proud of its reputation for high quality and on-time delivery. The pursuit of constant improvement has already awarded Zenith QS-9000 and ISO-9001 certifications.

"This is a tradition that is being continued without interruption in Manitowoc," says Tanner. "Our direction was set when the founders chose the name 'Zenith,' and we have not deviated from that original objective."

The company's vision is clearly stated in its promotional literature: "Zenith seeks to achieve the highest levels in the powder metal industry—to produce products representing the highest quality, productivity, technical advancement, and economic benefit."

# Dramm Corporation

*I*n the early 1940s Manitowoc florist John G. Dramm, with a gift for invention, designed a product that was to become the cornerstone of the Dramm Corporation. He called it the 400 Water Breaker.

Johnny, as everyone knew him, shared his invention with fellow growers and nurserymen. Basically a watering nozzle with 400 tiny holes that turns high-velocity water into a soft-flowing shower that is gentle to plants, the invention proved worthy. Word of mouth spread the news and requests for the new nozzle began filtering in.

Today the Dramm Corporation manufactures and distributes a complete line of professional greenhouse tools and equipment throughout the world. It is the most respected name within the industry.

The company's development, from a "basement operation" to a 55,000-square-foot facility employing over 50 people, was not without its tragedies. In 1951 Johnny died. He was only 47. His wife, Perdita, with two sons ages 12 and 18 and no Social Security benefits, struggled to keep the fledgling business going. Subcontracting the parts and assembly, Perdita—or Dt, as she was known—packed the orders and attended to all of the paperwork, using her lunch hours while she worked as a school librarian to drive to the post office and mail out the shipments. Taking no salary from the company, Perdita used the modest profits to put her two sons through college.

By the late 1950s John Peter, Johnny and Perdita's older son, was working out of his own basement, laying the groundwork for developing an extension handle for the 400 Water Breaker. By the early 1960s John was renting a small factory and doing the actual manufacturing of the Water Breaker and Handi Reach Handle, taking on some of the management

*Johnny and Perdita Dramm outside their florist shop, circa 1930.*

*RIGHT: The late John P. Dramm, a self-taught engineer, refines plans for a new product.*

functions of The Dramm Company. Although a marketing major (UW-Madison), he inherited his father's love for invention. Over the years, John evolved into a self-taught engineer, designing and building equipment and machines to manufacture the expanding menu of Dramm products.

While the original products were designed for the professionals working in greenhouses and nurseries, requests from the public were building. The avid home gardener wanted to use the same watering tools the "pros" were using. And the "pros" were all using Dramm. Johnny's utilitarian design now required a more attractive, refined look for the burgeoning retail market.

In 1967 younger brother Kurt William, with a degree in horticulture (UW-Madison) and experience in sales with Vaughn's Seed Company, joined and then later purchased The Dramm Company

from his mother, Perdita. The "born salesman" in the family, Kurt set about to develop new products and increase sales. There were then actually two separate companies—The Dramm Company and the John P. Dramm Manufacturing Company. But, being a family, they operated as one entity.

When, in 1978 at age 45, John P. Dramm, like his father before him, died at too early an age, the two companies became one under the name Dramm Corporation.

In an effort to increase sales, Kurt purchased German-made Pulsfog® machines, low-volume chemical applicators that greatly reduce the risk of exposure. He then added the Japanese Autofog™, advantageous because it requires no operator. With a history of being a leader in horticultural technology, the Dramm Corporation today manufactures and distributes a variety of sprayers, foggers, environmental controllers, and horticultural equipment.

A new facet in development at the Dramm Corporation is its Drammatic® Liquid Fish Fertilizer. Environmentally appealing because it is 100 percent organic, the low-impact fertilizer utilizes chopped-up fish. Something considered

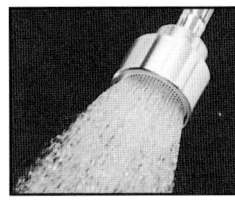

*ABOVE: Dramm's "Coldfogger" greenhouse chemical applicator treats 45,000 square feet in as little as 45 minutes.*

*LEFT: The Dramm Corporation's oldest product, the 400 Water Breaker, was invented by John G. Dramm.*

*ABOVE: Heidi Dramm Becker demonstrates the Dramm Rain Wand™ — the ideal tool for watering flower beds, gardens, and shrubs.*

*BOTTOM RIGHT: Drammatic® Organic Plant Food with Kelp is an example of Dramm's environmentally friendly fertilizer.*

waste and formerly dumped into landfills is now made into a useful and highly effective product. Native Americans apparently understood this secret when they taught the *Mayflower* Pilgrims to "plant" a fish in each hill of corn! A clean, state-of-the-art factory was newly completed in Algoma, Wisconsin, in 1999.

While keeping a position at the forefront of technology is essential, the 400 Water Breaker, in combination with a variety of extension handles, still remains the premier Dramm product. Its success attracts many imitators. Though copied worldwide, none of the competition has equaled the quality, craftsmanship, and durability of the original American-made product.

"Quality," Kurt Dramm says, "has been the hallmark of the Dramm Corporation throughout its over-50-year history."

Recently "the bender," one of the custom machines designed by John in the early years, was retired, replaced by an English-made counterpart. But the new machine, though expensive, couldn't do the job to the company's standards, and the original "bender" was re-engineered and brought back into service.

Perdita, after retiring from her school librarian job in 1972, devoted herself full time to the business. She continued to

work at the Dramm Corporation until her death in 1996 at age 89.

Family involvement, so integral to the growth and success of the company, is still a vital ingredient today. Andrew, one of John's sons, is director of marketing and product development, while son-in-law Kurt Becker is international sales director.

There's excitement in the dynamics of seeing a company move from a basement operation to a multimillion-dollar global corporation. This past decade has witnessed explosive growth. Combined with the firm footings of a strong family heritage, Kurt Dramm says his company is prepared and confident to move into the twenty-first century.

# Kahlenberg Brothers Company

*I*n 1895 two brothers, then in their early twenties, set up shop in Two Rivers to rebuild marine steam engines for local commercial fishermen. With that, William Robert (W.R.) and Otto Kahlenberg, Jr., launched Kahlenberg Brothers Company, a name well known in ports of call throughout the world. John L. Kahlenberg joined the firm several years later.

When he was just 16, W.R. built his first steam engine using the flywheel of his mother's sewing machine. That engine marked the first of many Kahlenberg engines manufactured over a period of more than 60 years. The earliest were steam-powered engines, but by 1900 the standard switched to gasoline-powered internal combustion engines, able to reverse without stopping from full speed ahead to full speed astern, a previously unheard-of maneuver for engines of any sort.

The innovative Kahlenbergs did not stop there. They also manufactured custom cast steel propellers and other accessories for Great Lakes fishing vessels. By 1907 they outgrew their original facilities and built the first portion of the plant they now occupy at 1700 Twelfth Street.

In 1911 the company developed its first semi-diesel engine, and the Kahlenberg name became known throughout the world. Commercial fleet owners welcomed these efficient engines since they no longer were able to procure sufficient quantities of the precious gasoline needed for World War I military vessels. (Semi-diesel

*The Kahlenberg plant, circa 1930.*

engines need gasoline only to start; they run on diesel fuel.) By 1920 these hardy semi-diesels completely replaced gasoline engines, and proved so reliable that General Douglas MacArthur requested as many Kahlenberg engines as possible to power the Pacific fleet during World War II.

After the boon of the war years, however, the lure of heavy-duty marine engines waned. The second generation of Kahlenbergs did not waver. W.R.'s sons, Roger W., George E., and William J., and nephew John B. focused on marine accessories and contract machining work to fuel their growth. They produced their last engine in 1964, but continued supplying parts well into the 1990s. After all, it is not uncommon for Kahlenberg engines to operate for 50 years, but occasionally they do need replacement parts.

The company's solid contract manufacturing division, launched during those postwar years, now represents approximately one-third of Kahlenberg Brothers' total business. It helps the firm weather the capricious marine industry, but the firm has never wavered from its original market. The remaining two-thirds of the business is equally split between some of the best propellers on the Great Lakes and the seven seas, and sound signals for luxury yachts and commercial freighters alike.

Additionally, Kahlenberg Brothers manufactures propeller shafts, muff couplings, and navigation aids.

The most notable of the company's products, however, are certainly its airhorns, the first of which sounded in the 1930s.

These airhorns do more than announce the presence of a marine

*ABOVE: Employees testing engines, circa 1915.*

*LEFT: The company's gasoline engine showroom, circa 1910.*

*John B. Kahlenberg (seated, front) represents the second generation of leadership in this venerable family-owned firm. Standing behind him (left to right) are Erick M. Kahlenberg (fourth generation), Karl K. Kahlenberg (third generation), and Steven B. Kahlenberg (fourth generation).*

vessel. The distinctive sound of Kahlenberg Airhorns is the result of a design that blends the richness of fine musical instruments with the volume and reliability required on the high seas and in crowded ports alike. Kahlenberg Airhorns will emit attention-getting blasts of sound, or may be programmed to play the skipper's favorites from up to eight gleaming trumpets. These phenomenal Chimetone "eight-bangers" in brushed brass, chrome plate, or white powdercoat play the "Star Spangled Banner," "Auld Lang Syne," "Anchors Aweigh," "Louie, Louie," and more than a dozen other tunes.

All Kahlenberg Brothers Sound Signals are tested in the company's unique Anoechic Test Chamber, and meet or exceed performance standards established by the International Maritime Organization. The chamber is just one of the highly technical features of the plant that, though considerably larger than it was in 1907, still stands watch over the Lake Michigan shoreline.

Occasionally, Kahlenberg Brothers' state-of-the-art testing facilities are called upon by others, as happened in early 1999, when three steam whistles of the ill-fated ocean liner the H.M.S. *Titanic* were cleaned and tested. The whistles are part of the Titanic Exposition Display in St. Paul, Minnesota. Kahlenberg Brothers was chosen because this is possibly the only company in the world that makes a triple steam whistle and has the machining capabilities to replicate the original whistles had that been necessary. Fortunately, in spite of the fact that the whistles had been under water for 81 years, it was determined that their tone would not be adversely affected. The whistles indeed sounded again.

Kahlenberg Brothers Company is phenomenal, both in terms of planning and production. Karl W., son of William J., joined the firm in 1955 and Fritz Kahlenberg came aboard in 1972 as the new chief engineer. They successfully piloted the firm through the turbulent 1980s when the oil industry virtually collapsed, taking the luxury yacht industry with it.

Now, as yachts are once again sailing the oceans and inland waterways and vessels of all sorts sound distinctive signals, signals that could only originate in Two Rivers, Wisconsin, John B. Kahlenberg, second generation, and Karl W. Kahlenberg, third generation, are preparing to turn Kahlenberg Brothers Company over to the fourth generation. Karl's son, Steven B. Kahlenberg, and Fritz's son, Erick M.

*One of a pair later shipped to Bayou La Batre, Alabama, this 1,000-pound, 60-inch, four-blade stainless steel propeller is being ground and bounced prior to pitching and polishing.*

Kahlenberg, have now been with the company seven years after graduating from their respective universities. This means that today, Kahlenberg Brothers Company epitomizes the ideals of its entrepreneurial founders, successfully transferring operations—and its exemplary reputation—from generation to generation to generation to generation.

# Holy Family Memorial Medical Center

A cornerstone was laid in a building atop Manitowoc's Gerpheide's Hill on September 22, 1898. The builders could not then have known that it would be a cornerstone for the community, as well as for Holy Family Hospital.

Just one year later, on September 28, 1899, Mother Alexia Fullmer and the Franciscan Sisters of Christian Charity opened Wisconsin's most modern hospital

*ABOVE: Mother Alexia Fullmer, superior general of the Franciscan Sisters of Christian Charity, 1898.*

*BELOW: The campus of Holy Family Hospital included the following buildings in 1967: 1) 1898 building; 2) 1924 building; 3) 1925 laundry; 4) 1929 addition; 5) nurses' home, completed in 1947; 6) 1948 and 1964 additions; 7) 1966 addition; and 8) priest's home.*

to serve the people of this busy lakeport town. The 45-bed, $75,000 hospital was the beginning of a partnership between the Franciscan Sisters of Christian Charity and the people of Manitowoc County that has endured throughout a century of change, a century in which the hospital experienced several metamorphoses, always to the benefit of the community.

By 1909 Holy Family had served 2,500 patients, regardless of age, race, religion, or financial ability. That same year the Sisters also established a training school for nurses, a forerunner to the Holy

*This undated photo shows Holy Family Hospital during its early years. Notice the garden in the lower left. This garden provided produce for patients, nursing students, employees, and Sisters from 1901 to 1961. Many Manitowoc citizens remember the Sisters working in the garden. The garden helped them get through the Depression and allowed them to feed all who came to their back door in need of food.*

Family Hospital School of Nursing which opened in 1920 and trained 871 nurses before it closed in 1976.

A 100-bed, $325,000 addition crowned the capital improvements of the 1920s. Yet, as impressive as the facility was, it would not have been possible without the extraordinary efforts of Holy Family Hospital's early volunteers who raised the funds that made the five-story structure possible.

The link between hospital and community was further solidified during the Great Depression. The Sisters tended a garden that fed their patients, themselves, and the hungry who came to their back door looking for sustenance. And the people of Manitowoc County generous-

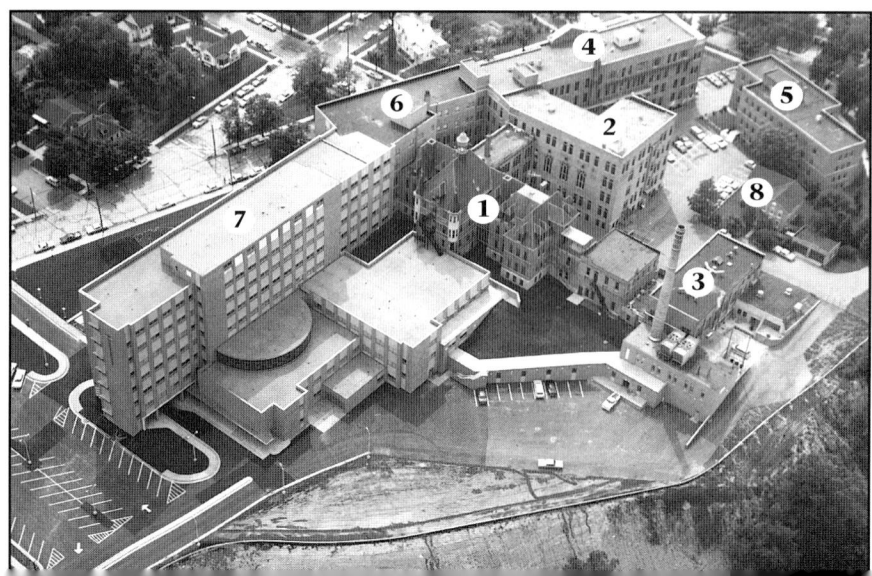

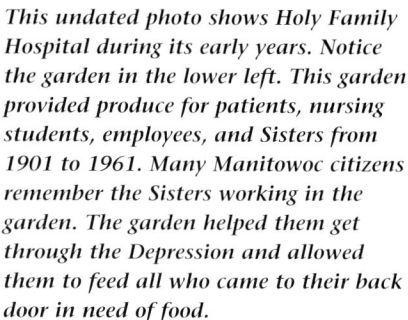

ly and faithfully paid their pledges to pay for the 1929 addition.

The 1940s were years of great change. World War II was the focal point of Manitowoc life. When the war ended and the baby boom began, Holy Family again expanded, this time adding an administrative and pediatric wing, bringing total available beds to 250.

During the 1950s and 1960s the hospital continued growing. In 1964 a seven-story, 170,000-square-foot addition was built. The role of volunteers also increased during these decades. They no longer sewed linens like many of the early volunteers who served in the Florence Nightingale Society of the 1920s, but they did serve patients, raise funds, and solidified the relationship between the hospital and the community.

During the 1970s increasing government regulations, third-party payors, advances in technology, and growth in services necessitated changes. Lay persons joined the governing board. Most of the original building was demolished in 1973, a laundry erected, and the chapel renovated. Medically, HFH instituted physician coverage of the emergency room 24 hours a day, seven days a week, enhancing emergency services for area citizens.

Hospital development during the 1980s progressed rapidly. To receive necessary state approval for the $18-million construction and renovation project, Holy Family made a heart-wrenching decision to give its nursing home license to St. Mary's Home for the Aged in Manitowoc. For the first time in its history, Holy Family did not have a service specifically for the elderly.

During this decade the hospital opened rural health clinics in Reedsville and St. Nazianz, established home health services, a hospice, and a chemical dependency unit. HFH also opened a comprehensive medical rehabilitation unit.

### Holy Family Memorial

- *Holy Family Memorial Medical Center*
  *Inpatient Facility —*
  *2300 Western Avenue*
  *Outpatient Facility —*
  *333 Reed Avenue*
- *Anesthesia Associates*
- *Sean Benham, M.D.*
- *Cancer Care Center*
- *Ear, Nose & Throat Associates*
- *Emergency Department Physicians*
- *Family Services Lakeshore*
- *Heart Center*
- *Lakeshore Pediatrics*
- *Lakeshore Urology*
- *Karl Larson, M.D.*
- *Alexandra Logan, M.D.*
- *Manitowoc Family Practice*
- *Manitowoc Surgical Associates*
- *Medical Arts Diagnostic Services*
- *Cecilio Mendoza, M.D.*
- *North End Drug & Home Medical Services*
- *Nutrition Plus and Diabetes Center*
- *Park Medical Center*
- *Reed Avenue Dialysis Center*
- *Rehab Plus*
- *Unified Ambulance & Care Van*
- *Wolfe-Snyder Drug*
- *Woodland Clinic*

In light of these momentous changes, in 1985 the hospital changed its name to Holy Family Medical Center.

The 1990s brought even greater challenges. Stand-alone medical facilities were quickly becoming economically unfeasible. To maintain the standard of health care available throughout Manitowoc County, Holy Family Medical Center merged with Manitowoc

Memorial Hospital in 1991. Memorial Hospital was dedicated on July 19, 1953, as a living memorial for all war veterans of Manitowoc County. An auxiliary, with 252 charter members, was established to serve patients of the 50-bed, $800,000 hospital, and to raise funds for its growth. Memorial Hospital eventually grew to 87 beds, with the first Laminar Air Flow operating room in Manitowoc County, a blood bank, and an extensive physical therapy department.

The two hospitals became Holy Family Memorial Medical Center. Inpatient care moved to the Western Avenue Campus and the Reed Avenue facility was dedicated to outpatient services. This alliance created a comprehensive health care network for the benefit of the people of Manitowoc County.

During the 1990s six clinics, many independent medical practitioners, several pharmacies, medical laboratories, therapy services, and emergency care providers consolidated their services within the Holy Family Memorial network. Family Services Lakeshore, Inc., a community outreach program that predates even the hospital, also joined forces with HFM. FSL offers home health services, respite care, adult day services, outpatient mental health and chemical dependency counseling, family and parenting programs, and sexual assault victim advocacy.

As the century comes to a close, Holy Family Memorial offers medically superior, cost-effective medical care. An excellent example is the Cancer Care Center, the centerpiece of an $8-million centennial building project, scheduled to open in the fall of 1999. Offering state-of-the-art cancer treatment here enables patients to remain near loved ones. At Holy Family Memorial, service is both their motivation and their commitment.

# Formrite Companies

Formrite of Two Rivers, Wisconsin, will celebrate its 50th anniversary in the year 2000. The story of Formrite is much like the short-lived histories of a number of other enterprises that burst upon the American manufacturing scene during the postwar economic boom of the 1950s—with a significant difference. Formrite survived.

During World War II Formrite founders Karl Wage, Don Surfus, and Joseph J. Birkenstock saw a need for something better in hydraulic piping than the 400- to 600-pound-per-square-inch systems then in use. After the war increased use of hydraulics in farm machinery and heavy equipment pushed working pressures beyond the 1200 psi range, highlighting a need for fabricated tube assemblies.

Of the few fabricators in the business there were even fewer willing to depart from their accustomed manufacturing practices to take on the ideas of Wage, Surfus, Birkenstock, and the other engineers and investors, all local residents, who joined them, namely Ray Young, Henry Schuette, and Wendel MacEachran.

On the strength of mere promises of potential business with Massey-Ferguson, Bucyrus Erie, and Hamilton Manufacturing, the Formrite entrepreneurs purchased their first fabrication plant in 1950—a former schoolhouse on 10th Street in Two Rivers.

From that humble beginning the firm quickly expanded into new buildings, and extended operations into Ohio, Illinois, and Canada. There was, in those years, a popular business philosophy that equated success with size. Corporate health was too often measured in terms of numbers—more products, more buildings, more employees—without much regard for the ability of sales and revenues to keep pace. When economic downturns came, as they did in the late 1970s and early 1980s, many companies shut down, or were gobbled up in bankruptcies, acquisitions, mergers, and not-so-friendly takeovers.

Reorganization came in 1988 as the founding managers and directors retired. A new board of directors and managers identified the company's "core" business, divesting themselves of non-core activities. This set the stage for reinvestments in up-to-date MRP (manufacturing resource planning) systems and CNC (computer numeric control) manufacturing equipment.

The results can be seen in reduction of production time between manufacturing order and delivery—from 30 days in 1992 to seven days in 1998. On-time delivery averaged only 30 percent of orders in 1992. Today the average is 96 percent and climbing.

The directors and managers of Formrite have always felt a strong responsibility for the economic health of Two Rivers and the surrounding community. Their successful efforts in refocusing the company have not only kept it alive, they have reenergized its personnel to maintain the company as a leader in the design and fabrication of structural and hydraulic tubing, systems, and components.

"It has been, and continues to be, a real challenge," says David Wage, executive vice president, "but we love every minute of it!"

*Formrite Companies of Two Rivers will celebrate its 50th anniversary in the year 2000.*

# Bill's Pick 'N' Save

Remember the "Mom and Pop" grocery stores of yesteryear? Can you recall the convenience of walking to the corner for a loaf of bread? Those neighborhood grocers were personal friends who went out of their way to stock what they knew we liked. Did that friendly concern for the customer disappear with the advent of the supermarket?

The answer is a resounding "No!" at Bill's Pick 'n' Save in Two Rivers. Owned and operated today by Tom and Debbie Czerwonka, Bill's Pick 'n' Save continues the customer-pleasing tradition of its founder, the late William H. Czerwonka, for whom the store is named.

Bill Czerwonka entered the retail grocery business in 1939, when he purchased the Clover Farm Store in Rosholt. It was a natural expansion of his farming experience and expertise. He moved his family to Two Rivers in 1962 and purchased the Red Owl Store on Washington Street.

In 1969 Bill purchased the newly constructed Red Owl Store on 22nd Street built by the Gamble Development Company. The building was designed to be a strip mall, or plaza, containing the Red Owl Store, a drugstore, and several other shops until 1974, when Czerwonka took over most of the footage to expand. A year later Tom, Bill's son and present operator, became manager.

More remodeling took place in 1978, and in 1983 the entire building was purchased from Gamble Development Company, an additional 6,000 square feet was added to the store, and the first electronic checkout scanning in the lakeshore area was introduced.

Bill Czerwonka retired in 1987

*ABOVE: Bill Czerwonka (left) and his meat manager stand behind the store's display case in 1943.*

*BELOW: Debbie and Tom Czerwonka oversee operations at today's Bill's Pick 'n' Save.*

discontinued services, "downsized," or moved away, Czerwonka added those products and services to his store.

In 1989 the present facade and additional floor space was added to the building, bringing the total to 40,500 square feet. Roundy's Foods of Milwaukee was contracted at that time as a major supplier, allowing the store to drop "Red Owl" for "Pick 'n' Save."

Since then the land itself (originally leased) has been purchased and the bakery and delicatessen

after 48 years as a grocer, and that same year was honored as "Grocer of the Year" by the Wisconsin Grocers Association. He died on November 16, 1998, at the age of 85.

In the early years Bill Czerwonka's Red Owl store managed to hold its own in competition with two larger stores, popular because of their meat and bakery products. Bill felt the only way he could compete would be to move or enlarge, according to his son Tom, so, as the other stores

expanded. All bakery goods are made from scratch by a dedicated crew who work each day from midnight to 8:00 a.m.

"My father was always trying to find out what the people wanted," says Tom Czerwonka. "He asked our customers what they wanted. Then he kept improving." The owners, managers, and employees of Bill's Pick 'n' Save in Two Rivers take great pride in continuing that tradition.

# JCPenney Company

"Penney's is here to stay," store manager David Biundo announces firmly. Located in the Lakeview Centre mall, the JCPenney Company is celebrating its 76th year in Manitowoc County.

James Cash Penney pioneered merchandising in the West at Kemmerer, Wyoming, with his "Golden Rule Store" in 1902. Building his business on quality and value, he established a merchandising empire through friendship, trust, and good customer service. Today JCPenney stores are a part of more than 1,300 communities all across America. And Penney stores can also be found today in Mexico, Chile, and Puerto Rico.

Manitowoc welcomed JCPenney in 1923 and the Two Rivers store was opened in 1941. When the Mid-Cities Mall (now Lakeview Centre) was built in 1968, the Manitowoc and Two Rivers stores were combined in May of that year and relocated in the mall, where it became—and continues as—the major retail "anchor" of the mall.

The design of the present store is identical to that of the Sheboygan store. Few people are aware that the Manitowoc facility has a second floor that has never been opened for trade. It is presently used for storage, maintenance, and offices. Complete with (walled-off) escalators, the additional space represents the company's far-sighted planning for a day when growth in the

lakeshore marketing area may create a demand for additional merchandise display and customer service.

"Catalog sales are especially big here," says Biundo. "In fact, JCPenney is among the first retailers to sell in three dimensions—store, catalog, and the Internet (http://www.jcpenney-inc.com)."

In 1996 the JCPenney Company, Inc., acquired the Eckerd Corporation, adding 2,800 drugstores to its other key services—department stores, catalog, and direct marketing. Although Penney does not operate a drugstore in the lakeshore area, it is a company, according to Biundo, "where the resources available to any one of our business segments can be used for the benefit of the whole."

JCPenney employees are called "associates." The culture of their workplace can be described as a climate of energy in which the Manitowoc Penney associates practice six "E-N-E-R-G-Y creating" principles:

1. EMPHASIZE the best in each other.
2. NEVER try to control each other.
3. ENCOURAGE ideas, have fun, be creative, share.

*James Cash Penney (shown in photo at left) established his first Golden Rule Store in Kemmerer, Wyoming, in 1902. This photo (above) of the store's second location was taken two years later.*

*BELOW: JCPenney's Manitowoc store has been the major retail anchor of today's Lakeview Centre since 1968.*

4. REPLACE competition with cooperation.
5. GIVE away what you have—watch it multiply.
6. YIELD the credit to others.

"We are a team," explains Biundo, "and there is no 'I' in team. It is not my store, my department, my success, or my failure. It's our team. And it's our community!"

# The Lighting Center

"*T*he light at the end of Franklin Street," is the way it's described in local radio advertisements. Truly, The Lighting Center of Manitowoc is an illuminating (pun intended) contribution to the area's economy and to the great diversity of services and products offered by Manitowoc and Two Rivers businesses and industries.

The Lighting Center was established in 1952 by Ed Skarda as Manitowoc Electric Supply. It was located in a Washington Street building shared

the company also provides free on-site consultations for home owners and small businesses as well as print layout service and free delivery anywhere in Wisconsin. More than 150 product lines are marketed and supplied by The Lighting Center compared to an average of 10 to 12 lines carried by most competitors.

Recycling is a fairly new service offered to major industrial customers by the environmentally conscious company. The Lighting Center serves as a collection agency for all fluorescent tubes and industrial light bulbs and transports these items to an area recycling plant.

In addition to the wide selection of products and services, The

Lighting Center is unique in the experience of its employees.

"Working in this field is not just a job," says CEO Bissonette. "It's a career. On-the-job training for all Lighting Center employees takes a minimum of three years, and often includes factory tours to familiarize our lighting consultants with the ongoing changes in the lighting industry."

The Lighting Center keeps a constant eye on the future, too. One of the company's products, a light therapy unit called the "sun box," is manufactured at the Franklin Street location. According to Bissonette, there has been a steady growth in

by Manitowoc Plumbing Supply. The firm moved to its present location in 1979. Wholesale electrical supplies were a mainstay then, but by 1989 the business was becoming a lighting showroom for homeowners and contractors.

Floyd Bissonette became owner and president in October 1995 and continued the move to specialization in lighting fixtures and related supplies. Today The Lighting Center boasts the largest lighting showroom in northeast Wisconsin.

Although 50 percent of The Lighting Center's customers are electrical and building contractors,

*ABOVE: Shown here are a few of the lighting products displayed in the largest lighting showroom in northeast Wisconsin.*

*TOP: The Lighting Center's present location is at 2310 Franklin Street in Manitowoc.*

demand for this product. That could lead to establishing a separate manufacturing division in the future.

Keeping pace with emerging electronic marketing strategies, The Lighting Center is experiencing a steady growth in Internet sales through its Web page: http://www.lightingcenterinc.com.

"Lighting technology changes rapidly," explains Bissonette. "We have to anticipate customer needs and upcoming innovations in the industry. This prepares us to be ready to make changes in our own operations and product lines on a moment's notice."

# VPI, LLC
## *Contract Manufacturing Division*

*I*f you were a non-managerial production worker and wanted to take golf lessons in your spare time, would your employer pay for those lessons? The answer would be "yes," if you were employed by Manitowoc's Contract Manufacturing Division of VPI (previously known as Vinyl Plastics, Inc.).

"It's not automatic," explains John Crawford, VPI vice president of human resources. "A request must be submitted. But few, if any, are ever turned down." That's true even when the self-improvement request does not seem to benefit the company directly.

"What we're really paying for in the long run," says Crawford, "is improvement of our employees equal to the emphasis we place on the constant improvement of manufacturing processes, procedures, quality, and customer service."

"People are our most important asset and deserve trust, respect, and recognition," according to the in-plant posted statement of VPI Values. "Involvement and teamwork will provide opportunities for all employees to contribute, learn, and grow."

VPI opened its Manitowoc plant at 2917 Division Street in 1983. The original 30,000 square feet was doubled in 1990 and tripled in 1992. A major remodeling in 1993 added another 2,400 square feet in office, locker, and lunchroom space.

During the 1980s the Sheboygan-based business was reorganized to allow each of its three separate product lines and markets to more effectively and efficiently control their own destinies. VPI became a "divisionalized" company with the Floor Products Division based in Sheboygan, the Sheet Products Division in Sheboygan Falls, and the Contract Manufacturing Division in Manitowoc. A separate Medical Products Division plant, representing the addition of a new

product line, is also located in Sheboygan. In 1997 VPI acquired American Mirrex Corporation and now also has facilities in Delaware City, Delaware, and Salisbury, Maryland. Each division is headed by a general manager and operates as an independent profit center, with centralized staff functions provided by the corporate staff in Sheboygan.

The VPI-Manitowoc division produces sound barrier and vinyl flooring materials for the automotive industry as well as research and development projects in other types of materials for automotive and specialty applications. This product line began as a joint effort between VPI and the K.W. Muth Company of Sheboygan in 1981 with the development of an automobile floor mat that wouldn't wear out!

As demand for the product began

to exceed the two companies' capacity, the Manitowoc division was born. On June 22, 1987, the one-millionth piece of automotive dash barrier material was delivered to K.W. Muth without a reject, and on September 25 of that year the Manitowoc Contract Manufacturing Division received the K.W. Muth

Company's first ever Outstanding Quality Achievement Award.

In 1995 the Manitowoc division was making new cars quieter and cleaner with sound barrier (installed against the car's firewall and under-dash) and floor matting material for Masland Industries (now Lear). By 1996 products from the Manitowoc

ABOVE: *VPI's Manitowoc facility is located at 2917 Division Street.*

LEFT: *The company's Manitowoc plant, opened in 1983 with 30,000 square feet, has been expanded more than threefold.*

division could be found in most models of Buick, Chevrolet, Dodge Ram, Ford, Geo, GMC, Oldsmobile, Pontiac, Suzuki, and Toyota. In 1999 the division was given the highest recognition at VPI—the President's Award for outstanding improvements in quality and effeciency. The division also became both QS-9000 and ISO-9000 compliant in 1999.

In addition to award-winning production excellence, an important priority at the Manitowoc

division has always been "safety first." The division was honored by the Society of the Plastics Industry (SPI) in 1988 for achieving a year of operation without a lost-time or restricted-activity accident. By June 15, 1992, VPI-Manitowoc employees had achieved two full years of production without a lost-time accident.

The Manitowoc division also continues to make contributions to the community. In 1993 the employees earned a United Way of Manitowoc Award for their efforts in the United Way fund drive. In 1994 the Manitowoc/Two Rivers Area Chamber of Commerce's first-quarter Small Business Award was presented to VPI's Manitowoc Contract Manufacturing Division. The VPI Foundation made a major

contribution to the Manitowoc Lincoln Park Zoological Society, provided some of the funding for Habitat for Humanity to move nine houses in Manitowoc to a new site, and continues to support the Manitowoc Museum, the Capitol Civic Centre, and the United Way.

The first in-house Lifelong Learning seminar for Manitowoc division employees and their spouses took place in September 1993, at the Holiday Inn in Manitowoc. This program, alluded to in the beginning of this article, is widely used and appreciated by employees. The company's Lifelong Learning Statement reads:

"It is the philosophy of VPI to promote training and education, and provide an opportunity for all employees to learn and grow in a rapidly changing business and social environment."

Research and development at the Manitowoc division is in the tradition of VPI uniqueness—bold innovation. VPI has survived and prospered through economic recessions and oil embargoes by experimenting with the use of recycled vinyl materials, seeking new applications for its products, and diversifying its product line. Its success can be directly attributed to a workplace climate that is reality, not theory, expressed in the VPI Mission Statement:

"VPI is an organization of people committed to continuous improvement of the products and services we provide to meet our customers' needs for custom compounding of filled thermoplastic materials utilizing recycling technology. We will achieve profitable growth in rapidly changing environments through the strategic marketing of new products, added value for existing products, and acquisitions which complement our manufacturing, marketing, and distribution skills."

# Copps Food Center

*T*he turbulent decade of the 1960s saw, among other things, the rapid spread of discount department stores throughout the North and West. For the most part these were large chains based in the South and East. Manitowoc's first discount department store was born and bred in Wisconsin.

The Copps Corporation began in Stevens Point in the year 1892 with E.M. Copps selling barrels of

"We lasted 107 years in this highly competitive market simply because, for four generations, we have asked all our people to relentlessly pursue the goal of customer satisfaction," says chairman Michael Copps.

Two things happened during the 1940s to change the direction of the business: Copps joined the International Grocers Alliance (IGA) and then in 1946 added retail stores. The latter happened

dise store opening in October 1965 in the building immediately south of the present location.

By 1983 the company had discontinued general merchandise to focus solely on groceries. A new building was constructed in Manitowoc just north of the previous facility, between Calumet and Custer streets, opening on October 31, 1985, as Copps Food Center. A major addition completed in 1997 provides space for expanded liquor, video rental, and floral departments.

Copps is constantly changing to keep up with its customers' needs, always staying on the cutting edge of what's new in the grocery business. Indeed, Copps' mission is to provide a uniquely satisfying shopping experi-

*Copps Food Center has been serving discerning Manitowoc County customers from its location at 3415 Custer Street since 1985.*

molasses and soap powder to grocers from a horse-drawn wagon. It is today the 15th-largest privately held company in the state and remains one of Wisconsin's few large corporations owned and managed by the same family for more than a century. The company operated as a grocery wholesaler before the turn of the century but is now a major force in both retail and wholesale groceries.

almost by accident. The owner of a large store decided to retire. Rather than risk losing the wholesale account, Copps purchased the store. Several more retail stores were purchased until Copps built its first "Foodliner" in Stevens Point in 1952.

That was followed by some experimentation with combination food and discount department stores, with Manitowoc's combination grocery and general merchan-

ence in which customers are offered products and services that exceed their expectations. It's a formula that has worked for 107 years!

Today the Copps Corporation owns and operates 20 corporate stores, and distributes to over 45 independent IGA grocery stores.

# Zaug's Vending & Food Service

We live in an era of coin machine service and it is a far cry from the days of the penny peanut vendor that stands as an antique in Allen Zaug's office. Zaug's Vending & Food Service today operates locations in Manitowoc and Wisconsin Rapids in addition to its commissary in Appleton.

A family business, Zaug's was founded in 1938 in New London by Roger Zaug, who passed away in 1973. Allen Zaug, son of the founder, continues as president of the corporation, which today serves more than 150 locations and 2,000 vending machines in Wisconsin with 24-hour, seven-day food service and maintenance.

A recognized and awarded leader in the industry, Zaug's introduces 25 new items to its menu every six months and has done so for the past half-decade. The practice has become part of the company's culture, as has Zaug's unique rotating menu which gives vending machine customers the variety of fresh food selections they are looking for. And Zaug's does this efficiently with a

*Owner Allen Zaug is flanked by his sons, Cary (left) and Gary Zaug.*

*Vending merchandisers (left to right) Ken Qualman, Roger Siehr, and Paul Dietrich at Dayco Eastman in Manitowoc.*

constant goal of improving quality and customer service. A fully prepared and packaged sandwich, for example, represents one unit. Production units increased from 25 per labor hour when the Appleton commissary opened in 1971, to the present output of 110-plus units.

Zaug's 150 employees (14 at Manitowoc) receive continuous training and take pride in performing their jobs with a constant eye on quality. Under its far-sighted management Zaug's has grown from vending peanuts and candy in 1938 to today's $15-million enterprise. Each day more than 8,400 fresh-

food items are prepared and delivered in the company's fleet of refrigerated trucks to the vending machines and cafeterias of lakeshore area hospitals, nursing homes, schools, and businesses.

Custom-order catering is also a Zaug's specialty. Since 1970 the firm has catered the monumental fast-food requirements of the Experimental Aircraft Association's annual convention in Oshkosh, where, for one week each year, a half-million aviation enthusiasts from all over the world gather.

Zaug's prepares its own food. A tour of the commissary reveals state-of-the-art food-preparation and packaging machinery in a spotless environment, arranged for efficient and ergonomically pleasant production.

Allen Zaug likes to speak of "fathering ideas." Employees and customers are eagerly listened to, and solicited for ideas and suggestions to improve service and the product line menu. Randy Schultz, vice president, agrees: "It's that constant openness to capitalize on new ideas and set trends that makes our food exceptional, and our service unique."

# Aurora Health Care

Despite the lure of the sunny South, the Manitowoc-Two Rivers area has a sizable population of elderly and retired persons. A tradition of strong family ties from middle-European immigrant settlers, passed down from generation to generation, is probably a significant factor in this phenomenon. Comprehensive health care, from the cradle to the grave, is also an accepted part of that tradition. Now, as the "Baby Boom" generation ages, and a new health-conscious generation emerges, a "next generation" of health care is required.

Providing that "Next Generation of Quality Health Care" is precisely the vision of Aurora Health Care behind the ground-breaking in December 1998 of a 72-bed medical center to replace the Two Rivers Community Hospital. The new Aurora Medical Center faces Lake Michigan on Memorial Drive between Manitowoc and Two Rivers.

Two Rivers Community Hospital was build in 1927, with a major addition in 1962. Aurora will continue to use it for a variety of non-acute care services. For instance, Hamilton Memorial Home, a long-term care facility adjacent to the current hospital, may expand into the existing building. The Visiting Nurse Association of Wisconsin also has offices in the

Two Rivers Community Hospital and, along with other support services, is expected to remain and expand there.

In addition to Aurora Medical Center's 180,000 square feet, a new Aurora satellite location for the Manitowoc Clinic opened in the fall of 1999 on the south side of Manitowoc, near the intersection of I-43 and Highway 151. Aurora also operates the 16-physician Two Rivers Clinic on Garfield Street and the 15-physician Manitowoc Clinic

on Reed Avenue. The central location of the new Aurora Medical Center was chosen for the purpose of providing convenient access for the patients and physicians of these clinics.

Aurora Health Care is a not-for-profit health care system of more than 18,000 employees serving the residents of eastern Wisconsin from 230 locations. Aurora's four regions include 12 hospitals and more than 80 clinics, the state's most comprehensive home health and social

*A new Aurora satellite location for the Manitowoc Clinic on the city's south side, near the intersection of I-43 and Highway 151, opened in the fall of 1999.*

*Ground was broken in December 1998 on the new Aurora Medical Center, expected to be operational by mid-2000. The 72-bed facility faces Lake Michigan on Aurora Memorial Drive (State Route 42) between Manitowoc and Two Rivers.*

service agency, and several long-term care facilities. Aurora's central region includes Manitowoc, Sheboygan, Calumet, Fond du Lac, and Winnebago counties.

"Our emphasis is on the future," says Aurora's central region executive vice president, Patrick J. Trotter. "We expect the medical center to be fully operational in mid-2000 with advanced technology and the latest in patient choices, services, and comfort."

# Comfort Inn

The hospitality business, for all the outward amenities, is highly competitive. What, then, are the attributes of a successful hotel?

"Every one of our guests is a person, not a room number," explains Bobbi Schuetze, general manager of the Comfort Inn of Manitowoc.

Classified as an economy hotel, the Comfort Inn serves its niche well. The two-story, 47-room hotel is located just off the Interstate 43 and Highway 151 interchange at the southwest corner of the city. This convenient location is ideal for the business travelers to whom the Comfort Inn caters. Clean, spacious rooms, all furnished with two queens or a king-size bed, as well as tables and chairs, make the Comfort Inn a comfortable choice for business travelers just stopping for the night, those working on long-term projects, and even families moving into the area.

The complimentary breakfast, served in a sun-washed room adjacent to the registration desk, features hot and cold cereals, muffins, bagels, yogurt, fresh fruit, juices, milk, coffee, and tea. Additionally, complimentary fruit, cookies, and beverages are available throughout the day. When guests book extended stays, the hotel furnishes their rooms with refrigerators and microwaves.

*ABOVE: The daily complimentary breakfast is served in a sunny room adjacent to the registration desk.*

*LEFT: The Comfort Inn's convenient location just off the I-43 and Highway 151 interchange is ideal for the business travelers to whom the hotel caters.*

"We're a franchise of Choice Hotels International, managed by Tharaldson Property Management of Fargo, North Dakota," says Bobbi, "and we live by the corporate mission statement: Creating an atmosphere which is so positive that each person who enters our hotel will become a regular guest and will recommend any Tharaldson Hotel."

"We have a hard-working, dedicated team here. We're professionals, and I like to think we have a knack for hospitality," Bobbi continues. "Our goal is to make our guests happy."

Sometimes that's a bit challenging. In addition to creating a home away from home for the business traveler, the Comfort Inn caters to many of Manitowoc's special guests, including the participants at various dog shows. Pets are welcome, of course, and a dog run has been constructed in the back of the property.

While the Comfort Inn boasts the most spacious guest rooms in the county, the amenities don't stop there. The entire hotel is renovated every five years. Carpets, quilts, and drapes in all the guest rooms and common areas are replaced, of course. Even bathroom floor tiling is redone. Television sets are also upgraded.

"We listen to our guests and upgrade accordingly," says Bobbi. And the guests notice. In an area where all guest rooms are booked during summer months but winter rooms are plentiful, the Comfort Inn is bustling.

"When we say, 'Satisfaction is guaranteed,' we mean it," explains the proud hotel manager.

# RBA, Inc.

When The Manitowoc Company moved its dry dock and shipbuilding interests to Sturgeon Bay in the 1970s, and its subsidiary, Manitowoc Engineering, moved its crane works to a new plant on Manitowoc's south side, a number of nostalgic old-timers felt that the heroic history of the "boat basin" had come to an end. Many citizens feared that the industrial area on the great loop of the Manitowoc River, in the center of the city, would become an eyesore of abandoned and decaying factory buildings.

That was not to be. Access to the area by rail, truck, and Great Lakes shipping for the assembly and transportation of heavy manufacturing was too good a resource to go unnoticed, and noticed it was by RBA (Ray Brickner Associates), Inc., of Sheboygan.

RBA, Inc., began in 1985 as an industrial mechanical contractor specializing in on-site repair, modification, demolition, and installation of process and material-handling equipment for the foundry, food, plastics, and steelmaking industries. Originally located in Sheboygan, the business grew until 1995 when it relocated to the former Manitowoc Shipbuilding facility

---

*BELOW: Sophisticated hydraulic and pneumatic material-handling systems are manufactured, fully assembled, finished, and tested within RBA's expansive fabrication and assembly bays.*

*Manitowoc's historic "boat basin" as it appeared in the late 1960s before ship repair and dry docking were moved to Sturgeon Bay. The large area in the river loop is now occupied by RBA, Inc. Photo by Daryl Cornick; courtesy, Manitowoc/Two Rivers Area Chamber of Commerce*

in Manitowoc's "City Centre" industrial basin.

After acquiring much of Manitowoc Engineering's largest machining and fabricating equipment, RBA purchased the entire one-million-square-foot facility in 1998. While RBA's original industrial mechanical contracting business continued to grow, more space was needed for the company's expanding business in subcontract machining, fabrication, welding, and assembly for the construction, marine, mining, automotive assembly, and metals industries.

Huge assemblies for mining machinery, especially, required large assembly sheds with sizable overhead cranes and access doors. For example, Large Assembly Bay No. 2 (above right) is serviced by two 125-ton overhead traveling cranes with a 55-foot hook height. Finished assemblies are moved out of the building through a door measuring 90 feet wide and 50 feet high.

It is difficult for the average citizen of Manitowoc, daily exposed to, or working in, a prosperous community balance of custom mechanical services and manufactured items, to visualize the magnitude of

*ABOVE: The firm's Assembly Bay No. 2 with its 50- by 90-foot access door. This picture was taken from the far shore of the Manitowoc River, across the water where submarines and carferries were once launched. Note how small the semi-tractor and trailer appear in the huge doorway.*

*LEFT: RBA's size capability is illustrated by comparing the workman on the lift platform with the caterpillar crawler track frame he is machining on one of the firm's six-inch twin horizontal boring mills.*

RBA's capabilities.

In Manitowoc, one occasionally sees a forklift truck moving a small pallet of carton merchandise, but RBA material-handling equipment moves semi-truck-size shipboard containers. Shiny new backhoes and graders are rather common sights at implement dealers, but RBA fabricates huge scoops and crawler tracks for draglines and the monstrous ore-moving trucks one never sees beyond the confines of an open-pit ore mine.

RBA capabilities reflect the oversize machinery and material needs of the firm's customers. Welding positioners of up to 20-foot by 40-ton capacity are manned by RBA's 30 in-house certified welders who are TIG weld, air arc, and torch experienced. They are equipped with welding machines ranging up to 655-amp capacity—1,000 amp submerged arc and 400 amp portable.

Welding is only one of RBA's many capabilities. Fixtures, jigs, and tooling required for the company's manufacturing is provided by RBA's own toolroom in order to ensure prompt production support.

Size is no substitute for quality, according to RBA managers. The company's skilled 70-plus work force expects to achieve ISO-9002 certification by the year 2000, and have already received many commendations and awards from satisfied customers and industrial associations.

So, once again, Manitowoc's historic "boat basin" hums with heavy manufacturing, thanks to RBA, Inc. A grateful city welcomes RBA as one of its newest community-minded members in the lakeshore area's diversified family of businesses and industries.

# WCUB AM 980 & OLDIES 92.1 FM

*H*ow would you like to eat breakfast with the owner of a popular radio station and be on the air at the same time? Lee Davis of "CUB" radio in Manitowoc has been hosting the WCUB "Breakfast Club" for more than 10 years from mobile transmitters set up on weekday mornings in McDonald's restaurants in Manitowoc and Two Rivers. All you have to do is sit down with Lee and he will quickly help you realize your dream of someday "being on the radio."

With four transmission towers on Viebahn Street and a 500-foot tower on Mirro Drive that serves several stations, WCUB's 5,000-watt radio broadcasting station (980 KHz. on the AM dial) got its start in 1952 when famed Chicago radio personality Eddie Allen chose Manitowoc to establish his own radio station. Jack Severson purchased WCUB in

*WCUB's Breakfast Club co-host interviews state representative Bob Ziegelbauer at McDonald's restaurant, where the show originates.*

again to the present WLTU. The station is now called "OLDIES 92.1 FM," and features hit music from the 1950s, 1960s, 1970s, and 1980s. An extensive library of popular artists and their recordings is maintained, using the latest digital technology to "clean" and restore the sound for listener enjoyment.

WCUB (AM) became a country music station in 1975 while it was still signing off the air at 6:00 p.m. each day. In the early 1980s the station became full time when it increased its power from 1,000 to 5,000 watts. This enabled 24-hour broadcasting and increased the station's coverage to approximately 17 counties in Wisconsin and a number of counties in Michigan. It has since broadcast in that mode continuously and has received numerous awards and recognitions from country music organizations and nationally known recording artists.

Three special emphases make WCUB unique among radio broadcasters in northeast Wisconsin. The first is the station's extensive and thorough coverage of motor sports.

This includes regular coverage of the many NASCAR racing events, the Indianapolis 500, and the Indy Race at Road America. The continuing popularity of this coverage is convincing proof that there is a surprisingly large number of auto racers and racing fans in the lakeshore area. Sports coverage also includes snowmobiling and skiing reports in season.

WCUB motor sports coverage is not limited to terra firma. The station regularly covers the annual Experimental Aircraft Association fly-in and convention in Oshkosh, the largest aviation show in the world.

The second unique emphasis is WCUB's pioneering tradition of sport fishing coverage. According to Lee Davis, previous owner Jack Severson liked to deep-sea fish in Lake Michigan. It was almost by accident that fishing reports originated when Severson, on his "Sport Fishing Machine," one day decided to radio back to the station where the fish were biting and what other fishermen were catching. It was aired and the station was flooded with calls from listeners wanting more information. Sport fishing reports became a regular feature and today WCUB is the source for such

*CUB Radio has been reporting on Lake Michigan fishing for almost 30 years.*

the early 1960s when Allen moved north to set up another radio station in Door County. Lee Davis became a partner in the operation in 1975 and sole owner about 15 years later when Severson retired.

It was during Severson's ownership that "simulcasts" began on WKUB (FM 92.1). The call letters were later changed to WKKB, then

news to a network of 20 to 25 radio stations around Lake Michigan, including Chicago.

The third unique emphasis is WCUB's consistent coverage and support of agricultural news and events. The station employs one of the state's five farm directors certified by the National Association of Farm Broadcasters—there are only 170 in the entire nation. Comprehensive farm news and agricultural coverage has been broadcast since 1979.

"CUB Radio" has been involved with the community since its inception. The company started CUB Charities, which in the 1970s pioneered raising money to provide a reward program for law enforcement agencies. CUB Charities also helped to establish the lakeshore area Crimestoppers program.

WCUB puts its facilities and personnel at the disposal of the Manitowoc/Two Rivers Area Chamber of Commerce when the

Chamber annually sponsors Aviation Day at the Manitowoc County Airport.

The station is also active in attracting and sponsoring big-name country music performers such as the Statler Brothers and others at Manitowoc's renowned Mecca for the performing arts, the Capitol Civic Centre. In addition, WCUB is actively engaged in a constant search for new country music talent. The station currently sponsors the True Value/Jimmy Dean Country Showdown, the largest talent search in the nation.

Extensive world, national, state, and local news is regularly broadcast by WCUB. The news department has won numerous awards over the years for outstanding news coverage.

*WCUB and OLDIES 92.1 personalities pose for an ad about CUB Radio's "classy stations."*

WCUB and WLTU have large and loyal audiences in many Wisconsin and Michigan counties, according to research commissioned by the stations and conducted by the Leede Research Group in October 1998. In Manitowoc County alone, WCUB reaches approximately 40,000 people each week and WLTU serves a weekly audience of approximately 20,000 people. This is especially good news for WCUB and WLTU advertisers. The stations' professional marketers pride themselves on finding and promoting those unique products and services that set advertisers apart from their competition.

"Keeping up with the changing technology in radio broadcasting is a real challenge," says owner-manager Lee Davis. "Right now we're busy planning and upgrading for the digital future. When digital radio comes to our area, we'll be ready."

# Radio Stations WOMT and WQTC

L akeshore commuters on their way to work tune their car radios to national and local news. People at home scribble down the "Cash Call Jackpot" hoping that theirs will be the next phone call from the radio station. Others call in vocal classifieds to the "Air Exchange." Still others call to question the guest speaker or to comment on the day's topic, on "Be My Guest." And many spend a pleasant Sunday evening listening to the big band music of "Sunday Night Bandstand." They're all listening to the radio station that continues to "say a lot for the lakeshore," WOMT in Manitowoc.

WOMT was put on the air by Francis and Lillian Kadow in the second story of the building on

Washington Street, facing Washington Park, now occupied by the Triumphant Christian Church. The Kadows were well known for their interests in, and promotion of, the fine arts and show business in general, and operated the movie theater, the Mikado, on the first floor. The call letters of the radio station, in fact, stood for "World's Only Mikado Theater." Today, according to Don Seehafer, president and general manager of Seehafer Broadcasting

---

*At Milwaukee County Stadium in 1993, Don Seehafer, president of SBC (second from left), stands with (left to right) Bill Haig, vice president of the Milwaukee Brewers; Phil Garner, manager of the team; Ben Jakel, station manager of WOMT; and Mark Seehafer, vice president of SBC.*

Corporation (SBC), the present owner, the call letters stand for "We Offer More Things."

The year was 1926, only six years after pioneering radio station 8MK (later WWJ) began America's first daily broadcasting in Detroit. President Warren G. Harding had a radio installed in the White House in 1922, but it remained for President Calvin Coolidge to deliver the first presidential radio broadcast. The Kadows were keenly interested in this new entertainment and communication medium and WOMT made its debut a year before President Coolidge signed the bill creating the Federal Radio Commission, the forerunner of the present Federal Communications Commission (FCC). WOMT was

only the third station on the air in the state of Wisconsin.

There were some later-to-be-famous people born in 1926—Marilyn Monroe, Tony Bennett, Queen Elizabeth II, and Fidel Castro, to name a few. The evangelist Aimee Temple McPherson was drawing crowds as she held revival meetings around the nation, and

RIGHT: Don Seehafer, president and general manager of Seehafer Broadcasting Corporation; Jay Mitchell, president of Jay Mitchell & Associates, Fairfield, Iowa; Philip LeNoble, president of Executive Decision Systems, Inc., Littleton, Colorado; and Paul Stenstrom, president of Market Tech, Houston, Texas (left to right) attend the National Association of Broadcasters Radio Show '92 in New Orleans.

BELOW: Don and Jean Seehafer pose with popular national radio talk show host Rush Limbaugh at the NAB Radio Convention '94 in Dallas. Limbaugh is aired on Seehafer's AM radio station in Wausau, WXCO.

Isadora Duncan had just fled to France after scandalizing New Yorkers with her avant-garde dancing. WOMT news broadcasts that year announced the deaths of silent film star Rudolph Valentino and Appleton native, magician Harry Houdini.

Also in WOMT news in 1926 was the first North Pole flight of Richard Byrd and Floyd Bennett, and a tribute to Gertrude Ederle of New York, who became the first American woman to swim the English Channel.

The Kadows retained ownership of WOMT until 1967, when Wisconsin Fuel & Light purchased the station and moved its studios to its North 10th Street office complex. Seehafer Broadcasting took official ownership on January 1, 1970, and moved the studios to a new facility at 3730 Mangin Street, the present location. In 73 years WOMT has had only three owners.

Today WOMT is noted for its news, weather, and community-oriented feature programs and especially for its outstanding sports coverage. WOMT has broadcast Green Bay Packer games for the past 40 years, and the Milwaukee Brewers since the team came to Milwaukee in 1970. The UW Badgers, Marquette Golden Eagles, and Milwaukee Bucks have also been carried for many years by WOMT.

The station continues to give the same professional coverage to local high school sports as well. Manitowoc Lincoln Ships sporting events have been broadcast for 50 years, the Roncalli Jets since 1969, and the Manitowoc Lutheran Lancers for the past 25 years.

WOMT (1240 Mhz. on the AM band) has been a CBS affiliate for 25 years and Don Seehafer serves on the CBS Affiliates board of directors.

In 1980 WOMT purchased station WQTC in Two Rivers and moved the studios to the Mangin Street location in Manitowoc. WQTC (FM) went on the air in 1965 and is currently a "classic rock" station. Two Rivers Raiders high school football and basketball games are aired by WQTC.

Today a third generation of TV-accustomed children are growing up, for the most part, unaware that radio is the technological foundation of television. Gone are the "Golden Days" when radio listeners used their imaginations to mentally visualize what they were hearing. Nevertheless, radio remains an indispensable medium of information, an emergency channel of communication, and, yes, still a source of entertainment. These roles are taken seriously by WOMT and WQTC as they carry on a tradition of dependability in the lakeshore area.

Somewhere in the Manitowoc or Two Rivers area a very young future electronics technician is at her father's basement workbench putting together the pieces of a kit she received as a Christmas present. She has strung a thin wire all the way from the attic, down two flights of stairs, and now, holding an earphone to the side of her head with one hand, she probes with the other hand the powerless charcoal "crystal" in the primitive radio assembled for her sixth-grade science project.

"Dad! Dad! Come listen! I got WOMT!"

# Lakeside Foods, Inc.

*I*n 1883 Albert Landreth relocated from Philadelphia, Pennsylvania, to the Midwest, with the realization that Wisconsin's rich soil could produce a superior pea. He began his operation out of the kitchen of a small hotel on the Lake Michigan shoreline of Manitowoc, Wisconsin. Those early experiments with the canning of green peas led to the creation of Wisconsin's first commercial canning company in 1887, established on the site of the hotel. The Albert Landreth Seed Company's early focus was split evenly between seed production and pea processing. However, by 1896 it became apparent that the canning industry held much room for growth, and the firm staked its future in canning, thus diminishing its role as a seed producer.

In 1907 the Albert Landreth Seed Company merged with the Wisconsin Pea Canners Company to ensure its place in the quickly expanding canning industry. In 1922 a group of investors purchased the business and renamed it Lakeside Packing Company. Today, after one final name change, that corporation is known as Lakeside Foods, Inc.

Up until the 1950s Lakeside's emphasis had been on its own quality brand labels, including "Lakeside," "Hobby," and "Eureka" brands. It was at this time that the company set out on a new mission to become a private-label-only supplier. With this fundamental change, Lakeside was positioning itself to better focus its resources on satisfying the production, quality, and service needs of many of the leading food retailers and wholesale distributors of the era.

*ABOVE: Lakeside Foods' processing plant in Manitowoc is one of nine such facilities in Wisconsin and Minnesota.*

*LEFT: Albert Landreth established Wisconsin's first commercial canning company in 1887.*

This was the most substantial change in the firm's direction since Albert Landreth decided to focus on pea canning rather than seed production back in 1896. This private-label focus continues to distinguish Lakeside Foods today, with virtually all of the company's products being sold under its customers' brand names.

Lakeside Foods, with an average annual employment of 900 people, has always sought to grow through diversification in the food-processing industry. Its involvement in the USDA meat program began in 1975. In 1982 Lakeside entered the frozen vegetable market. While Lakeside Foods' foundation was built on pea processing, its product line has expanded into a diverse line of canned and frozen vegeta-bles, canned meats, whipped topping, jellies and preserves, microwaveable meals, meal starter kits, complete home meals, and salsa, picante, and other sauces.

Today Lakeside Foods is poised to continue its success into the twenty-first century. The company has nine processing plants and five distribution centers throughout Wisconsin and Minnesota manufacturing a substantial line of products that feed people throughout the United States as well as 14 countries around the world. Lakeside Foods will continue to look to the future with its great potential, but the company will always be built around the people and the principles that were set forth 112 years ago in a small midwestern town on the shores of Lake Michigan.

# Notes

## Chapter One

1. Ralph G. Plumb, *A History of Manitowoc County* (Manitowoc: Brandt Printing and Binding Co., 1904), 15.
2. John Nagle, *History of Manitowoc County, Wisconsin* (Manitowoc: Manitowoc County Historical Society, 1878), 4.
3. Ibid., 6.
4. Plumb, 29.
5. Nagle, 5. The Manitowoc County Centennial Committee, *The Manitowoc County: Story of a Century 1848-1948* (Manitowoc: 1948 and 1970); Robert C. Nesbit, *Wisconsin, A History* (Madison: The State Historical Society of Wisconsin and the University of Wisconsin Press, 1973); and Dr. Louis Falge, *History of Manitowoc County, Wisconsin*, Vol. I (Chicago: Goodspeed Historical Association Publishers, 1911).

## Chapter Two

1. Plumb, 33.
2. Nagle, 14.
3. Plumb, 35.
4. Ibid., 56-57.
5. Ibid., 56.
6. Ibid.
7. Ibid.
8. Ibid., 243.
9. Ibid., 244.
10. Ibid., 245.
11. Ibid., 246.
12. Ibid., 195-197.
13. Ibid., 200-209.
14. Ibid., 208-209, and Falge, 38.
15. Nagle, 6-7.
16. Plumb, 35-36, and Nagle, 9,12.
17. Plumb, 38.
18. Ibid., 27.
19. Otto Gass, "The History of the City of Manitowoc, Wisconsin: Its Pioneer and Early Industries Prior to 1850" Occupational Monograph #52, 1984 Series, Manitowoc County Historical Society. (Hereafter cited by monograph and series #s.)
20. Arthur H. Lohman, "Early Days in Two Rivers, Wisconsin" Occupational Monograph #50, 1983 Series.
21. Ibid.
22. Gass, 8.
23. Caroline Hubbard, "History of the City of Manitowoc from 1850 to 1860" Occupational Monograph #56, 1985 Series.
24. Plumb, 37-39.
25. Ibid., 282.
26. Nagle, 13.
27. Plumb, 270.
28. Ibid., 271.
29. Ibid., 86.
30. Ibid., 89-99.
31. Ibid.
32. Ibid., 257.
33. Ibid., 255-259.
34. Ibid., 157-160.
35. Ibid., 70.
36. Ibid., 71.

## Chapter Three

1. For a complete and scholarly treatment of Manitowoc County during the Civil War, see Kerry A. Trask, *The Fire Within: A Civil War Narrative from Wisconsin* (Kent, Ohio: Kent State University Press, 1995). Falge, Vol. I, 454.
2. Ibid., 229-230.
3. Ibid., 454.
4. Ibid., 251-2, and Trask.
5. Ibid., 455.
6. Ibid.
7. Ibid., 257-259.
8. Ibid., 455.
9. Letters of Edwin R. Smith, in "Former Manitowoc County Superintendent of Schools' Civil War Letters Have Historic Merit," Occupational Monograph #61, 1987 Series, 5.
10. "Frederic Charles Buerstatte, A Diary of a Soldier in the Civil War," in *Newsletter*, Manitowoc County Historical Society, Vol. IX, #2, March 1975, 6-9.
11. Ibid.
12. Ibid.
13. Falge, 255.
14. "Edward Salomon, Wisconsin's Civil War Governor," in *Newsletter*, Manitowoc County Historical Society, Vol. XII, #4, September 1978, 86-87.
15. Richard N. Current, *The History of Wisconsin, The Civil War Era*, Vol. II (Madison: The State Historical Society of Wisconsin, 1976), 315-323.
16. Ibid., 329-331.
17. Ibid., 321-323.
18. Falge, 151.
19. Current, 477, 481.
20. Falge, 432.
21. "Shipbuilding in Manitowoc," in *Creative Wisconsin*, Vol. 6, #1, 29-52.
22. *Manitowoc Industries*.
23. Falge, 151-154.
24. Ibid., 136.
25. Ibid., 455.
26. Lawrence Bohn and Edward Ehlert, "Railroads and Railroading in Manitowoc County," Occupational Monograph, #19, 1973 Series.
27. Lawrence Bohn, "The Steam Locomotive and Manitowoc," Ibid., 4.
28. "The Carferry Industry," in *Manitowoc Industries*.
29. Ibid.
30. Falge, 130.
31. Ibid., 131.
32. Barbara Prinkman, "The Manitowoc Seating Company," *Manitowoc Industries*.
33. *Story of a Century*, Manitowoc County Centennial, 1948, 61.
34. *Manitowoc Industries*, 24-26.
35. Dan Juchniewich, "The American Hamilton Industries of Two Rivers, Wisconsin 1880-1980," Occupational Monograph #42, 1980 Series.
36. Ibid.
37. Ibid.
38. Ibid.
39. Ibid.
40. Ray Bertler, "Brickmaking, A Manitowoc Industry From the 1850s to About 1948," Occupational Monograph #32, 1977 Series.
41. Ibid.
42. Leonora Kadow, "The History of Aluminum," Occupational Monograph #18, 1972 Series.
43. Ibid.
44. Edward Ehlert, "Manitowoc County—A Leader in the Manufacture of Farm Machinery," Occupational Monograph #8, 1969 Series.
45. Ibid.
46. Ibid.
47. Ibid.
48. Edward Ehlert, "The Development of the Dairy Industry in Manitowoc County, Wisconsin," Occupational Monograph #11, 1970 Series.
49. "Rohde's Dairy was Started in Newton in 1884," and "Fischl's Dairy," in *Newsletter*, Manitowoc County Historical Society, Vol. 14, #4, September 1980, 16,17.
50. Edward Ehlert, "Food Processing—A Manitowoc Triumph," Occupational Monograph #10, 1970 Series.
51. *Story of a Century*, 65.
52. *Manitowoc Industries*, 2-7.
53. Falge, 455-457.

## Chapter Four

1. Falge, 358, and Edward Ehlert, Chief R.E. Herzog and Assistant Chief George F. Denk, "The History of the Manitowoc Fire Department," Occupational Monograph #29, 1976 Series.
2. Walter Vogl, "Forest Fires in Manitowoc County—1871," Occupational Monograph #58, 1986 Series, 1-4.
3. Ibid.
4. Ibid., 6.
5. Ibid.
6. Ibid., 7-8.
7. Falge, 363.
8. Ibid., 363-364.
9. Ibid.
10. *Story of a Century*, 130.
11. Falge, 417-418.
12. Ibid.
13. Ibid., 366.
14. Ibid.
15. Ibid., 367.
16. Ibid., 368.
17. Ibid., 421-423.
18. Ibid., 423, 177.
19. Ibid., 184.
20. Plumb, 227-228.
21. Ibid.
22. Ibid., 232-233.
23. Ibid.
24. Ibid., 110.
25. Ibid.
26. *Story of a Century*, 234-235.
27. Ibid.
28. Ibid., 236.
29. Ibid.
30. Ibid.
31. Falge, 237.
32. Ibid., 238.
33. Ibid.
34. Joseph Zahorik, "A History of the Manitowoc County Fair," *Newsletter*, Manitowoc County Historical Society, Vol. III, #5, November 1969; and "The Manitowoc County Fair," 21st Annual Exhibit, Premium List, September 14, 15, 16, 1904, Collection of the State Historical Society, Madison, Wisconsin.
35. Marcie Baer, "The Billy Schulz Indoor Circus," Occupational Monograph #43, 1981 Series.
36. Ruth Pech Gillespie, "Ceske Slovanska Lipa Opera House," Occupational Monograph #24, 1974 Series.
37. Ibid.
38. John Harmon, "Turner Hall, Early Manitowoc County History," Ibid.
39. Ibid.
40. Robert A. Niquette, "The Two Rivers Opera House," Occupational Monograph #44, 1981 Series.
41. Ibid.
42. Ibid.
43. Ibid.
44. "Walter Peters, Memoirs of His Days in Manitowoc," Ibid.
45. Brochure from the Two Rivers Historical Museum.
46. Georgia M. Fay, "The Schroeder Brothers Company of Two Rivers 1891-1991, A Family Tradition of Retail Business," Occupational Monograph #69, 1991 Series.
47. Ibid.
48. "The Manitowoc County Fair," Program 1904.
49. Ibid.
50. Ibid.
51. Falge, 365.
52. Ibid., and Edward Ehlert, "The History of Banking in Manitowoc County," Occupational Monograph, #12, 1970 Series.
53. Ehlert, and Marjorie Barnes Thompson, "The Failure of the Bank of Manitowoc," Occupational Monograph #31, 1977 Series.
54. Ibid.
55. Ibid., and Fay.
56. Edward Ehlert, "Courts and the Legal Profession in Manitowoc County, Wisconsin," Occupational Monograph #36, 1978 Series.
57. Ibid.
58. Edward Ehlert, "A History of Medicine in the Early Years," Occupational Monograph #6, 1968 Series.
59. Falge, 200.
60. Ibid., 207.
61. Ibid.
62. Ibid.
63. Ehlert,"Medicine," and Falge.
64. Sister Richarda Gilsdorf, "Happenings in the Founding of Holy Family Hospital, Manitowoc," *Newsletter*, Vol. IX, #5, November 1975, Manitowoc County Historical Society.
65. Ibid.
66. *A Century of Caring*, 1899-1999, Holy Family Hospital, Manitowoc.
67. Ibid., 8.

**220**

68. Ibid.
69. *Story of a Century*, 44-46.
70. Ibid.
71. Falge, 458.

**Chapter Five**
1. Marcie Baer, L.A. Murray, "The Polish Influence on Manitowoc County History," Occupational Monograph #41, 1980 Series; and Plumb, 212-213.
2. Baer.
3. Ibid.
4. Camille Dushek, Mrs. George Pribyl, Clarence Spevacheck, Dan Juchniewich, et al, "Bohemians Prominent in Manitowoc County History," Occupational Monograph #38, 1979 Series.
5. Alfred D. Sumberg, Dora Graff, Jeffrey Lauda, et al, "The Manitowoc County Jewish Community," Occupational Monograph #45, 1981 Series.
6. Ibid.
7. Ibid.
8. Ibid.
9. Ibid.
10. Ibid.
11. Ibid.
12. Ibid.
13. Frederick I. Olson, "The Milwaukee Socialists, 1897-1941" (Ph.D. Dissertation, Harvard University, 1952), 230-239.
14. Lloyd Velicer, "Municipal Ownership and the Manitowoc Wisconsin Socialists 1905-1917," Occupational Monograph #35, 1978 Series.
15. Ibid.
16. Ibid.
17. Ibid.
18. Ibid.
19. Ibid.
20. "Manitowoc Public Utilities, 1914-1964, 50 Years of Power and Progress," Manitowoc Public Utilities.
21. Ibid.
22. Plumb, as quoted in Ibid.
23. Manitowoc Public Utilities.
24. "Brewing," *Manitowoc Industries*, 9-11.
25. *Story of a Century*, 31-32.
26. Leonora Kadow, "The History of Aluminum," Occupational Monograph #18, 1972 Series.
27. Juchniewich.
28. Ibid.
29. Ibid.
30. Robert Dufek, "Paragon Industries, Two Rivers, Wisconsin," *Manitowoc Industries*, 111-115.
31. Bill Haberman, "Manitowoc Portland Cement Company," *Manitowoc Industries*, 76.
32. "Eggers Plywood Company," Ibid., 24-26.
33. "Imperial Eastman," Ibid., 125-127.
34. Ted Frieder, "Lakeside Packing Company," Ibid., 232-235.
35. Dennis Kujawa, "A.M. Richter Sons Company," in Ibid., 269-271.
36. Michael Brauer, "Consumer's Steel Company, Inc." Ibid., 193.

37. "The Manitowoc Company, 75 Years of Growth and Diversification," The Manitowoc Company.
38. Lyle Gorder, "The Manitowoc Equipment Works of Manitowoc, Wisconsin," Ibid., 179-183.
39. *Story of a Century*, 47.
40. Ibid.
41. Paul V. Glad, *History of Wisconsin, A New Era and Depression, 1914-1940*, Vol. 5 (Madison: The State Historical Society of Wisconsin, 1990), 25.
42. Kadow, "Aluminum..."
43. "Hamilton..."
44. Dufek.
45. "Shipbuilding in Manitowoc."
46. Ibid.
47. Ibid.
48. Ibid.
49. Ibid.
50. Francis M. Kadow, "Opinion Molders Prominent in Manitowoc's History," Occupational Monograph #21, 1973 Series.
51. Ibid.
52. Ibid.
53. Ed Arndorfer, "Retired Radio Pioneer Recalls Long, Sometimes Exciting Career," *Newsletter*, Manitowoc County Historical Society, Vol. 12, #2, March 1978.
54. "Some Reminiscences of Anita Biesemeyer Gamble," *Newsletter*, Manitowoc County Historical Society, Vol. 12, #2, March 1978.
55. Ibid.
56. Ibid.
57. *Story of a Century*.
58. Ibid.
59. "Thomas J. Walsh, Native of Two Rivers: His Role in 'Teapot Dome Scandal' of 1920s," reprint from January 31, 1974, *Manitowoc-Two Rivers Herald Times Reporter*, *Newsletter*, Vol. IX, #1, January 1975.
60. Ibid.
61. Ibid.
62. "Thorstein Veblen, Manitowoc County's Famous Son," reprint from *Manitowoc Herald-Times*, June 14, 1948, *Newsletter*, Vol. 14, #2, March 1980.
63. Ibid.
64. *Century*, 133.
65. Thomas Rider, "Invincible Metal Furniture Company," *Manitowoc Industries*, 217-223.
66. *Century*, 134.
67. Ibid.
68. Ibid.
69. Ibid., 139.
70. Ibid.
71. Ibid.
72. Robert Janda, "Entertainment Tonight, An Account of Bands in Manitowoc County Since 1900," Occupational Monograph #28, 1976 Series.
73. Ibid.

**Chapter Six**
1. Ehlert, "Banking..."
2. Glad, 413-420.

3. Ibid.
4. *Century*, 30,78.
5. "The Manitowoc Company."
6. Ibid.
7. Ibid.
8. Kadow, "History of Aluminum..."
9. Glad, 494.
10. Glad, and *Century*, 98.
11. *Century*, 98-103.
12. Ehlert, "Banking..."
13. Ibid.
14. Ibid.
15. Ibid.
16. Ibid.
17. *Century*, 111.
18. Ibid.
19. Ibid.
20. Ibid., 108-109.
21. Ibid.
22. Ibid., 104-105.
23. Ibid., 58.
24. Ibid., 47.
25. Ibid., 48.
26. Ibid.
27. Ibid.
28. Ibid.
29. Ibid., 122-123.
30. Ibid.
31. Ibid., 124-125.
32. Kadow, "Aluminum..."
33. "The Manitowoc Company, 75 Years..." 22.
34. Ibid., 23.
35. Ibid.
36. Ibid., 29.
37. Ibid., 28-29.
38. Ibid.
39. Ibid.
40. Ibid.
41. Ibid., 30.
42. *Century*.
43. Fay.
44. Kean Leiker, "Report on Lube Devices, Inc." *Manitowoc Industries*, 245.
45. Lyle Gorder, "Chermake Sausage Company," Ibid., 187.
46. "Early Industry of Manitowoc County," Ibid., 205-210.
47. Charles Faskow, "The Metal Ware Corporation," Ibid., 261-264.
48. Edward Ehlert, "The History of Manitowoc's Secondary Schools," Occupational Monograph #17, 1972 Series.
49. Ibid., 7.
50. Ibid., 10-12.
51. Ibid., 13.
52. Ibid., 11.
53. Ibid., 12.
54. Edward Ehlert, "The History of 'Learnin' in Manitowoc County," Occupational Monograph #14, 1971 Series, 9.
55. Ibid.
56. "The Silver Lake College Story: Historical Overview," Archives, Silver Lake College, Manitowoc, Wisconsin.
57. Ibid.
58. Ibid.
59. Information from Campus, University of Wisconsin College, Manitowoc.
60. Edward Ehlert, "Public Libraries of Manitowoc County From 1852 to the Present," Occupational Monograph #26,

1975 Series.
61. Information from the Lester Public Library, the Kiel Public Library, and the Manitowoc Public Library.

**Chapter Seven**
1. Bay-Lake Regional Planning Commission, "Manitowoc County Economic Analysis," and "Manitowoc County Population Characteristics," 1995.
2. *A Century of Caring...*, 33.
3. Ibid., 38.
4. "The City of Two Rivers Proudly Presents," *Manitowoc Herald-Times*, December 13, 1963.
5. "Aurora Breaks Ground for new TR Hospital," *Herald Times Reporter*, December 22, 1998.
6. Ibid.
7. Fay.
8. "Experience Manitowoc County," Promotional Brochure, Manitowoc County.
9. "The Hamilton Story."
10. "Mirro Aluminum Centennial," Brochure.
11. Ellen D. Langill, *Spanning a Century, Henry Nagy and the Story of Spancrete* (Milwaukee: Chestnut Publishers, Inc., 1999), 75-76.
12. Ibid.
13. "Manitowoc Public Utilities..."
14. "20th Anniversary, Point Beach Nuclear Power Plant," Brochure.
15. Ibid.
16. "Capitol Civic Centre, Manitowoc," Brochure.
17. Ibid.
18. Ibid.
19. Herald Times Reporter, *Manitowoc County Memories*, 1995, 127.
20. "Two Rivers, Wisconsin," Promotional Brochure.
21. "Wisconsin Maritime Museum," Brochure.
22. "Wisconsin's Largest Maritime Museum," Brochure.
23. "Pinecrest Historical Village," Brochure.
24. "Manitowoc County," Brochure.
25. Ibid.
26. Ibid., and Susan Talbot-Stanaway, "Jensen's Work Celebrated Land and Life of Midwest," *Voyageur*.
27. Ibid.
28. Ibid., and Ludington Daily News, *Ludington's Carferries*, 1997, 118-125.
29. "Experiencing Manitowoc County."
30. Ibid.
31. "Population Characteristics..."

# Corporate Sponsor Index

# General Index

MANITO

T

1  Post Office, Chas. Esslinger, P. M
2  Court House.
3  Ward Schools.
4  Turner Hall.
5  Fire Engine Houses.
6  Flouring Mill, Truman & Cooper.
7  Oriental Flouring Mill, J. Schuette.
8  Wisconsin Central Flouring Mill, Fleigler & Haupt.
9  Richards' Iron Works, H. C. Richards.
10  Eagle Brewery, W. Rahr's Sons.
12  Elevator.
13  A. F. & A. C. Dunkes, Engine Building and Mill Furnishing Works
14  Manitowoc Axe Manufacturing Works, Jos. Gillott & Sons.
15  Saw Mill and Lumber Yard, Geo. Pankratz.
16  Tannery, L. Sherman & Son.
17  Tannery, Henry Vits.
18  Farm Machinery Manufactory, Smalley Mfg. Co., Props.
19  Carriage and Wagon Manufactory, Andrew Hanson.
20  Williams House, A. D. Smith, Prop.
21  North Western House, M. Kettenhofen, Prop.
22  Miller House, J. L. Miller, Prop.

23  North House, William Witt, Prop.
24  First National Bank, C. C. Barnes, Pres't, C. Luling, Cashier
25  Bank, T. C. Shove & Co.

### BUSINESS REFERENCES.

O. Torrison, Dry and Fancy Goods, Notions and Carpets, Clothing,
     Boots and Shoes, Hats and Caps, Groceries and Produce, Torri-
     son's Block.
J. Schuette & Bros., Dry and Fancy Goods, Notions and Carpets, Cloth-
     ing, Boots and Shoes, Hats and Caps, Groceries and Produce, 216
     and 218 South Eighth St.
Fred. Heineman, Books and Stationery, 217 North Eighth St.
John Franz, Notary Public and Insurance, Franz's Block.
L. T. Mohrhusen, Saloon and Restaurant, 323 Quay St.
Ed. Weinschenk, Saloon, 219 Washington St.
Hans Christensen, Saloon and Billiards, Franze's Block.
T. C. Buerstatte, Druggist, 219 South Eighth St.
Alfred Manheimer, Tobacco and Cigars, 122 South Eighth St.
H. & W. Wollmer, Jewelers, 124 South Eighth St.
C. Beers, Harbor Saloon and Pool Room, 102 South Eighth St.
Chris. Koerke, Saloon and Billiards, 111 North Eighth St.

A   P
B   M
C   N
D   N
E   Ep
F   Ca
G   H
H
J   Ca
K   P